On the fringe of a Soviet-occupied forest stronghold in the north of Finland, Finnish ski troopers lie against a snowy hummock with their bayoneted rifles at the ready. Bitter weather and hostile Arctic terrain bedeviled the foreign troops —German, Russian, British and French —who fought with and against the Scandinavians between 1935 and 1945.

BATTLES FOR SCANDINAVIA

TARGET NATIONS ON THE CREST OF EUROPE

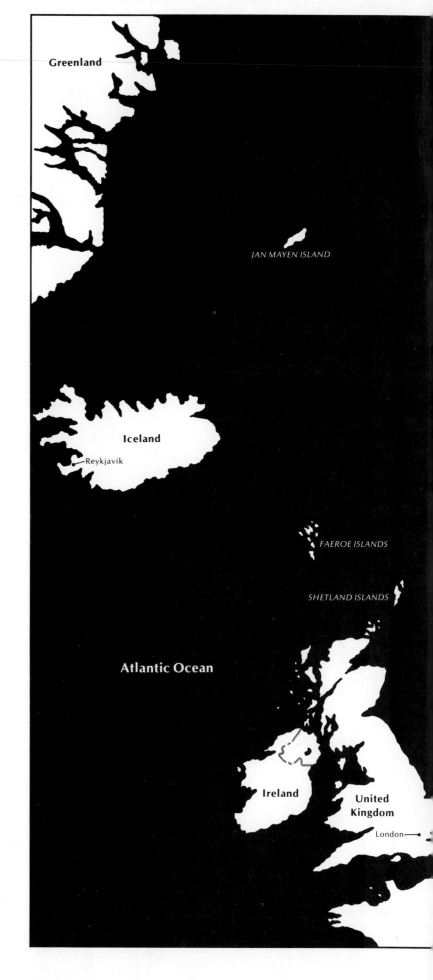

The four nations of Scandinavia—Denmark, Norway, Sweden and Finland—hoped to remain neutral in World War II. But the Arctic crest from Petsamo in Finland to Narvik in Norway was rich in iron, nickel, copper and molybdenum—the stuff of arms and armor. For the Germans, the long Norwegian coast afforded sheltered waters from which Britain and British shipping might be attacked. The airfields of Denmark provided a steppingstone to Norway. Finland and its gulf offered a passageway between Germany and the Soviet Union. For all these reasons, the major European combatants of the War converged on Scandinavia.

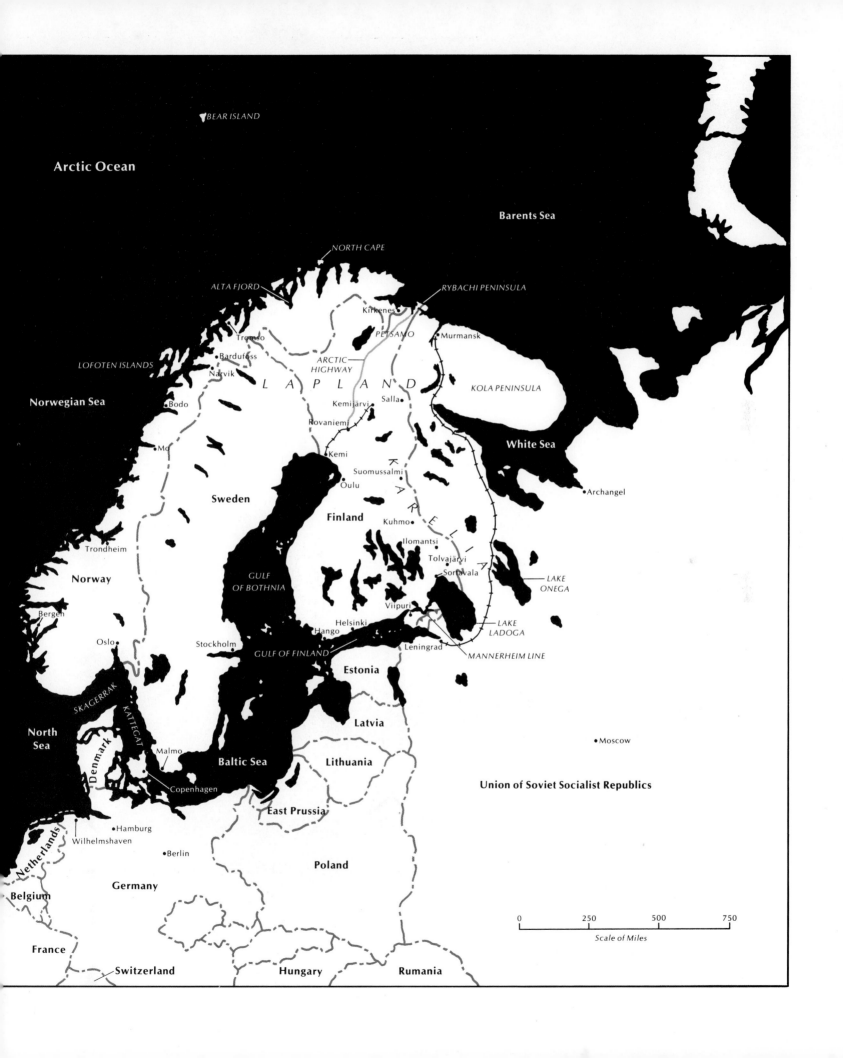

Arctic Ocean

Barents Sea

BEAR ISLAND

NORTH CAPE

ALTA FJORD

RYBACHI PENINSULA

Kirkenes

Tromso

PETSAMO

Murmansk

Bardufoss

ARCTIC
HIGHWAY

KOLA PENINSULA

LOFOTEN ISLANDS

Narvik

L A P L A N D

Norwegian Sea

Bodo

Kemijärvi

Salla

Rovaniemi

White Sea

Mo

Kemi

K
A
R
E
L
I
A

Sweden

Suomussalmi

Oulu

Archangel

Finland

Kuhmo

Ilomantsi

Trondheim

Tolvajärvi

LAKE
ONEGA

Norway

Sortavala

GULF
OF BOTHNIA

Viipuri

Bergen

Helsinki

LAKE
LADOGA

Hango

Oslo

Stockholm

Leningrad

GULF OF FINLAND

MANNERHEIM LINE

Estonia

Moscow

Latvia

SKAGERRAK

KATTEGAT

North
Sea

Denmark

Malmo

Lithuania

Baltic Sea

Union of Soviet Socialist Republics

Copenhagen

East Prussia

Hamburg

Wilhelmshaven

Berlin

Netherlands

Poland

Belgium

Germany

France

Switzerland

Hungary

Rumania

| 0 | 250 | 500 | 750 |

Scale of Miles

Other Publications:
LIBRARY OF HEALTH
CLASSICS OF THE OLD WEST
THE EPIC OF FLIGHT
THE GOOD COOK
THE SEAFARERS
THE ENCYCLOPEDIA OF COLLECTIBLES
THE GREAT CITIES
HOME REPAIR AND IMPROVEMENT
THE WORLD'S WILD PLACES
THE TIME-LIFE LIBRARY OF BOATING
HUMAN BEHAVIOR
THE ART OF SEWING
THE OLD WEST
THE EMERGENCE OF MAN
THE AMERICAN WILDERNESS
THE TIME-LIFE ENCYCLOPEDIA OF GARDENING
LIFE LIBRARY OF PHOTOGRAPHY
THIS FABULOUS CENTURY
FOODS OF THE WORLD
TIME-LIFE LIBRARY OF AMERICA
TIME-LIFE LIBRARY OF ART
GREAT AGES OF MAN
LIFE SCIENCE LIBRARY
THE LIFE HISTORY OF THE UNITED STATES
TIME READING PROGRAM
LIFE NATURE LIBRARY
LIFE WORLD LIBRARY
FAMILY LIBRARY:
    HOW THINGS WORK IN YOUR HOME
    THE TIME-LIFE BOOK OF THE FAMILY CAR
    THE TIME-LIFE FAMILY LEGAL GUIDE
    THE TIME-LIFE BOOK OF FAMILY FINANCE

This volume is one of a series that chronicles
in full the events of the Second World War.
Previous books in the series include:

Prelude to War
Blitzkrieg
The Battle of Britain
The Rising Sun
The Battle of the Atlantic
Russia Besieged
The War in the Desert
The Home Front: U.S.A.
China-Burma-India
Island Fighting
The Italian Campaign
Partisans and Guerrillas
The Second Front
Liberation
Return to the Philippines
The Air War in Europe
The Resistance
The Battle of the Bulge
The Road to Tokyo
Red Army Resurgent
The Nazis
Across the Rhine
War under the Pacific
War in the Outposts
The Soviet Juggernaut
Japan at War
The Mediterranean

WORLD WAR II · TIME-LIFE BOOKS · ALEXANDRIA, VIRGINIA

BY JOHN R. ELTING
AND THE EDITORS OF TIME-LIFE BOOKS

BATTLES FOR SCANDINAVIA

Time-Life Books Inc.
is a wholly owned subsidiary of
TIME INCORPORATED

Founder: Henry R. Luce 1898-1967

Editor-in-Chief: Henry Anatole Grunwald
President: J. Richard Munro
Chairman of the Board: Ralph P. Davidson
Executive Vice President: Clifford J. Grum
Chairman, Executive Committee: James R. Shepley
Editorial Director: Ralph Graves
Group Vice President, Books: Joan D. Manley
Vice Chairman: Arthur Temple

TIME-LIFE BOOKS INC.

Managing Editor: Jerry Korn
Executive Editor: David Maness
Assistant Managing Editors: Dale M. Brown
(planning), George Constable, Martin Mann,
John Paul Porter, Gerry Schremp (acting)
Art Director: Tom Suzuki
Chief of Research: David L. Harrison
Director of Photography: Robert G. Mason
Assistant Art Director: Arnold C. Holeywell
Assistant Chief of Research: Carolyn L. Sackett
Assistant Director of Photography: Dolores A. Littles

Chairman: John D. McSweeney
President: Carl G. Jaeger
Executive Vice Presidents: John Steven Maxwell,
David J. Walsh
Vice Presidents: George Artandi (comptroller);
Stephen L. Bair (legal counsel); Peter G. Barnes;
Nicholas Benton (public relations); John L. Canova;
Beatrice T. Dobie (personnel); Carol Flaumenhaft
(consumer affairs); James L. Mercer (Europe/South
Pacific); Herbert Sorkin (production); Paul R. Stewart
(marketing)

WORLD WAR II

Editorial Staff for Battles for Scandinavia
Editor: Anne Horan
Designer: Herbert H. Quarmby
Chief Researcher: Philip Brandt George
Picture Editor: Peggy Sawyer
Text Editors: Richard D. Kovar, Brian McGinn,
Robert Menaker
Staff Writers: Donald Davison Cantlay,
Roger E. Herst, Brooke Stoddard, David S. Thomson
Researchers: Harris Andrews III, Kristin Baker,
LaVerle Berry, Loretta Y. Britten, Mary G. Burns,
Jane Hanna, Jayne T. Wise
Art Assistant: Mikio Togashi
Editorial Assistant: Constance Strawbridge

Special Contributors
Christina S. Draper, Alexandra Gleysteen,
Lettie S. Multhauf (translations)

Editorial Production
Production Editor: Douglas B. Graham
Operations Manager: Gennaro C. Esposito,
Gordon E. Buck (assistant)
Assistant Production Editor: Feliciano Madrid
Quality Control: Robert L. Young (director),
James J. Cox (assistant), Daniel J. McSweeney,
Michael G. Wight (associates)
Art Coordinator: Anne B. Landry
Copy Staff: Susan B. Galloway (chief), Ann Bartunek,
Allan Fallow, Barbara F. Quarmby, Celia Beattie
Picture Department: Betty Hughes Weatherley
Traffic: Kimberly K. Lewis

Correspondents: Elisabeth Kraemer (Bonn); Margot
Hapgood, Dorothy Bacon, Lesley Coleman (London);
Susan Jonas, Lucy T. Voulgaris (New York); Maria
Vincenza Aloisi, Josephine du Brusle (Paris); Ann
Natanson (Rome). Valuable assistance was also
provided by: Helga Kohl, Martha Mader (Bonn);
Katrina Van Duyn (Copenhagen); Lance Keyworth,
Risto Meanpaa (Helsinki); Judy Aspinall, Brian K.
Davis, Karin B. Pearce (London); Felix Rosenthal
(Moscow); Carolyn T. Chubet, Miriam Hsia, Christina
Lieberman (New York); Dag Christensen, Bent
Onsager (Oslo); M. T. Hirschkoff (Paris); Mimi
Murphy (Rome); Mary Johnson (Stockholm); Traudl
Lessing (Vienna).

The Author: COLONEL JOHN R. ELTING, USA (Ret.),
was an intelligence officer with the 8th Armored Division in Europe during World War II. A former Associate Professor of Military Art and Engineering at West
Point, he is the author of The Battle of Bunker's Hill,
The Battles of Saratoga and Military History and Atlas
of the Napoleonic Wars, and was associate editor of
The West Point Atlas of American Wars. He has
served as chief consultant for other volumes in the
World War II series.

The Consultant: DONALD MACINTYRE served with
the Royal Navy during World War II as a commander
of destroyers and convoy escort groups in the North
Atlantic. Since his retirement in 1954 he has written
more than a score of books on naval historical subjects, including U-Boat Killer, Narvik and Battle for
the Mediterranean, and has served as consultant on
the World War II series volumes The Battle of the Atlantic and The Mediterranean.

Library of Congress Cataloguing in Publication Data

Elting, John Robert.
  Battles for Scandinavia.

  (World War II; v. 28)
  Bibliography: p.
  Includes index.
  1. World War, 1939-1945—Scandinavia.   2. World
War, 1939-1945—Finland.   3. Scandinavia—History—
20th century.   4. Finland—History—1939-
I. Time-Life Books. II. Title. III. Series.
D754.S29E47   940.53'48   81-5698
ISBN 0-8094-3397-4
ISBN 0-8094-3396-6 (lib. bdg.)
ISBN 0-8094-3395-8 (retail ed.)

For information about any Time-Life book, please write:

Reader Information
Time-Life Books
541 North Fairbanks Court
Chicago, Illinois 60611

CONTENTS

A MODEL SCANDINAVIAN HERO

On a gleaming charger, Field Marshal Gustaf Mannerheim reviews Finnish tanks as they clank through the city of Viipuri en route to the Russian front in 1939.

AN IMPOSING LEADER FOR A RESOLUTE PEOPLE

In the uniform of a Finnish military academy cadet in the 1880s, Gustaf Mannerheim exhibits soldierly bearing and clear-eyed determination.

No individual was better cut out to lead his countrymen through the violent nightmare that World War II brought to Scandinavia than Gustaf Mannerheim of Finland. Yet it is hard to imagine a personality and a background less likely than his to produce a popular hero.

Mannerheim was an aristocrat in a world turning toward democracy, a conservative in an age of revolution. He was a person of such forbidding self-control and hauteur that one aide described him as "a prisoner of his own splendor," and another marveled that he "even drank in such a way that he stayed sober." Still, this imposing nobleman—he stood 6 feet 2 inches tall—was destined to lead Finland, and symbolically all of Scandinavia, in its first head-on collision with the combatants of the War. In doing so he won a permanent place in the hearts of the people he led.

Contrasts ran as deep in the times as in Mannerheim. In 1867, when he was born, Finland was a grand duchy of the Russian Empire—but its leading families, including his, traced their lineage to Sweden. The Finns gradually were beginning to assert a spirit of nationalism; against the imperial fiat that Russian be taught in the schools, they persisted in speaking Swedish or Finnish. And, against imperial insistence on the primacy of the Russian Orthodox Church, they persisted in worshipping as Lutherans.

As a young baron-to-be, Mannerheim grew up on a large estate, holding himself aloof from the Finns and looking upon them with youthful arrogance. At 16 he wrote archly: "I look forward happily to that moment when I can turn my back forever on Finland." As a member of the Swedish-speaking aristocracy, he had entree to the courts of Saint Petersburg and Stockholm, and at 20 he did leave Finland for czarist Russia.

Nevertheless, he returned in maturer years to play a crucial role in Finland's birth as a nation. By 1939, when the former duchy went to war with the Soviet Union, no other leader was so widely acclaimed among the Finns, and none more brilliantly reflected the resolute will with which Scandinavians met the intrusions of World War II.

At the front during World War II, Mannerheim consults with his officers. For his valor, a German general called him ''the last of the grand knights.''

REWARDING DECADES OF SERVICE TO THE CZAR

Mannerheim's military career began with a blot that would have ended almost anyone else's—his expulsion from a Finnish military academy for going AWOL. "Without realizing it," he wrote later, "I thus took a step that was to be of enormous importance for my future." His noble blood and social connections won him a second chance: entree to another and more prestigious institution, the famed Nikolaevski Cavalry School in Saint Petersburg, where the sons of the Russian nobility trained. Mannerheim seems to have excelled there on his own merits; when he graduated in 1889, he was near the top of his class.

The following decades were the happiest of Mannerheim's life. As a cavalry officer in the imperial palace guard, he spent most of those years serving the Czar. He mingled with princes and grand dukes at the Winter Palace in Saint Petersburg— the historic imperial capital that would become Leningrad—and when Nicholas II was crowned in 1895, he was one of four officers chosen to stand guard on the steps of the cathedral altar. Mannerheim drew other agreeable assignments as well. He traveled across Europe to buy thoroughbred horses for the imperial stables, and he made a two-year journey through Central Asia, exploring trade and military prospects for the Russian Empire.

When Russia entered World War I in alliance with Britain and France, Mannerheim saw action as a high imperial officer. By 1917 he had risen to lieutenant general and corps commander—just in time to see the world for which he fought swept away by the Russian Revolution. He had to flee for his life, and chose to return to Finland.

Shown with his regimental officers, Major General Mannerheim (far left), a rising czarist officer, stands at ease under a portrait of Nicholas II in a photograph taken in 1913.

Sent to China in 1908, Mannerheim (far right) attends a diplomatic banquet in Lanchow, an ancient city on the Yellow River. On this mission he mapped a 5,000-mile trade route from Turkestan to Peking.

Wearing a black papachka—the fur hat that was fashionable among soldiers as well as civilians in Imperial Russia—Major General Mannerheim receives a report from aides in Austria-Hungary in 1915.

BRINGING PEACE TO A FREE FINLAND

At a time when any czarist officer might be shot on sight by revolutionaries, Mannerheim fled in style. He crossed Russia in a private railway car, and in full uniform.

The Finland to which he returned was on the brink of civil war. The abdication of Czar Nicholas II theoretically had cut Finland's tie to Russia. But the Finns were torn over the issue of how to establish a new form of government.

Those Finns who leaned in the direction of the radicals who had taken over Russia styled themselves Reds. Those advocating a parliamentary form of government were known as Whites. Feelings ran so high that the two sides took up arms against each other. When they did, the Whites needed a leader. Offering his services, Mannerheim took over the White troops. In three and a half months he had brought the civil war to a close.

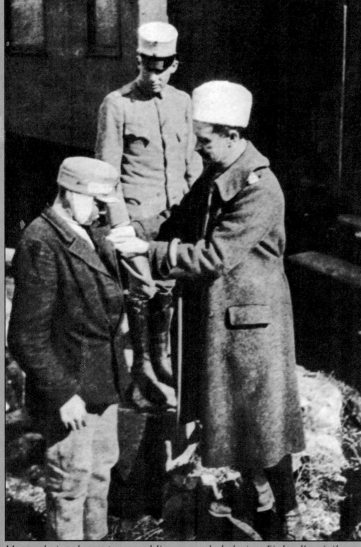

Mannerheim decorates a soldier wounded during Finland's civil war.

In a cobblestone square, Mannerheim leads his troops in salute to the Mayor of

Helsinki at the end of the civil war in May 1918. He continued wearing a fur hat, but had it made of white fur to distinguish himself from the Communist Reds.

Mannerheim, seated next to Sweden's King Gustaf V, rides through Stockholm in February 1919. The King, as well as other rulers of the Western world, regarded Mannerheim as a stabilizing influence in Scandinavia.

WORLD EMISSARY BETWEEN THE WARS

During the years that followed World War I and Finland's internal war, Mannerheim settled in the nation he had once spurned, serving variously as regent and as a goodwill ambassador who traveled over much of the world.

After the wars, one of Mannerheim's first acts was to secure a loan from American banks for the purchase of American wheat. As a result, the Finns were able to have white bread, which had previously been a rarity in Finland; it came to be known as "Mannerheim bread." As an emissary, he was welcomed as a hero everywhere he went. "I can tell you, General," said the King of Sweden, "it is only since your victory that we have peace in the country"; Sweden, too, had been fearful of a Communist take-over. And as a private citizen, Mannerheim endowed a child-welfare association to rear and educate the children of men who had died in the fighting—whether they fought for the Red or the White Army.

Even with all those activities, Mannerheim still found time to travel for pleasure, for study and for sport. He became chairman of the Finnish Red Cross, and made a trip to Switzerland for a firsthand look at that organization in the country where it had been founded. For many years he stalked deer and antelope every autumn in the mountains of Austria. And during a visit to Nepal in 1937—when he had reached the age of 69—Mannerheim bagged his first tiger.

Bowing, Mannerheim shakes the hand of a child at an orphanage in southwestern Finland. In the years after World War I, he inspired the founding of more than 500 such homes.

With his royal host, the Maharaja of Nepal, Mannerheim stands over a 10-foot tiger he shot on a 1937 hunting trip to the Himalayas.

Resplendent in the full-dress uniform of a Finnish field marshal, Mannerheim treads a path that has been strewn with spring flowers. The occasion was the celebration of his 70th birthday on June 4, 1937.

Standing on a carpet of snow, Mannerheim delivers a personal word of thanks to one of the 11,500 volunteers from other countries who had come to fight for Finland in the opening months of World War II.

"RACING THE STORM" OF CONFLICT TO COME

In 1931 Finland called Mannerheim out of retirement to make him chairman of a newly created Defense Council. In his own phrase, he spent the 1930s "racing the storm" of war. Relations with the Stalinist regime in Russia continued to be uneasy, and as the decade wore on the eastward expansion of Adolf Hitler's Germany increased the strain.

Traveling on behalf of his nation, Mannerheim used the Defense Council post to acquaint himself with the development of arms in England, France and Germany—although Finland had almost no funds with which to buy arms.

By November 1939 the race was lost; the Soviet Union invaded Finland, and Finland girded itself to fight back against overwhelming odds. To the surprise of no one, Mannerheim—at the age of 72—found himself once again commander in chief of Finland's armed forces.

1

"We cannot move Leningrad, so we must move the border"
Mobilizing behind the Mannerheim Line
"One Finn is always worth 10 Russians"
An invasion stalled by ingenious booby traps
When "White Death" stalked the Red Army
Chopping up the enemy like kindling
Retreat of a bruised behemoth
A general who dared Stalin's wrath
Dress rehearsal for an all-out assault
High cost for an uneasy peace

"We must be able to bar entrance to the Gulf of Finland," declared Soviet Premier Josef Stalin in a tone unlikely to invite argument. Stalin's listeners were a delegation of wary Finnish diplomats summoned to Moscow to meet with him and his Foreign Minister, Vyacheslav M. Molotov, on October 14, 1939. "We are on good terms now with Germany," the Russian dictator commented. Then, with grim prescience, he added, "But everything in this world may change." The ostensible reason for the meeting in Moscow was to discuss what Molotov called "certain concrete questions of a political nature." But Stalin had more than questions on his mind; he had demands to make.

Some two months earlier, the Soviet Union and Germany had signed a nonagression pact that neatly divided Poland—and for that matter all of Eastern Europe—between them. Adolf Hitler, assured that the Red Army would not stand in his way, then sent the German war machine rolling into Poland on September 1—the act that brought declarations of war from France and Great Britain and the onset of World War II. Two and a half weeks later, with Polish defenses a shambles, Stalin sent four armies across Poland's naked eastern border and easily acquired 77,000 square miles of land on his western frontier.

Eager to put as much territory as possible between the Soviet Union and the conflagration that would soon engulf all of Western Europe, and to obtain bases from which to launch offensives of his own, Stalin then compelled the tiny Baltic republics of Latvia, Lithuania and Estonia to sign treaties that, in effect, accorded the Soviet Union carte blanche to occupy their territory.

Now he was looking to the north. To prevent an unfriendly navy from sweeping up the Gulf of Finland and onto his own shores, he wanted control of the gulf. Specifically, he wanted Sursaari and four other islands in the gulf outright, and he wanted to lease Hango Peninsula at the entrance to the gulf for a Navy base. He also wanted the Finns to yield nearly 750 square miles of territory across the Karelian Isthmus, the thin strip of land that joined the two countries between the gulf and Lake Ladoga. The cession of land on the isthmus, said Stalin with a curious twist of logic, as though the Finns were somehow a threat to Soviet security, would put Leningrad more than 40 miles from the Russo-Finnish border instead of the present 20—beyond the range

A WAR THAT WINTER BROUGHT

of Finnish guns. "We cannot move Leningrad," said Stalin, "so we must move the border." Finally, Stalin wanted the western half of the Rybachi Peninsula on the Barents Sea, 60 miles west of the port of Murmansk. In return, he proposed to cede 2,135 square miles of East Karelia, a tract he could afford to spare because it consisted of virtually nothing but woods, lakes and swampland.

But the Finns were not fooled. Stalin did not have to tell his listeners that control of the Rybachi Peninsula, together with Hango on the Gulf of Finland and the gains he had already made in Estonia, would give him a choke hold over Finland. In spite of the bonhomie of the dictator's conciliatory remarks, the Finnish diplomats knew they would be in for some tough negotiating.

Their delegation was led by Juho Paasikivi, who was the Finnish Minister to Sweden and a man experienced in dickering with the Russians. Two decades earlier, he had negotiated with the Bolsheviks the treaty that had given the Finns the territory of Petsamo. Now, in October 1939, he stood up to Stalin. Paasikivi pointed out that for the Finnish government to agree to relinquish any territory would require changing the country's constitution. He explained further that the Finns would find it particularly difficult to give up the Hango Peninsula and the portion of the Karelian Isthmus that the Russians were demanding.

Such transactions were "nothing, really," Stalin rejoined. "Look at Hitler. The Poznań frontier was too close to Berlin for him, so he took an extra 186 miles."

"We want to continue in peace and remain apart from all incidents," answered Paasikivi. But he stood no chance against Stalin. For weeks the Finnish diplomat and his colleagues shuttled between Moscow and Helsinki, meeting offer with counteroffer again and again—and all in vain. In early November, Molotov broke off the negotiations, remarking ominously, "We civilians can see no further in the matter; now it is the turn of the military to have their say."

Molotov's warning was the opening chord in a dirge of death and destruction that would eventually reverberate across all Europe and bring the major combatants of World War II face to face in Scandinavia. So far, the four small nations that made up that northern corner of Europe—Finland, Sweden, Norway and Denmark—had escaped being drawn into the great powers' quarrels. Sweden, Norway and Denmark had sat out World War I as neutrals; they hoped to do so again. The Finns had fought in World War I—but their land was then part of the Russian Empire. Now, as an independent nation, Finland hoped to remain neutral. But it would not be spared.

At first glance, Scandinavia would hardly seem worth the attention of Europe's warring nations. On the east, 700 miles of tundra, forest and swamp stretch from the Arctic Ocean south to Leningrad; on the west, 1,500 miles of fjords and headlands zigzag from the Skagerrak, the arm of the North Sea that separates Norway and Denmark, to Petsamo in northern Finland. Almost a third of Scandinavia lies above the Arctic Circle; most of it is empty land, harsh and barely habitable, its long winters and short summers punctuated by savage storms.

Still, Scandinavia rated high in the plans of Josef Stalin and Adolf Hitler—and, by extension, of Winston Churchill. Stalin was interested mainly in Finland's value as a buffer state. Hitler had more material concerns: Finland was a veritable mother lode of nickel, copper, molybdenum and cobalt. Norway's coastline, with its myriad fjords, would make a perfect base for raids against England. Even more important was Norway's value as a pipeline of raw materials from Sweden, particularly the high-grade iron ore that met more than half the requirements of Germany's arms industry. Eight million tons of Swedish iron ore were imported into Germany annually. Securing the flow of ore weighed heavily on Hitler's mind, and even before the outbreak of war he had planned to incorporate Denmark, Norway and Sweden into the Reich. "If they don't like it," he proclaimed, "they can try to drive me out."

At the time, the prospect that any of the three might drive out Hitler's armies was unthinkable. Norway had a military force of only 19,000 men, and they were ill trained and ill equipped. Denmark was even worse off, with a token force of about 15,000. Sweden had a respectable 100,000-man army, but it would be no match for the Germans' 2.5 million men—particularly if the nations that surrounded Sweden were occupied first.

In all Scandinavia, only Sweden would escape invasion by one or more of the major powers, and even Sweden escaped only by turning itself into an armed camp. Norway and Denmark fell quickly to invading armies, then endured the yoke of occupation for a full five years. Finland suffered a different fate. That small nation of four million citizens not only had to fight for its existence against the acquisitive demands of the Soviet Union, but after 1941 it became a boulevard of war for the Soviets and Germans. It lay athwart the path by which Hitler aggressively sought to block the Soviet Union's vital gateways to the West—the city of Leningrad and the seaports on Russia's Arctic coast. As a result, nearly three million troops saw action on Finnish soil—far more than in any other Scandinavian nation.

In the autumn of 1939, Stalin expected Finland to be an easy conquest. His illusion was encouraged by a number of misreadings, many of them fostered by Otto Kuusinen, spokesman for a group of Finnish Communists who had been living in exile in Moscow since 1918. Kuusinen and his sympathizers hoped to establish a Communist state in Finland and, prompted by their own wishful thinking, they asserted that the country was ready to be taken. The Finns themselves earnestly wanted to avoid war, but after a generation of independence they were by no means disposed to knuckle under. Indeed, they took advantage of the drawn-out negotiations in Moscow to shore up their defenses in every way they could.

The Finns had precious little to start with: 100 airplanes, and scarcely enough gasoline to fuel them for a month; a single tank company (indeed, tanks were such a novelty in

Finland that many Finnish soldiers had never even seen one); and a collection of machine guns and mortars, rifles and artillery dating from World War I and in some cases as far back as 1877. They had few modern antitank or antiaircraft guns, and no field radios. The one new weapon the Finns possessed was the 9mm Suomi submachine gun; it could fire up to 900 rounds per minute and was deadly at short range—capabilities that made it well suited to fighting in the dense forests of Finland.

Finland's greatest asset was its manpower—a defense force of approximately 300,000 men. The nation had a volunteer militia of another 100,000 men, and a women's auxiliary, 100,000 strong, known as the Lotta Svärd. Virtually all these men and women were physically fit. Most of them lived in rural areas, where the harsh climate bred self-reliance, resourcefulness and physical stamina. They were fond of skiing and were skilled at hunting. They were also well trained in military exercises: Since 1932 all 20-year-old males had been required to do 350 days' military service. Finns in general had a formidable tradition as fighting men; ever since the 18th Century, when they fought the Imperial Russia of Peter the Great, they had congratulated themselves that "one Finn is always worth 10 Russians." Finally, the Finns were well led; they looked to Field Marshal Gustaf Mannerheim, the brilliant and charismatic strategist who had quelled the civil war that erupted in the wake of Finnish independence in 1917, and who remained the cynosure of the nation's hopes.

With Mannerheim again inspiring them, the Finns mobilized soberly throughout October and November. Troops were strategically placed to husband the nation's strength. Nine small, independent units, none larger than a battalion, were stretched to cover the 625-mile eastern frontier from Petsamo south to the town of Ilomantsi—a zone that the Finnish general staff deemed least likely for the Soviet armies to tackle. Two divisions took position on a 60-mile line that ran from Ilomantsi south to the shore of Lake Ladoga, an area of broken forest and rolling hills that tanks and infantry could maneuver in. The largest concentration of Finnish troops—seven divisions of 14,200 men each—was posted on the Karelian Isthmus, while a 10th division began to form at Oulu on the Gulf of Bothnia.

The Karelian Isthmus seemed the likeliest place for a Rus-

As Premier Josef Stalin stands by with Finnish Communist Otto Kuusinen to his left, Soviet Foreign Minister Vyacheslav M. Molotov signs a treaty legitimizing the Soviet grab for Finnish territory in 1939. The treaty established a puppet government with Kuusinen as its figurehead.

sian assault, not only because Stalin had put it high on his list of demands, but because its geography made it inviting. The isthmus is only 70 miles across at its widest point and, except for some lakes and marshes that might obstruct the passage of tanks, is fairly level and open.

Long alert to its vulnerability, the Finns had fortified the isthmus as early as the 1920s, and as recently as the summer of 1939 more than 100,000 citizens had voluntarily used their vacations to improve and extend its defenses. The fortifications were known as the Mannerheim Line, for the national hero who had helped to conceive them, and it was there the Finns knew they would have to make their stand.

The Mannerheim Line was based on a military concept of static defense held over from World War I. It consisted of an 88-mile-long string of 66 strong points, each consisting of two or more concrete pillboxes or bunkers sited to block every road and stretch of open ground. Where possible, the strong points were concealed in woods and outcroppings. The best of them had three machine guns, two or three rifle squads and a team that directed artillery fire. The strong points were linked by a continuous trench system intended to give cover for troops, and the main line was screened by a picket line of dirt-and-timber emplacements that lay between it and the Russian frontier. Minefields and rows of boulders lay along all of the routes that incoming tanks might be likely to take.

Yet the Mannerheim Line was outmoded and weak. At least half the strong points were more than 10 years old and could not be expected to stand up to a direct artillery hit. Its greatest virtue was the sense of security it gave the Finns.

The Russians watched as the Finnish defense preparations went forward—and soon trumped up a pretext for moving against them. On November 26, Molotov sent a note to the Finnish Ambassador to the Soviet Union, accusing the Finns of shelling the village of Mainila, about 20 miles northwest of Leningrad, and asserting that four Russians had been killed and nine wounded. Molotov then suggested that Finnish troops on the isthmus be pulled back 12 to 16 miles "to preclude a repetition of provocative acts."

In fact, the Finns had been carrying out training maneuvers on the isthmus, but they had deliberately held their artillery out of range of the frontier to avoid any incidents. Now, trying to keep the peace, they agreed to withdraw their troops from the isthmus area, provided the Soviets would withdraw from their side of the border as well. The Finns also proposed that the incident be investigated by a joint committee, in accordance with the terms of a border agreement the two countries had signed in 1928.

Molotov rejected both offers on November 28, accusing the Finnish government of harboring "deep hostility" and declaring that the border agreement was no longer valid. The Finns then offered to withdraw most of their forces on the isthmus unilaterally and said they would be willing to open negotiations on Stalin's earlier demands.

The offer fell on deaf ears. Stalin and his military advisers had made the decision to fight. "We thought that all we had to do was raise our voice a little bit," recalled a rising commissar by the name of Nikita S. Khrushchev. "If that didn't work, we would fire one shot and the Finns would put up their hands."

The Soviets were in for a rude surprise. The Finns would

A French-built MS 406 fighter—one of 191 aircraft given or sold to Finland by France, Britain, Sweden and the United States during the winter of 1939-1940—taxis along the primitive surface of a Finnish airfield. The swastika on the fuselage, the emblem of the Finnish Air Force, was a good-luck symbol chosen by a Swedish nobleman who in 1918 had given Finland one of its first planes.

fight—and with the same tenacity that they had shown at the conference table. Mustering every resource at their command—men, women, their meager matériel, their native ingenuity—the Finns would do battle with the colossal Red Army on its own terms through freezing cold and snow, conditions that ultimately gave the struggle its name: the Winter War.

By the end of November the Soviets had moved into position to attack. The Seventh Army's 10 infantry divisions and six tank brigades (240,000 men, 1,500 tanks and 900 guns, supported by 300 planes) under General Kirill A. Meretskov stood ready to plunge headlong toward the Finnish fortifications on the Karelian Isthmus to take Viipuri, Finland's second-largest city, and cut the railway to Sortavala, an im-

portant junction on the north shore of Lake Ladoga. This move was intended to split Finnish forces and enable the Soviets to head toward Helsinki, the capital.

The Soviet Eighth Army's seven infantry divisions and one tank brigade (150,000 men, 545 tanks, 520 guns and 200 planes) advanced westward around Lake Ladoga, where they were to link up with the Seventh Army. Farther north, the Ninth Army with five infantry divisions (95,000 men, 275 tanks and 360 guns) drove for the Swedish frontier at the head of the Gulf of Bothnia, intending to cut Finland's land communications with Sweden. In the Arctic the Fourteenth Army's three infantry divisions (55,000 men, 165 tanks and 220 guns) were to take the Petsamo region and move down the Arctic Highway, a 300-mile-long road (and the only one) that ran from Petsamo to Rovaniemi. From

Wielding pickaxes and shovels, Finnish civilians construct embankments along the Mannerheim Line in the summer of 1939. Citing the popular eagerness to volunteer for the backbreaking work, Mannerheim said of the Finnish people that "they had an earlier and stronger premonition than government or parliament" of the danger that was rapidly approaching.

Rovaniemi the Fourteenth Army was to turn westward to the Swedish border. Some 170 aircraft supported the Ninth and Fourteenth Armies.

At 7 a.m. on November 30, six hundred Russian guns opened fire without warning along the isthmus front. A half hour later, Soviet tanks and infantry moved forward. At 9:30 that morning, the Soviets bombed a number of cities, including Helsinki and Viipuri.

Although the Finns were fully expecting a Soviet invasion, the weight and scope of the one that came, according to Marshal Mannerheim, commander in chief of Finland's armed forces, "exceeded our worst apprehensions." Mannerheim had intended that the units holding the Finnish outposts in front of the Mannerheim Line would fight a delaying action, inflicting the heaviest possible casualties on the enemy before withdrawing. But all along the frontier his screening forces were overwhelmed by the Red Army's massed assaults. Many of the troops panicked and fled at their first sight of tanks; others bravely but vainly stood fast with their antitank guns, only to be overrun. By nightfall, the Soviets had penetrated as deep as five miles into Finnish territory and seemed unstoppable.

The following morning, as if to add insult to the casualties his armies were inflicting, Stalin announced that he had concluded a treaty of friendship, assistance and cooperation with what he called the "Democratic People's Republic of Finland," headed by Otto Kuusinen, leader of the Moscow-based Finnish exiles.

The news of the invasion sent shudders through the Western world—and prompted some efforts to restore the peace. The United States and Sweden sent word through diplomatic channels that they would be willing to mediate Stalin's dispute with Finland. Stalin rebuffed their offers, alleging that he was not at war with Finland but simply responding to a request from a legitimate Finnish government for assistance. The would-be negotiators had no rejoinder. Meanwhile the Soviet juggernaut rolled on.

As the enemy tanks came at them, the Finns were forced to retreat more rapidly than they had planned. Still, they managed to cause the Soviets some trouble. In some places they burned all buildings that might shelter the invaders; in others they set booby traps. Watches, wallets, radios, bicycles, suitcases and record players—anything that might appeal to the peasant soldiers of the Red Army—were rigged to explode at the lightest touch. The booby traps were more ingenious than lethal; they did not kill great numbers of unsuspecting soldiers, but they did serve to harass the Russian advance.

Then, inexplicably, on December 6, the isthmus front fell strangely quiet as the Russian commander Meretskov pulled up just short of the Mannerheim Line. Meretskov would later blame the Finnish booby traps for his army's sudden standstill, claiming that his men were afraid to advance. It is more probable that after a seven-day march he had to pause to regroup his troops and bring up his heavy artillery. Whatever the reason, the halt was to last for 10 days. For the Finns the lull was heaven-sent; it gave them time to regroup themselves.

Their countrymen defending other sites had no such respite. Along the northern shoreline of Lake Ladoga, the Soviet Eighth Army had crossed the border and was advancing westward toward the railhead at Sortavala and the towns of Tolvajärvi and Ilomantsi to the north. To the right of the Eighth Army, the Ninth Army was advancing westward from the border in three columns toward the largest population centers in its path. The southern column, the 54th Division, was headed toward the town of Kuhmo; the center column, the 163rd and 44th Divisions, drove for Suomussalmi, a village located on the junction of two roads that ran from Finland to the Soviet border; the northernmost column, the 122nd Division, moved toward the town of Salla. In the far north, the Soviets' Fourteenth Army easily wrested the Petsamo area from its defenders—one company of infantry and four antique fieldpieces, which were normally used only to fire ceremonial salutes.

The Finns seemed to be everywhere in retreat; not only were their military forces yielding to the Soviet thrust, but thousands of civilians were fleeing down narrow, snow-clogged frontier roads with whatever belongings they could snatch up. The Soviet leaders, confident that the fighting would be over in a few days, went so far as to admonish their field commanders not to cross the Swedish border when their forces reached it.

But Mannerheim was of no mind to quit, and at this critical moment he got help from an unexpected, if typically

Finnish, source. Paavo Talvela was an industrialist, a director of the Finnish Cellulose Association and a member of the government's Arms Procurement Commission. He was also a colonel in the reserve, and had watched with dismay the beating the Finns had taken during the past few days. Talvela prevailed upon his friend General Rudolf Waldén, who functioned as Mannerheim's alter ego in the Finnish cabinet, to get him an appointment with the marshal. Waldén obliged, and the three men met in a Helsinki hotel room. Talvela paced back and forth, thundering that "the Finnish Army is running away." He warned Mannerheim that the Soviets must be stopped on the eastern frontier, north of Lake Ladoga, lest they break through and launch an attack on the Mannerheim Line from the rear.

Throughout the diatribe, General Waldén looked on with astonishment; no one ever talked to the imperious Mannerheim that way, and he trembled to think of the consequences. He was even more astonished when Mannerheim suffered the harangue with perfect calm—and then acceded to Talvela's request for a command. He gave the reserve colonel a makeshift force of a regiment and three battalions and sent them to the town of Tolvajärvi, on the western shore of the lake by the same name. There Talvela made camp, barely a mile from Kotissari Island, where the enemy's advance guard stood.

When Talvela took them over, the Finnish forces in the area had been retreating westward for nearly a week under constant fire. They were mentally and physically exhausted. Nevertheless, Talvela was determined to make a stand.

"To improve the spirits of the men and get control of the situation," as he put it, he ordered a raid shortly before midnight on December 8. Slipping across the frozen lake, his men caught the Russians half-asleep and completely off guard. The Finns opened up with their rifles and Suomi submachine guns, fired a few bursts and disappeared into the woods. The bewildered Russians fired wildly, hitting only thin air. The next morning, the Finns returned to the safety of their camp at Tolvajärvi, exhausted but exhilarated. Talvela had his morale builder, and the Soviets had had their first taste of the hit-and-run style of fighting that the Finns would refine into a deadly art.

Having once introduced the tactic, the Finns repeated it again and again. They attacked by day and by night, denying the Russians rest. Almost invisible in the woods in white winter camouflage gear and ghost-silent on skis, the Finns hit and vanished. Expert skiers and woodsmen all, they hunted the Russians as they had once hunted game, and with such unfailing marksmanship that some Russians began to call them *Belaya Smert*—the White Death. "They were able to get their man at distances of 800 to 1,000 yards," one Red Army officer remembered. "They fired but rarely, and never missed." Because silence was so vital, the Finnish soldier sometimes carried no firearm at all, only a *puukko* knife—the traditional Finnish huntsman's tool with a deadly four-inch blade.

One Finnish sharpshooter was able to knock out a Soviet machine-gun nest by shooting through a narrow slit in the gun's armored shield. "There was an opening in the shield about one half inch high and two and one half inches wide for aiming," an admiring fellow soldier recounted. "I could hardly see it, but obviously the man with the gun saw it better. We heard a shot and the Russian's helmet rolled on the ground."

The Finns did not confine their harassment to machine-gun nests, but went after field kitchens and supply trucks—a practice that deprived the Russians of warm food. According to one tale, a canny Finn had some dangerous sport at the expense of a Soviet commissary; he donned a Russian uniform and took hot meals from a Soviet field kitchen back to his comrades for more than two weeks without being caught. Similarly, a group of Finnish soldiers used Red Army uniforms and signal flags to impersonate traffic controllers. After they had sent one particularly large supply convoy into their own lines, unknowing Soviet officers on the scene actually thanked the Finns for relieving a traffic jam.

In addition to their desperate ingenuity, the Finns had inhospitable weather and rugged terrain in their favor. The Russians found the border areas, where much of the heaviest fighting of the Winter War would take place, a bewildering maze of woods and frozen lands and swamps, buried under snow and whipped by blizzards. "The Finnish woods are altogether unlike our Ukraine," wrote one homesick soldier. "The stars wink—frigid, still. The snow falls silently, straight in the eye. The firing of the guns sounds like a long, drawn-out echo from afar, as if from a tube." Though the

In a Helsinki street, Christmas shoppers caught by an air-raid alert dash for shelter. Such raids, beginning abruptly in late 1939, induced the Finns to improvise for protection; the Cabinet moved its regular meetings from the vulnerable Parliament building to a vault in the Bank of Finland.

Russians could easily move troops and supplies up to the frontier via the Murmansk railroad, which ran from Leningrad to Murmansk on the Barents Sea, most of the roads leading from the Soviet Union into Finland were nothing but single-lane tracks. Trucks stalled in snowdrifts. Tanks skidded on icy curves and plunged into gullies. Not even the infantrymen could make much headway on the tracks, for not enough of them had been supplied with skis, and fewer still knew how to ski.

The terrain enabled the Finns to perfect another deadly tactic, one of carving a large enemy force into bite-sized chunks. They would pin down an advancing column from a favorable spot such as a slight hill behind a frozen lake that gave their machine gunners a good field of fire. Barbed wire laid in the snow between tree stumps would block the Russian infantry; camouflaged holes in the lake ice would entrap their tanks. While the Russians struggled to extricate themselves, a Finnish force would take the enemy column flank and rear, breaking in between its units, cutting it off from its base, penning the Russians into constantly shrinking pockets. The Finns called each pocket with men thus entrapped a *motti*, after their name for a stack of wood ready to be chopped into kindling. Soviet troops caught in a *motti* were usually doomed, though they scrabbled trenches in the frozen ground with amazing speed and used their tanks as pillboxes. They fought desperately for as long as they could. But cold and hunger killed them as surely as bullets.

Using the *motti* tactic with deadly effect, Colonel Talvela moved out from Tolvajärvi on December 12 and quickly entrapped the 139th Infantry Division. The Soviets sent the 75th Division to the aid of the 139th; Talvela dealt it the same blow. By December 23, he had driven the survivors of the two divisions all the way to the Aittojoki River, 15 miles east of Tolvajärvi, where they established a defensive position. The Soviets listed 4,000 men dead; an even greater number were wounded and countless others were missing along the snow-covered flanks of the Tolvajärvi-Aittojoki road. The Finns' losses were slight by comparison: 630 dead, 1,320 wounded.

Meanwhile, the Russian 163rd Division had taken the junction village of Suomussalmi on December 7. Regrouping, the Finns launched a series of counterattacks near the village that would inflict on the Soviets their most stunning comeuppance of the Winter War.

While the Soviets were digging in at Suomussalmi, elements of the Finnish 9th Division, under Colonel Hjalmar Siilasvuo, cut the road behind them, surrounded their positions and held them in place until Finnish reinforcements could arrive. By Christmas Day, Colonel Siilasvuo had five new battalions as well as two modern antitank guns and eight 76.2mm guns. The latter were vintage 1902, but they were better than nothing.

The Soviet command had long since dispatched relief for the beleaguered 163rd—the 44th Motorized Division under General A. I. Vinogradov. But Vinogradov was incompetent; not only did he arrive late on the scene, but at the

mere sight of sniping Finnish ski troops he froze. Believing that he was under attack by superior forces, Vinogradov ordered his men to dig in all along the road, four to five miles east of the division he was supposed to relieve.

On Christmas Eve, the 163rd attempted to break out—without success. Already frostbitten, the Russian soldiers floundered through chest-high snow and a relentless rain of snipers' bullets that drove them back into their freezing holes, where they either perished or were flushed out by the Finns. "With hand grenades, pistols and bayonets, we forced our way through the enemy positions," Siilasvuo later recalled. "Not even their tanks frightened our boys, although they had no weapons to use against them." By December 28, the 163rd Division had ceased to exist. The Finns then hunted down the stragglers, taking 500 prisoners and, more important, capturing 11 tanks.

Now the Finns could turn their attention to the bungling 44th Motorized Division, cold and hungry but still a formidable fighting force of 18,000 men and 40 or more tanks.

While Finnish scouts probed the 44th's defenses, Finnish engineers plowed open a "snow road" along a parallel chain of small lakes five miles to the south of the Soviet positions. All along the road they set up assembly areas where heated shelters and hot food were available. From these places, trails led forward to concealed attack positions near weak points in the 44th's defenses. Warm and well-fed, the Finns were able to beat back the enemy almost everywhere he attempted to break out.

By January 8, the battle was all but over: A total of 27,500 Russians had fallen to Finnish bullets or Finnish weather; another 1,300 had been taken prisoner. The Allied world cheered the Finnish Davids for routing the Russian Goliath; American newspapers ran daily accounts with headlines exclaiming "Finns Smash a Red Division" and "Finns Smash a New Division." Stalin raged against his generals, scoring them for incompetency, and inevitably heads rolled. The hapless General Vinogradov, who had managed to escape, was the first to feel Stalin's wrath. He was executed, ostensibly for "the loss of 55 field kitchens to the enemy"—but actually because of the tactical bungling that had cost the Soviets so dearly.

As the Finns were picking apart the invaders at Suomus-salmi, the rest of the Soviet Ninth Army was faring little better. Advancing westward from the town of Salla, which it had captured in mid-December, a regiment of the 122nd Infantry Division was caught in a swirl of Finnish ski detachments that routed and harried them back toward Salla. The 88th Division, which had come to the 122nd's support in early December, had retreated into the same pocket; both divisions would remain there throughout the Winter War.

The Finnish high command made Colonel Siilasvuo a brigadier general for his role in the Suomussalmi victory. He promptly turned his attention to the Soviet 54th Infantry Division, swooping down upon it near Kuhmo. Again the Russians dug in along a road. The pinned-down troops had to be resupplied by airdrops. The Finns had too few antiaircraft guns to prevent the Red Air Force from parachuting food, ammunition and fuel to their comrades. The best they could do was force the Russians to fly at night. Then Finnish cunning came into play: Learning to recognize the sound of Soviet supply planes, the Finns took to firing signal flares to lure the planes off course—and bring the airdrops into their own zones.

To rescue the 54th Division, the Soviets decided to challenge the Finns at their own game and send in a brigade made up of skiers. But the high command made some fatal mistakes. It failed to supply the brigade with white camouflage uniforms. And it neglected to train the men to maintain their weapons properly against the frost; clogged with frozen oil, the weapons often could not be fired. A few of the skiers managed to ambush a Finnish column—but then their whole brigade was scattered and annihilated like the tank and infantry divisions that had preceded them. The demise of the rescue brigade allowed General Siilasvuo to break the 54th itself into several *mottis*. He devoted the rest of the winter to whittling the division down into eversmaller pieces.

Near Sortavala, two divisions of the Soviet Eighth Army would wind up sharing the fate of their Ninth Army comrades. The 18th and 168th Divisions were shoving four Finnish battalions around when a heavy snowfall gave the nimble Finns an opportunity to retaliate. Screened by a blinding curtain of white, the Finns slipped silently through the woods, and surrounded and annihilated the 18th Division and a supporting tank brigade. They then were able to surround the 168th and reduce it to a remnant of starving tatterdemalions.

Meanwhile, the Soviet Fourteenth Army, which had occupied Finland's Arctic coastline, had begun moving down the Arctic Highway, with orders to take Rovaniemi, 300 miles to the south. By the middle of the month, however, a Finnish battalion had once more exploited the rough terrain and harsh winter to establish a defensive line at the town of Höyhenjärvi, only 50 miles down the road.

While his fellow commanders to the north were learning firsthand of the Finns' tenacity and ingenuity, General Meretskov was planning to renew his stalled drive against the Mannerheim Line. He planned to feint a major drive along the eastern end of the line to draw off the Finnish reserves, then attack at the western end at a 10-mile gap between the Summojoki River and Lake Moulaanjärvi. The area, which lay in the province of Viipuri, was referred to by the Finns as the "Viipuri Gateway" because from the beginning of history unwelcome invaders had driven through it into the heart of Finland.

Meretskov opened his main assault on the Mannerheim Line on December 17. For four thunderous days, wave after wave of Soviet infantry and tanks drove against its western half, trying to break through to the Viipuri road. The infantry came on in close formation, the traditional Russian style, stepping over the dead, apparently indifferent to exploding land mines and the Finns' deadly enfilade. Cooperation between the different Soviet military arms was so totally lacking that Mannerheim likened the attack to a performance by a "badly conducted orchestra in which the instruments were played out of time."

Here, as elsewhere, the Finns, although outnumbered about 4 to 1, defeated the Russians by canny tactics and sheer desperate courage. Whenever Soviet tanks managed to break into the Finnish lines, they met "tank destroyers"—single Finnish soldiers or two-man teams who used 6- to 13-pound charges of high explosives or Molotov cocktails against them. When explosives were not available, the Finns jammed heavy logs between the tracks and wheels of a tank to stop it. One soldier, a Captain Kuiri, was credited with immobilizing four tanks in that manner. One way or another, the Finns knocked out 239 tanks across the isthmus front and captured a dozen more in serviceable condition.

By December 20, Meretskov was ready to give up his offensive. He began pulling his troops back under cover of a heavy air and artillery bombardment. Except for minor skirmishing and artillery fire, the isthmus front would remain quiet for a month while the Soviets reorganized and pondered their next move.

In the Kremlin, Stalin was furious. To be sure, no one had expected the Finns to put up such a determined fight. But by Stalin's lights that did not excuse the disgraceful performance of the Red Army. Clearly he would have to order a major reorganization of the Soviet armed forces. But first, he cast about for a scapegoat. He found one in Marshal Kliment E. Voroshilov, an old drinking companion and now his Commissar of Defense. In early January, Stalin summoned the hapless Voroshilov to his *dacha* outside Moscow, along with a coterie of Soviet officials that included the ubiquitous Molotov; General Meretskov, brought back to Moscow from the front; General Nikolai N. Voronov, the Red Army's foremost artillery expert; and General Semyon K. Timoshenko, commander of the Kiev Military District, who was accompanied by his political commissar, Nikita Khrushchev.

The occasion was an extraordinary one in this already extraordinary winter. During dinner, Stalin suddenly jumped up and began shouting at Voroshilov. His ineptness as a commander, said Stalin, was largely responsible for Soviet losses against Finland. To the astonishment of all those present, Voroshilov answered the accusation with bitter recrimination, angrily retorting that the setbacks were due to mistakes committed earlier by Stalin himself. "You have only yourself to blame for this," he shouted, his face turning beet-red. "You're the one who annihilated the Old Guard of the Army; you had our best generals killed"—a reckless reference to purges Stalin had ordered in 1937 to rid the Red Army of the last vestiges of opposition to his rule. Voroshilov then picked up a platter with a roast suckling pig on it and smashed it on the dinner table.

"It was the only time in my life I ever witnessed such an outburst," recalled Khrushchev, with monumental understatement. Perhaps as unexpected as the ferocity of the outburst was the tameness of Stalin's reaction. He relieved Voroshilov of his command—but instead of having him killed, he inexplicably kept his old comrade around as an adviser to the Soviet high command. Voroshilov somehow managed to avoid Stalin's displeasure thereafter; he would die peacefully at the age of 89—30 years after he had dared the dictator's wrath.

As his new commander in Finland, Stalin named Timoshenko, who had commanded the Red Army's sweep into eastern Poland the previous September. Timoshenko also was to head a new Soviet military council; its objective was to breach the Mannerheim Line before the spring thaw, when Finland would be transformed from a frozen highway into an impassable morass.

Timoshenko had no quarrel with Meretskov's basic plan of attack. But he was determined that this time his men would be better prepared to wage a winter war. To make certain that victory did not elude them again, he beefed up the Soviet forces along the Mannerheim Line and to the north of Lake Ladoga. The Soviets had initially attacked Finland with 540,000 men; now Timoshenko would have 900,000 troops at his call.

Behind their lines, Russian soldiers went through intensive training in assault tactics. Timoshenko had Finnish fortifications reproduced behind his lines so the spearhead 123rd Division and 35th Tank Brigade could rehearse their attacks in conditions approximating those they would encounter in Finland. Tank crews were taught to wait for infantry support instead of rushing into a fray with their flanks exposed. Tank crews also had defenses against Finnish antitank tactics drummed into them; they learned to cover one another against the wily Finnish "tank destroyers" as well as against more conventional antitank guns. Armored sleds, which could be pulled or pushed by tanks, were manufactured to carry infantry squads into battle. Sappers were equipped with ski-mounted shields to protect them while they demolished antitank traps. Enough ammunition and supplies to support 500,000 troops were stockpiled on the isthmus. New roads leading up to the Mannerheim Line were created by plowing snow onto impassable terrain, then pumping water over the snow. The water froze in a matter of minutes, producing icy highways that could support heavy tank and truck traffic.

To soften up the Finns for the impending attack, Timoshenko ordered the 2,800 artillery pieces on the isthmus to increase their fire. Heavy guns were brought up to within a few hundred yards of Finnish strong points and sited to fire directly into Finnish gun embrasures. Soviet observation balloons directed fire on the roads and trails immediately behind the Mannerheim Line. The artillery bombardment was supplemented by intimidating air attacks: During January of 1940, the Soviets mounted 4,000 bomber sorties and nearly 3,500 strafing runs.

The bombing was generally inaccurate, but its cumulative effect over several weeks left most of the area behind the Mannerheim Line in ruins. It also eroded the Finns' morale and deprived them of what little they had in the way of comforts. They could not heat their dugouts or tents by day because the least trace of smoke brought down artillery or strafing aircraft. With cooking fires also forbidden, they got only one hot meal a day, and that brought up after dark by horse-drawn sleds that carried away the day's casualties on the return trip.

On the 1st of February, the Russians began powerful tank-and-infantry probes across the Karelian Isthmus to further wear down the Finnish forces before launching their main offensive. These were well-planned operations with artillery support; Mannerheim said that although they "exceeded anything our troops had hitherto experienced, we were soon to learn that this was only a beginning."

At a town on the Gulf of Finland, Soviet engineers examine antitank obstacles along the Mannerheim Line. The Soviets exaggerated the size and strength of the fortifications in an attempt to explain to Russian citizens why it took their forces so long to break through.

The attacks were methodically executed: Under cover of artillery and aerial bombardment, Soviet engineers blew away some of the boulders and concrete structures that served as Finnish antitank obstacles; Russian fire was concentrated on the gaps that were created; columns of heavy tanks then burst through, followed by flame-throwing tanks. Masses of infantry surged forward while as many as 200 aircraft strafed Finnish communications and artillery positions. No sooner was one attack beaten back than another was launched with fresh troops. It was now obvious, Mannerheim conceded, that "the Russians had learned to orchestrate cooperation between the different arms."

The effect on the Finns was devastating. Many of their concrete bunkers were blown open and had to be abandoned. Their artillery, so far the mainstay of their defense, had used up almost all of its ammunition. This meant the Finns could neither counter Russian artillery fire nor shell areas where the Russian reserves were waiting; only direct infantry-tank assaults merited firing the precious shells. The Finnish soldiers became so tired that it was not uncommon to see a man fall asleep in the middle of a fire fight. Finnish casualties mounted so fast that it became a challenge just to keep the front lines manned.

Russian losses ran into the thousands, by one reckoning. But the Russians had an unending supply of replacements. "In a couple of days," said one disbelieving Finn, "we captured prisoners belonging to 20 replacement detachments."

On February 10, fresh Soviet units moved into position for Timoshenko's major offensive. As in December, the main attack would be on the western side of the isthmus, with secondary attacks up the center and along the shore of Lake Ladoga. The well-rehearsed 123rd Infantry Division and 35th Tank Brigade were ready to strike at Summa, at the center of the Finnish defenses—specifically, five bunkers located between Lake Summa and an iced-over swamp near the main road to Viipuri.

At 8 a.m. on February 11, the Russian artillery opened up. For every mile of its front, the Seventh Army averaged 80 guns, some of them firing monstrous 11-inch shells. For more than two hours the bombardment thundered. The Finns' earth-and-timber field fortifications were crushed like matchsticks; concrete bunkers were wrecked. Immediately behind the barrage, Russian infantry and tanks attacked.

Facing the Soviets' spearhead division was the 2nd Battalion of the Finnish 9th Infantry Regiment. Although ravaged by weeks of enemy bombardment, the 2nd Battalion held, strewing its position with Russian dead until the late afternoon. Then, its heavy weapons knocked out and half of its 650 men casualties, the battalion fell back 1,000 yards.

Over the next two and a half weeks, the Soviets repeatedly made short, powerful assaults, wedging deeper and deeper into the Finnish defenses. From time to time the Finns counterattacked successfully and regained some ground, but they could not hold it against the massed armor the Soviets were hurling at them. Gradually, grudgingly, the battered Finns retreated.

By now the Finnish infantry—which started the war with 150,000 men—had suffered perhaps as many as 50,000 casualties. Desperately, the Army conscripted men previously rejected because of age or mental or physical disability; it recalled wounded men from convalescence, and formed combat units from teen-age schoolboy volunteers. These green troops were often more hindrance than help. One raw antitank crew that was thrown into action straggled back to report that when they reached the front lines, they found they did not know how to sight their weapons. Before they could fire, Russian tanks had overrun their position and wiped out half the company.

The Russians made their own blunders. As the Finns fell back toward Viipuri, General Meretskov loosed his cavalry in pursuit, but this proved to be an instant and literal flop: The cavalry commander had neglected to have his horses roughshod for winter service, and the unfortunate creatures slipped and fell on the icy roads.

Meanwhile, another threat was developing: The Russians had begun to move across the ice of the frozen Gulf of Finland in an attempt to outflank the Mannerheim Line and attack Viipuri from the west. Expecting such a move, the Finns had fortified several of the islands in the gulf, but by now the Russians had perfected a system of attack. In the gulf and on Lake Ladoga—where the Finns also had several island outposts—the Soviets bombarded each island heavily, then ringed it with tanks that supported an infantry assault.

"We could not stop the enemy," said one Finnish soldier trapped on an island strong point. "It was impossible to operate logically; it was each and every man for himself.''

Many of the Finns told tales of harrowing escapes across the ice. One, Sergeant Heikki Savolainen, stayed at his post until the barrel of his machine gun turned red-hot and bent from prolonged use. Then, with two fingers of one hand shot away by a Russian sharpshooter, he fled. ''I found a pair of skis and started skiing north,'' he recalled. ''It was hard to hold onto the ski pole with just three fingers, but I felt no pain. There was only one thought on my mind—to get out of this alive.''

By March 5 the Seventh Army had swept aside the island strong points and gained a foothold on the north shore of Viipuri Bay, enabling it to cut the important coastal road west of the city. East of Viipuri, Finnish engineers had opened up a sluice canal to impede the enemy. But Russian infantrymen waded through the three-foot-deep water in sub-zero weather to push home the attack. South of the city, the Finns checked one drive by setting a suburb on fire. It was a tactic of last resort, and it served only to forestall the inevitable.

Mannerheim's army still had the will for successful local counterattacks, but its artillery ammunition was almost exhausted and every available man was already in action. The spring thaw, due in two or three weeks, would halt the fighting, but meanwhile—as Talvela, who had been promoted to brigadier general after his victory at Tolvajärvi, put it—''everything is hanging by a thread.'' If any part of the Finnish defenses gave way, the Soviets could unravel the entire

From the deck of the Swedish liner Gripsholm, Finnish-Americans wave an enthusiastic farewell as they leave New York Harbor for Finland on December 12, 1939. They were the first of 300 Americans to join some 11,500 volunteer fighters who rushed from all over Europe— Sweden, Norway, Denmark and Hungary, among other nations — to enlist in the cause of Finland in its struggle against the Soviet Union.

Army with ease. Mannerheim knew the game was up. "The last minutes are at hand," he told officials in Helsinki. Finland had already lost 25,000 killed and more than 43,000 wounded—roughly one Finn of every four who fought. And Mannerheim felt compelled to recommend that his country try to end the war by negotiation. On March 6, 1940, the Finns sent a delegation to Moscow to sue for peace.

The Soviet Union also was eager to end the fighting. Finland had become a costly nuisance. The campaign had cost the Soviets at least 200,000 dead and 300,000 wounded, and possibly double those numbers; estimates varied widely, and the Soviets released no official figures. In any case, the campaign had delivered a shattering blow to Soviet military prestige. Moreover, the British and the French had promised to send the Finns planes, arms and munitions, and they were talking of sending men as well. Stalin did not want to face a war with the Western Allies. He junked the puppet government he had installed under Otto Kuusinen and sent Molotov to the negotiating table.

Disavowing the Finnish Communists was probably the Soviets' most generous concession. They demanded—and got—12 per cent of Finland's territory: most of the province of Viipuri, with the vital cities of Viipuri and Sortavala; the heights of Salla on the eastern frontier, which would give the Soviets an excellent outpost from which to monitor any moves against the Murmansk railroad, 90 miles away; the Finnish portion of the Rybachi Peninsula; Sursaari and its neighboring islands, which could be used to defend Leningrad, or to launch raids into the western Baltic; and a 30-year lease on the peninsula of Hango and its vital port, where the Russians intended to build a naval base. These were considerably stiffer terms than Stalin had offered in October. At that time he had demanded less territory and had been prepared to soften the Finns' losses by giving them part of East Karelia. Not the least of the hardships imposed by the treaty was the fact that 200,000 Finns living in the ceded territory would have to resettle within 12 days or be absorbed into the Soviet system; 200,000 or more Finns had already been uprooted in the three months since the beginning of the war.

The Soviets said they would evacuate the Petsamo region in the north, but demanded the right to open a consulate there and to transport goods through Petsamo to and from Norway free of all inspections and fees. The Finns were forbidden to station either armed aircraft or warships, save for small patrol craft, at Petsamo. Coupled with the cession of the Rybachi Peninsula, this clause gave the Soviets the leverage over Finland they had been seeking all along.

One final provision was especially jarring to the Finns. They were required to begin immediately constructing a rail line from Kemijärvi—then the eastern terminus of a line that ran from the Gulf of Bothnia—to Salla, where it would connect with a line the Soviets were building from the Murmansk railroad. When completed, the Soviets were to have free access to the new line, which neatly bisected Finland from east to west.

Strangely, there was one issue that the Russians did not press: Finnish defense—the right to maintain an army, keep weapons and build fortifications. With woeful lack of foresight, Molotov went so far as to declare that the U.S.S.R. was not afraid of anything Finland might do militarily. Yet virtually every other concession the Finns asked for was denied them. When Juho Paasikivi, once more negotiating for the Finns, requested monetary compensation for the lost territories, Molotov maliciously hinted in reply that Stalin could always resurrect the Kuusinen government and negotiate with it. Paasikivi persisted, citing the precedent of Peter the Great, who had paid substantial compensation when similarly negotiating for territory in 1721. "Fine," retorted Molotov, with stinging sarcasm. "Write a letter to Peter the Great. If he orders it, then we will pay compensation."

There was no use in arguing further. Reluctantly, the Finnish delegation sent a telegram to Helsinki asking authority to settle on the Soviets' terms. The government agreed—but grudgingly. "May the hand wither that is forced to sign such a paper as this," said Finnish President Kyösti Kallio bitterly as he put his signature to it. (The statement was tragically prophetic. Kallio suffered a paralytic stroke and was dead within the year.)

On March 13 at 11 a.m. the Winter War ended. The land of 60,000 lakes fell quiet, but it was an elusive quiet that would be broken in 15 months' time. During that uneasy respite, it would be the turn of Finland's Scandinavian neighbors to feel the effect of designs on their lands by two other great powers, Germany and Great Britain.

SPOILS FOR GHOST SOLDIERS

AFTERMATH OF A "MIRACLE" IN THE SNOW

The Finns regarded their victory in the Battle of Suomussalmi as a miracle. With scarcely a third of the enemy's strength, they counted 30 times as many Russian dead as they had lost themselves. Seldom in modern times had a battle resulted in such one-sided annihilation. "But this is war," wrote one Finn with prophetic detachment; "It could have been us."

As they gathered up the booty left behind by the invaders (almost the entire equipage of two Soviet divisions), even the soberest of the Finns had reason to smile at examples of Russian naïveté. They found Russian-made skis and thousands of packaged copies of a *Manual of Ski-Fighting*, a 277-page book that gave step-by-step instructions on such techniques as how to throw a grenade while wearing skis, how to stab with the bayonet while wearing skis, and how to ski across country while lugging a machine gun mounted on a pair of runners. "You don't beat an enemy by thinking up clever ideas like that," scoffed one Finn.

In grim fact, the manual's instructions reflected one of the underlying causes of the Russian debacle. The Soviet soldiers were predominantly from the Russian steppes, and hopelessly out of their element in the hilly forests of Finland. Not only were the Finns fighting on home ground, where skiing was so much a way of life that no instruction seemed called for; they also knew instinctively that the very slipperiness that made skis useful for mobility rendered them a hazard in close combat. The Finnish troops took off their skis before fighting.

The neutral world received the news of Suomussalmi with somber curiosity. The New York *Herald Tribune* in February 1940 published a photographer's record of the battle's aftermath with a description that read in part: "Those frozen, uplifted hands, those stiff-crooked knees, those lifeless faces, with snow sifting gently over them, and behind them the machines, the tanks and big guns, monstrous, horrible and stranded—these are the portraits of the dead." A selection of those photographs appears here and on the following pages.

Finnish Colonel Hjalmar Siilasvuo pauses near Suomussalmi, which he and 11,500 of his countrymen held against more than 30,000 Russians.

Finnish soldiers collect Russian dead for burial. Many more corpses lay hidden beneath drifts of snow and were not discovered until the spring melt

Mopping up after the Battle of Suomussalmi, three warmly clad Finnish soldiers stack up captured Russian skis. The Finns considered the skis to be of such inferior quality that they used them only as firewood.

Seated beneath captured Soviet banners emblazoned with portraits of Stalin, a group of Finnish officers chuckle over copies of the Russian Manual of Ski-Fighting. Said one Finn derisively: ''If you see a man walking along the road with a pair of skis on his back, that is a Russian.''

Finns inspect a four-barreled Soviet antiaircraft machine gun mounted on a truck. "I wish the Russians had brought more machine guns," one Finnish officer sardonically observed. "We could do with a few more."

Frozen stiff, a Russian battle casualty lies in the snow beside his artillery tractor, one of 20 the Finns seized from the Soviet 44th Division.

PRISONERS TAKEN BY THE TRAINLOAD

Soviet captives stand by the freight cars that transported them from Suomussalmi to a Finnish prisoner-of-war camp. The Russians, unaccustomed to forest fighting, were more bewildered than bitter over their defeat. Explained one: "We couldn't see the Finns."

Aboard the spanking-new 13,000-ton German heavy cruiser *Blücher*, Rear Admiral Oskar Kummetz peered through the mist that shrouded the outlines of Oslo Fjord at 4:10 on the morning of April 9, 1940. At precisely the same moment, five other task forces of the German Navy were slipping through other entrances to Norway, carrying 8,850 soldiers up similar fjords to surprise and overwhelm the ports of Narvik, Trondheim, Bergen, Egersund and Kristiansand. To the south, a corps of the German Army was poised to invade Denmark by land, air and sea. Admiral Kummetz, leading 16 ships toward the Norwegian capital at Oslo, still 15 miles ahead, had the most crucial assignment of all: He was ordered to seize the government and force Norway into immediate surrender.

This German undertaking, after seven quiet months of ''phony war'' on the Western Front, was a gamble for high stakes against high odds—an ambitious assault along a 1,000-mile front that extended from Copenhagen in the south to Narvik, well above the Arctic Circle. If it succeeded, Germany stood to gain possession of Norway's ports and Denmark's airfields; both could serve as bases from which to attack Great Britain. If it failed, the German forces would be isolated from one another, and Britain—which, as German intelligence knew all too well, had its own designs on Norway—would be able to reap the harvest of Germany's hasty sowing.

Thus far, it seemed, Kummetz had been lucky; the fog that obscured his vision also concealed the progress of his flotilla. He had had only one accident, and that to all appearances a minor one. Just after 11 p.m., at the very entrance to Oslo Fjord, some 60 miles south of the capital, a small Norwegian patrol boat, the *Pol III,* had collided in the fog with one of the destroyers in Kummetz' force, doing considerable damage to the *Pol III.* Her captain tried to back off, but the German vessel fired on her and the captain, wounded in the blast, fell overboard and drowned. The rest of the crew took to lifeboats and made for shore. Other Norwegian patrol boats came to the aid of the *Pol III,* towed her back to port and radioed a report of the incident to Oslo. Kummetz, however, could not have known of the report—and if he had, it doubtless would have made no difference; the German fleet proceeded with all deliberate speed toward the sleeping Norwegian capital.

2

Hitler's high-stakes gamble on a 1,000-mile front
A neutral seaway that frustrated Churchill
An invasion cloaked in secrecy and deception
Britain's plan for securing Norway
Alarm signal from a lost destroyer
Fatal shots from Oslo's museum fortress
Bold ruses at Bergen and Trondheim
A fast-talking German general takes Narvik
Consolidating a costly foothold

THE GRAB FOR NORWAY

Now, five hours later, Kummetz turned his attention to the chart before him. On the island of Kaholmen, which bisected this part of the fjord, stood Oscarsborg Fortress, so old the chart listed it as a museum; facing it on one shore was a battery at Dröbak. The fortress' weapons were old, but by no means museum pieces: They were potent, Krupp-built 11-inch guns dating from 1900. Kummetz looked up again. No light showed from Oscarsborg to suggest that it had been awakened from a century of neutral sleep. Kummetz relaxed, and at 4:15 a.m. the *Blücher* eased toward the forts. The first phase of Germany's surprise assault on Scandinavia was only moments away.

The Germans themselves were in for a surprise, for they were to find themselves face to face with British ships before the day was done. Planning independently, both Great Britain and Germany had been racing to secure Norwegian ports and Norwegian resources. And quite by coincidence, they would arrive offshore almost simultaneously. The encounter was to bring Britain and Germany into their first major combat of World War II.

The Norwegians had no more interest in the Allied-Axis quarrel than had the Finns. They hoped to sit out the War as neutrals. But geography had earned their nation the unwelcome attention of the combatants. Norway's western coastline is a mountain wall, cracked by narrow, winding fjords, some stretching 100 miles inland. Offshore, from the vicinity of Stavanger at the southern tip of Norway to the North Cape, lies a 1,200-mile-long complex chain of islands, skerries and reefs. And between this rocky chain and the mainland is a sheltered, deep-water channel known to sailors as the Leads and claimed by Norway as territorial waters. So long as Norway remained neutral, merchant ships of all nations might pass freely through the Leads, safe from all hazards but the natural ones of rock and reef.

In 1940 the Leads not only channeled large quantities of Swedish iron ore to Germany, but allowed German surface raiders and submarines to break out into the Atlantic from any of a hundred unwatchable channels to prey on Britain's vital supply lines. To Winston Churchill, First Lord of the Admiralty, this was intolerable. He wanted to stop the movement of iron ore by laying minefields across the Leads and seizing ships thus forced into international waters—

even at the cost of committing an act of war against Norway and inviting Germany to invade Scandinavia. "We can certainly take and hold whatever islands or suitable points on the Norwegian coast we choose," he argued to the War Cabinet in December 1939. "Small nations must not tie our hands when we are fighting for their rights and freedom."

The British Cabinet firmly turned thumbs down on this audacious proposal, but then the international outcry at the Soviet Army's invasion of Finland gave Churchill an idea for a different tactic. An Allied expeditionary force, ostensibly on its way to rescue the Finns, would land at Narvik, the Norwegian transshipment port for Swedish ore. The expeditionary force would occupy the port, and would seize for Britain the railroad that led to the iron mines just across the border.

Churchill's disingenuous rescue proposal attracted only grudging interest from the Finnish government and none at all from the other Scandinavians, who had no desire to be overrun by British and French troops, much less the Germans. They would be sure to follow. Nevertheless, by March of 1940 Churchill had won the cooperation of the Allies. Norway and Sweden would be formally notified that in allowing Germany to use the Leads for the iron-ore traffic, they had forfeited their rights as neutrals. The British would then mine strategic areas of the Norwegian Leads without further ado. "The operation, being so small and innocent," Churchill decreed with tongue firmly in cheek, "may be called *Wilfred*"—the name of a popular children's comic strip featuring three animal characters, the youngest and most guileless of which was named Wilfred.

Wilfred's mischief was to be followed by another undertaking that not even Churchill could disguise as nonbelligerent: Plan *R4*, a hair-trigger operation to land six battalions of British troops to seize the ports of Bergen, Trondheim and Narvik, and destroy the airfield at Stavanger. It would be set in motion just as soon as "the Germans set foot on Norwegian soil, or there is clear evidence that they intend to do so," said the official proposal in words cannily couched to leave room for a loose interpretation. Narvik had priority, in Churchill's view, because depriving Germany of iron ore would starve its all-important steel industry—and hence its war effort—of its most vital raw material. Because he expected no more than token opposition from the Norwegian government, Churchill did not include the occupation of Oslo in his plans.

After many delays, Operation *Wilfred* was finally scheduled to begin on April 8; Plan *R4*, Churchill confidently expected, would be triggered almost immediately thereafter. The orders were that a few hours after the minefields had been laid across the Leads, one battalion of the 24th Guards Brigade would sail from the Navy base at Rosyth in the Firth of Forth, cross the North Sea and seize the port of Narvik. The rest of the brigade would follow, occupy the city and take possession of the ore railway to the Swedish frontier. Some supply and administrative units and French reinforcements would come next, and Narvik would be converted into an Allied naval base with a garrison of approximately 18,000 men.

Strangely, Allied intelligence had still not made the discovery that *Wilfred* was in a race with a German operation called *Weserübung*—"Weser Exercise," named after the river that runs by the German port of Bremerhaven and flows into the North Sea.

Like Churchill, Admiral Erich Raeder, Commander in Chief of the German Navy, had long had his eye on Norway, and for strategic reasons of his own. The Royal Navy had virtually penned his ships inside the Baltic by blocking the English Channel and patrolling the North Sea from the Shetland Islands north of Scotland to the Skagerrak at the foot of Norway. Germany's capital ships were too few to challenge the Royal Navy's blockade directly, and Germany could muster barely 30 U-boats to send out into the high seas. Lacking strength to meet the Royal Navy in open battle, Raeder was waging a hit-and-run campaign of attrition against British merchant shipping. In this, however, European geography put him in the awkward position of having to fight from the bottom of a sack. His raiders had to make a long, dangerous run to reach the Atlantic shipping lanes, and had used up much of their fuel and other supplies by the time they got there.

German possession of air and naval bases in Norway would force the northern end of the British blockade westward toward the line of the Shetlands, the Faeroe Islands and Iceland. Obtaining such bases, whether by force or diplomacy, posed the double risk of losing Norway's neutral

ore channel plus an almost certain clash with the vastly superior Royal Navy. But throughout the fall of 1939 and the early winter of 1940, as Churchill's appeals to the Cabinet made it increasingly evident that the British were coming closer to disregarding Norwegian neutrality, Adolf Hitler and his advisers decided the risks had to be taken.

In January, Hitler ordered the OKW, the German High Command, to work up a general plan for invading Norway. In a few weeks it came up with one that called for seizing a number of strategic ports, among them Oslo, Kristiansand, Stavanger, Bergen, Trondheim and Narvik, as the first objective. (To this list Copenhagen would later be added, on the ground that the conquest of Norway would depend on securing Denmark and its airfields.) It was to be an entirely new type of military operation, involving the close coordination of land, sea and air forces over great distances.

All that remained was to work out the logistics. For that step Hitler summoned to his headquarters Lieut. General Nikolaus von Falkenhorst, a broad-shouldered man who had been operations officer of the German volunteer division that fought in Finland in 1918. More recently Falkenhorst had commanded troops in the invasion of Poland. Meeting him now for the first time, Hitler gave him five hours to develop a detailed plan for seizing Norway. "I had no idea what Norway was like," the general recalled. His first step was to buy a Baedeker travel guide. With that and the OKW proposal to help him, he roughed out a scheme

German troops bound for Norway line up to board the cruiser Admiral Hipper at the mouth of the Weser River on April 6, 1940. Normally manned by a crew of 830, the ship carried 900 extra men for the invasion.

for delivering the men, the matériel and the transports that an invasion of Norway would require.

Hitler was delighted. He gave Falkenhorst the job of preparing the invasion and commanding the forces that would carry it out. Later he designated April 9 (when the Baltic ports should be free of ice) as *Weser* Day, and 4:15 a.m. Norwegian time as *Weser* Hour.

Logistics for the invasion were of herculean proportions that might well have intimidated a lesser man than Falkenhorst. The 8,850 soldiers of the seaborne assault forces had to be assembled in port and packed aboard 71 vessels—without allowing their presence to be detected even by their fellow Germans, much less by enemy reconnaissance. To refuel the warships and supply the troops, freighters and tankers (which moved at a slower pace than warships) would have to set out in advance if they were to be on hand at *Weser* Hour. Every departure had to be timed with care. If the ships sailed too soon some accident might reveal their mission; if too late, they would still be at sea on *Weser* Day and would make easy targets for British warships.

For the Navy men who would carry the initial landing force on board their ships, there were heart-stopping risks. Their objectives lay at the end of narrow fjords guarded by forts, gun batteries and—unless total surprise could be achieved—minefields. These hazards would have to be run in darkness without the benefit of local pilots. Instead, masquerade and bluff would be the Germans' chief weapons. Each captain received secret instructions just before sailing to pass his ship off as British; if challenged by any Norwegian ship he was to answer in English, using the name of a British warship, and state his business as "Calling for short visit. No hostile intent."

Diplomatic preparations for *Weserübung* were equally complex and secretive. The German Ambassadors to Denmark and Norway were not to be informed until the last moment. Two Army officers—Brigadier General Kurt Himer, chief of staff of the 31st Corps, which was to invade Denmark, and Lieut. Colonel Hartwig Pohlman, operations officer of Falkenhorst's Gruppe XXI—would be sent to Copenhagen and Oslo respectively. As secret "Plenipotentiaries of the Wehrmacht," they were to advise and assist the ambassadors. These officers would set forth on April 7 in civilian clothes, sending their uniforms separately as diplomatic baggage—which could not be opened for inspection by customs officers. After making a last reconnaissance, Himer and Pohlman would brief their respective Ambassadors at 11 p.m. on the 8th.

In order to achieve the greatest shock effect possible, at approximately 4:00 the next morning, as German troops began landing, the Ambassadors would notify the Danish and Norwegian governments of the situation and demand that they submit peacefully to German occupation. Every effort would be made to get tacit control of the royal families and central governments of the two nations. Initial demands were to be kept to the minimum necessary for the success of the operation; the Ambassadors would promise economic aid and a high degree of internal sovereignty in return for cooperation. At the same time, the commanders of the various German landing forces would attempt to establish agreements with the local military and civilian authorities before orders from their central governments could reach them. The Swedish government would be informed it was expected to remain strictly neutral and to hold its Naval vessels within its territorial waters.

Throughout the months of February and March, while preparations for the operation went forward, the most exacting secrecy was maintained. But not even in strictly policed Nazi Germany could an operation of this size be completely concealed. Rumors inevitably began to seep across Europe. By April 2 the Swedish government had received vague reports of troops and ships being concentrated in north German ports. A day or two later a Dutch assistant military attaché in Berlin passed on to the Danes and the Norwegians the information that something was afoot in the same ports. Ironically, the warnings went everywhere unheeded. The Swedes did nothing at all; the Danish Foreign Minister concluded that any German move would be directed against Norway, and the Norwegians believed the Germans might have a plan to take over bases in western Denmark. It never occurred to anyone that a massive strike was under way on all fronts.

Ships of the German armada had begun to cast off for their several destinations on April 3. Over the next few days, 26 merchantmen set out carrying 8,105 tons of Army stores, 2,660 vehicles and 1,641 horses. Four tankers went out with fuel for the warships that would be carrying the invasion force. At 5:10 a.m. on April 7 the heavy cruiser *Admiral Hipper* and 14 destroyers slipped out into the dark seaway for Trondheim and Narvik, escorted by the battle cruisers *Scharnhorst* and *Gneisenau.* That evening at Kiel the cruisers *Blücher, Lützow* and *Emden,* with eight minesweepers, two armed whaling ships and three torpedo boats, sailed with their troops for Oslo. Around midnight two cruisers, the *Köln* and the *Königsberg,* a gunnery training ship, a storeship and eight torpedo boats departed from Wilhelmshaven for Bergen.

Early on the 8th, the light cruiser *Karlsruhe,* the auxiliary *Tsingtau* and 10 torpedo boats left for Kristiansand, and four minesweepers headed for Egersund, a terminal of the telephone and telegraph cable from England. Ahead of them 28 submarines were forming a protective screen across the western approaches to Norway while long-range Luftwaffe reconnaissance planes fanned out across the North Sea. Below the Danish border, Lieut. General Leonhard Kaupisch mustered the 31st Corps, and an odd collection of armed icebreakers, minesweepers, merchant ships and launches had gathered to support him.

The *Weserübung* planners had done all they could. Now everything depended on the skill and courage of the assault troops and the blind chance of battle.

Even as the German ships set out, the Allies' Operation *Wilfred* was going forward under the command of Vice Admiral William "Jock" Whitworth, a veteran of World War I. On the 4th of April, 16 submarines had begun moving from the North Sea into the Skagerrak and the Kattegat, the two bodies of water connecting the North Sea and the Baltic at the foot of Scandinavia. The next day Whitworth himself sailed northeast from the Royal Navy base at Scapa Flow on the battle cruiser *Renown,* with eight destroyers as escorts and another four carrying mines to be laid across the Leads outside the fjord at Narvik.

On the morning of April 7 came the first hint of trouble: The Royal Air Force reported sighting a considerable German Naval force in the North Sea. But the British misread the Germans' intent. Supposing that the presence of the German ships portended a raid against the blockade and an attempted breakout into the Atlantic, the Admiralty alerted Admiral Sir Charles Forbes, Commander in Chief of the Home Fleet, who soon was steaming northeast from Scapa Flow to intercept the Germans. With Forbes, who sailed aboard the flagship *Rodney,* went one other battleship, one battle cruiser, three cruisers and 12 destroyers.

The Home Fleet's mission did nothing to alter the plans for *Wilfred* or *R4.* Admiral Whitworth, in charge of *Wilfred,* continued toward Narvik with no sense that anything was amiss. The cruisers and transports designated for *R4* lay at the Navy base at Rosyth in the Firth of Forth and off Greenock in the Clyde River, some of them already loaded with the garrison troops intended for Narvik, Trondheim, Bergen and Stavanger. Their orders were to sail on April 8 if the Germans reacted to the mining of the Leads.

In the North Sea it was snowing heavily, and somewhere off Trondheim, about halfway up the Norwegian coast, Whitworth's flotilla suffered a mishap that seamen have always feared: The destroyer *Glowworm* lost a sailor overboard in the churning sea. The ship dropped back to search for him. Whitworth and the remaining 11 destroyers proceeded without the *Glowworm,* and late on the night of April 7 arrived at the entrance to Vest Fjord, 40 miles from Narvik. The four minelayers peeled off to lay their minefield, while the *Renown* and her escorting destroyers spent the rest of the night patrolling the entrance to the fjord, against the chance that Norwegian coastal defense ships based at Narvik might come out to challenge the intruders. So far as Whitworth was able to tell, Operation *Wilfred* was going perfectly well.

Meanwhile, Admiral Forbes steamed northward with the Home Fleet, earnestly expecting to intercept the reported German ships before they could reach the convoy lanes of the North Atlantic. He searched in vain; he had sailed right past one prong of the German force in the stormy night, and pounded furiously northward away from them.

It was the *Glowworm,* separated from Jock Whitworth's Narvik-bound squadron, that found the Germans. At about 8 a.m. on April 8 off Trondheim, she came up behind first one and then another destroyer. Lieut. Commander Gerard Broadmead Roope immediately engaged, damaging one destroyer and scaring the other away. The first destroyer's radioman tapped out a frantic call for help, and within an hour the 13,000-ton German heavy cruiser *Admiral Hipper,* which had been waiting for the next day's *Weser* Hour off Trondheim, bore down, with its guns firing, on the 1,345-ton *Glowworm*.

No escape was possible. So Commander Roope decided on a suicidal *beau geste*. He threw up a smoke screen and turned as if to flee. The *Hipper's* commanding officer was fooled. He ordered the *Hipper* in pursuit and charged toward the smoke screen—only to find the *Glowworm's* sharp bow thrusting toward him at top speed. The *Hipper* took a glancing blow that tore away 130 feet of her armor belt and her starboard tubes, and left her listing under the weight of 500 tons of ingested seawater. Moments later the *Glowworm* went down. Displaying a chivalry that would not last long in this war, the *Hipper* pulled the *Glowworm's* survivors from the icy waters. Commander Roope was not among those saved; his grip failed at the very moment of rescue, and he tumbled backward into the sea.

The first Anglo-German fire of the battle for Scandinavia had been exchanged. That much was known to the Admiralty in London. But after 9 a.m., when the *Glowworm*, disregarding radio silence, had apprised headquarters of her predicament, nothing more could be discerned. The information—and the mystery of the ensuing silence—threw the Admiralty into a state of frenzied activity. A spate of orders and counterorders was made more confusing by the fact that the Admiralty could radio Admiral Forbes with the Home Fleet and Admiral Whitworth on the *Wilfred* mission, but they could not answer for fear that the Germans would discover their locations. The results were a series of misunderstandings and one missed opportunity after another.

First the *Renown* and three accompanying destroyers were ordered to steam south from the Lofoten Islands (a course that took them out of the path of the German task force heading for Narvik) and search for the *Glowworm*. The eight destroyers that had been laying mines and guarding the entrance to Narvik were ordered to join them. They got as far as the *Glowworm's* last reported position, west of Trondheim, but found nothing; the *Glowworm* had already sunk, and the *Hipper*, waiting for *Weser* Hour, was circling west of Trondheim with four destroyers. So in the late afternoon the *Renown* and her escort were ordered by the Admiralty to turn around and head north again to resume their vigil off Narvik.

Forbes and the Home Fleet, meanwhile, had received word that aerial reconnaissance had once more spotted German ships at sea, and they were heading west. The sighting was of the *Hipper* and her escorts, but their westward course reinforced the notion the British had held all along that the German ships were attempting to break out into the Atlantic. Forbes therefore changed his course from northeast to northwest, hoping to intercept the Germans. But bad weather shielded both forces, and now Forbes and the Germans crossed each other's paths for a second time without knowing it. After dark, the *Hipper* completed her circling and made a run for the coast and Trondheim. Forbes held his northwest course.

By this time frustration had caused the Admiralty to abandon its carefully planned strategy and blindly concentrate its resources on locating the elusive German squadron. As early as 2 p.m. on April 8, Churchill had canceled Plan *R4* to free more ships to pursue the Germans. He ordered the four cruisers that had been waiting at Rosyth with the infantry to put their troops ashore and join the Home Fleet at sea.

To say that this unexpected order was messily executed

The Royal Navy destroyer Glowworm, seen from the bridge of the Admiral Hipper off Trondheim, lays a smoke screen and appears ready to flee. Moments later, the warship turned to starboard and rammed the Hipper.

would be an understatement. Not one of the infantry battalions was allowed to unload its 90 tons of supplies properly. The 1/5th Battalion of the Royal Leicestershire Regiment was given one hour to get off the cruiser *Devonshire;* its supplies—carefully loaded in tactical order, ready for combat—were dumped on the dock in a heap. Still, the Royal Leicestershires were luckier than some. The 1/4th Battalion of the Royal Lincolnshire Regiment was ashore getting some physical exercise when the order came; the *Berwick's* crew tossed some of the battalion's equipment onto the wharf and sailed, leaving the men of the Royal Lincolnshire wearing the shorts they were training in. The 1/4th King's Own Yorkshire Light Infantry found themselves watching helplessly as the *York* sailed with all of their signal equipment and both of their trench mortars still on board.

Almost unnoticed in the excitement was a report that should have enlightened the British as to the Germans' real intentions. At noon the Polish submarine *Orzel*—one of 16 Allied submarines patrolling in the Skagerrak—had challenged and sunk the German freighter *Rio de Janeiro.* To the astonishment of the *Orzel's* officers and crewmen, they saw in the resulting flotsam quantities of military stores as well as horses and uniformed German soldiers—and reported as much to the Admiralty. But the Admiralty was too distracted to think of passing on the news to Forbes. He was not to find out about the report from the *Orzel* until 11 o'clock that night.

Meanwhile, the Norwegian coast guard picked up the *Rio de Janeiro's* survivors and took them ashore, where they were questioned by the police chief of the port of Lillesand. The Germans obligingly volunteered that they were bound for Bergen to help Norway resist an Allied invasion. The police chief reported this bizarre half-truth to Oslo, where it was not only discussed by the Storting, the Norwegian parliament, but was carried on the evening news broadcasts. No one believed the story. According to Storting President Carl Hambro, it was taken as "merely another bit of amazing and amusing evidence of the willingness of Germans to believe anything they were told by their superiors." And so the Storting adjourned at 9 p.m. without taking any action other than alerting the country's meager defense forces along the coast.

In Copenhagen, too, the story that German soldiers and

horses had been found swimming in the Skagerrak provoked more curiosity than concern. But the Danes had another bit of excitement closer to home: Scores of ships were reported to be moving north from German waters. Newspapers and political party leaders besieged Foreign Minister Dr. Peter Munch for reassurance. He consulted with the German embassy in Copenhagen, and then assured everyone—party leaders, journalists, Army officers and King Christian himself—that he had the personal pledge of the German Ambassador that Germany had "no warlike intentions" toward Denmark. So the Danes, like the Norwegians and the British, went to bed on the night of April 8 with no idea that a massive German invasion force was positioned off Scandinavian shores, ready to close in.

Admiral Kummetz, leading the Naval units bound for Oslo, was still eyeing the Oscarsborg Fortress in Oslo Fjord at 4:21 on the morning of April 9 when suddenly a lone searchlight blazed out from the mainland on the opposite shore, bathing the flagship in ghostly white. At point-blank range the huge guns of the fortress opened up; 700-pound shells crashed into the *Blücher's* port side and then into the *Lützow* just behind her. Simultaneously came another blast from the mainland battery at Dröbak, damaging both ships on their starboard sides. The *Blücher's* steering gear and aircraft hangar were wrecked by the first shots, and she blundered forward erratically while flames fed by aviation fuel raged aft. They burned away the fog, revealing a torpedo battery built into Oscarsborg Fortress. It had been there for 50 years without showing up on the German charts.

In discounting Oscarsborg as a threat, Admiral Kummetz had not reckoned with the character of Colonel Birger Eriksen, its commander. Eriksen gave his gunners one simple order: Fire. Two of the ancient torpedoes ran straight to their mark and exploded on contact, reducing the brand-new *Blücher* to a floating inferno.

Captain Kurt Zoepffel, who was conning the *Blücher* at that moment, recorded: "Suddenly, an earsplitting roar of thunder rends the air. The glare of guns pierces the darkness. I can see three flashes simultaneously. We are under fire from two sides; the guns seem only 500 yards away. Soon bright flames are leaping from the ship." In a moment the *Blücher's* store of bombs and ammunition began to explode, the engines stopped and the ship heeled over. When at last the order was given to abandon, wounded and dead men were already rolling into the water, and many of the landing troops were trapped below deck. Admiral Kummetz and some 1,300 survivors were rescued by the Norwegians, taken ashore and imprisoned. But more than 1,000 Germans died in the explosions and the flaming oil. For days after the incident, their blackened bodies could be seen floating in the fjord.

Just behind the *Blücher*, Captain August Thiele of the

cruiser *Lützow*, having no idea that the museum-like fortress and its torpedoes could have been the source of the *Blücher's* explosive demise, concluded that the flagship had hit a minefield. For the safety of his own and the remaining ships, Thiele ordered all engines reversed. Under his command, the *Lützow* and the remaining consorts retired 12 miles south to an alternate landing site at Sonsbukten, on the eastern shore of the fjord. The bid to take Oslo from the sea was lost.

The other German assault groups had better luck. In Denmark, Copenhagen had quickly fallen to a well-coordinated air, land and sea assault *(pages 56-71),* and Luftwaffe planes were already marshaling on Danish airfields to support the landings in Norway.

The Kristiansand Naval base, at the southern tip of Norway, put up a better fight, twice driving back the cruiser *Karlsruhe* with its shore batteries. But a Luftwaffe bomber group moved in to support the attack, and by 11 o'clock that morning the German landing force had entered the harbor and seized the base.

At Bergen, to the north, the cruisers *Köln* and *Königsberg* and the smaller ships they were escorting met a challenge when a Norwegian torpedo boat hailed them and asked their destination. The Germans replied in English, according to plan; the Norwegian captain was rattled, and he wavered just long enough to let the enemy cruisers sweep by. The searchlights of Bergen's main fort failed to work when someone tried to switch them on. In the darkness one battery of guns discharged a few shells; three of them hit the *Königsberg* and knocked out her power, causing her to drop out of the action. But the rest of the flotilla slipped easily into Bergen harbor. The landing force took the city in a rush, unopposed by any infantry.

Trondheim, a superb port that commands Norway's land and coastal sea routes, proved an easy conquest. The heavy cruiser *Hipper* led four destroyers straight down the broad fjord in a 25-knot charge toward the city docks. A patrol boat challenged them once, but the *Hipper* answered in English: "Ordered to Trondheim by government. No hostile intent," and pressed right on. As she neared the harbor, a shore battery fired—belatedly—and the *Hipper* answered with a salvo that blinded the batteries, and their shots fell wide. By 5:25 a.m. the German ships were unloading 1,700

Capsized and burning, the German heavy cruiser Blücher (top) lies in the Oslo Fjord where the torpedoes of the Oscarsborg Fortress brought the ship to a halt. The Germans later erected a monument at the site (bottom) in memory of the more than 1,000 crewmen of the Blücher who had drowned or been burned to death "For Führer and Fatherland."

men of the 3rd Mountain Division on the Trondheim docks. The Germans' remaining target was Narvik—the most distant and exposed of the Norwegian ports, and the one that would prove most difficult to take. Leading the expedition was Brigadier General Eduard Dietl, a leather-tough Austrian mountaineer and a first-rate soldier. Dietl had been a crony of Hitler's during the Nazis' early street-fighting days, and long association and loyalty had made him one of the Führer's favorite generals. More to the point, he had attended winter maneuvers in Norway before the War and knew something of what awaited him.

As *Weser* Hour approached on the morning of April 9, Dietl stood impassively at the elbow of Commodore Friedrich Bonte aboard the *Wilhelm Heidkamp,* the lead destroyer of nine threading their way to Narvik via Vest Fjord and Ofot Fjord. Each ship carried 200 seasoned soldiers. Leaving one destroyer to stand picket duty, Bonte sent two more to land troops at Ramnes and Havnes, two sites that, according to the German charts, had coastal batteries guarding the entrance to Ofot Fjord. Another three destroyers with 600 men headed north to seize a Norwegian arms depot eight miles above Narvik. Bonte guided the *Wilhelm Heidkamp* and the remaining two destroyers in the direction of Narvik itself.

Bonte was within sight of the port at 4:15 a.m. when he spotted two 40-year-old ironclad coastal defense ships, the *Eidsvold* and the *Norge.* Both were antiquated, but they bristled with heavy guns; the thin-skinned German destroyers would be no match for them. Playing for time, Bonte dispatched a staff officer in a motorboat flying a flag of truce toward the *Eidsvold* to demand her surrender. The Norwegian captain refused, but he waited politely while the German emissary returned to his motorboat. Then a pistol barked and a red flare soared from the motorboat and burst among the snowflakes, signaling that the Norwegians meant to fight. Commodore Bonte, a gentleman sailor of the old Imperial Navy, groaned as he turned to the grim-visaged General Dietl: "Do we have to do this?" Dietl hissed a reply. Bonte heard the word *"Schiessen!"*—Fire!—and took it as an order. Four German torpedoes shot from their tubes while the Norwegian crews frantically cranked their unwieldy guns into position. Three of the torpedoes found their mark: The *Eidsvold* split in two and sank as her maga-

zine exploded, and the captain and 175 men were dragged to their deaths.

The other Norwegian coastal vessel, the *Norge,* put up a tougher fight. Upon hearing the explosion that destroyed her sister ship, the *Norge's* captain maneuvered her past the vessels in the crowded harbor and into firing position just as the German destroyer *Bernd von Arnim* was beginning to land troops on the pier. The *Norge's* gunners fired, but they were inexperienced marksmen. Their first salvo was low; their second was too high, and crashed into the town they were trying to defend. The *Arnim* returned the fire. Six torpedoes sped toward the *Norge.* Four malfunctioned and dived too deep, but two ran erratically on the surface and exploded. They were enough to capsize the *Norge,* and 101 more Norwegian sailors died.

The *Wilhelm Heidkamp* had now reached the pier, and General Dietl set about seizing the town. Springing ashore on the heels of his troopers, he was met by the German consul, who conducted him to the garrison commander, an elderly Colonel Konrad Sundlo. The colonel wavered at the sight of the menacing Germans, and Dietl talked him into realizing that his only option was to surrender his 430-

Holding his baton of rank, Admiral Erich Raeder—architect and commander of Germany's reborn Navy—inspects the battleship Tirpitz lying at berth in captured Trondheim during the summer of 1942.

man command and spare the town from the German guns. Dietl's men, meanwhile, swiftly occupied strategic points, setting up machine-gun posts and crowding Norwegian Army troops out of their own positions. About 200 men of the garrison brazened their way past the German troops and escaped along the railway line. But at 7:10 a.m. Dietl was able to radio Hamburg that his two battalions held Narvik and its adjoining Army base.

Far to the south of these events, Admiral Forbes and the British Home Fleet had spent the night on a wild-goose chase. As early as 8 p.m. Forbes had begun to have second thoughts about the supposed German breakout into the Atlantic; the absence of any ships in his path, and new reports that ships had been sighted in the Skagerrak and the Kattegat, led him to turn his attention at last to the Norwegian coast instead of out to sea. He divided his force in two. With his flagship *Rodney* and most of the fleet, he turned south and headed for the Skagerrak. He sent one battle cruiser, one cruiser and a few destroyers north to reinforce the *Renown,* which was still making her way to Narvik.

The tactics were well taken—but too late. Before the reinforcements reached him, Admiral Whitworth and the *Renown* had found the Germans and engaged in battle. At 3:37 a.m. on April 9 off the Lofoten Islands, Whitworth had sighted the battle cruisers *Gneisenau* and *Scharnhorst,* which were lurking 50 miles offshore in support of the invasion fleet. Whitworth opened fire on the nearer of the two, the *Gneisenau,* putting her main armament-control system out of action and damaging her forward gun turret. The *Gneisenau* broke off the action, and with the *Scharnhorst* fled into a snow squall. The *Renown* pursued, but was not able to catch up.

By the time the *Renown* gave up the pursuit it was 4 a.m., and *Weser* Hour had come for the Germans. One after another, ports along the length of the Norwegian coast were passing under German control. One of them was Egersund, the terminus of the undersea communications cable connecting England with Scandinavia. All Norway was in a state of confusion, and such reports as the British Admiralty received throughout the day were sporadic and conflicting. On the strength of a press report that a single German ship had landed a small force at Narvik, the Admiralty ordered

the 2nd Destroyer Flotilla—five vessels under the command of Captain B. A. W. Warburton-Lee—to detach itself from Whitworth and the *Renown* and "proceed to Narvik and sink or capture enemy ship." If possible, the destroyers also were to put a landing party ashore and take the town.

Reaching Vest Fjord about 4 o'clock on the afternoon of April 9, Warburton-Lee took his ship, the *Hardy,* partway in and sent ashore Lieutenant Geoffrey Stanning, a bespectacled youth who served as his secretary and spoke German, a language that most of the local people could understand. From some men and boys Stanning gathered that a number of destroyers had gone by the night before—four, five, maybe six of them, and considerably bigger than Stanning's, said one of the boys.

Given that report, Warburton-Lee reflected that there might be mines and submarines as well as shore batteries to contend with. For half an hour he pondered what message he should send to London, unsure whether to sortie into Narvik at once, or wait for reinforcements. At last he sent a coded message to the Admiralty. After listing the forces reported to be in Narvik, the report concluded: "Intend attacking at dawn, high water."

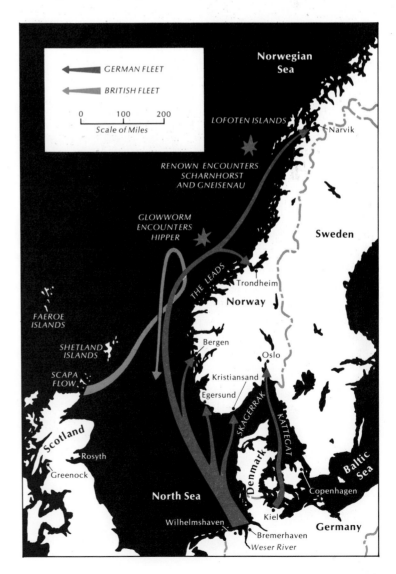

On April 8, 1940, the British destroyer Glowworm—straggling behind an escorted flotilla of British minelayers en route to Narvik—tangled fatally with the German heavy cruiser Admiral Hipper, the leader of one of six German assault forces (red) that would strike simultaneously at Norway's major ports the next morning. The Glowworm's distress call summoned the British Home Fleet (gray) on a fruitless search, and drew the minelaying force south from Narvik. In the series of near misses that followed, the battle cruiser Renown, part of the minelayers' escort, came upon the German battle cruisers Gneisenau and Scharnhorst near the Lofoten Islands. The skirmish that resulted was inconclusive.

And that is what he did, creeping through fog and snow that kept him hidden all the way into Narvik harbor. Leaving the destroyers *Hotspur* and *Hostile* to guard his rear and engage any German-held shore batteries, Warburton-Lee took the *Hardy* in a wide curve through the crowded harbor. Two more destroyers, the *Hunter* and the *Havock,* followed at intervals. They saw five German destroyers and hit them all, blowing up Commodore Bonte's flagship and killing him before he knew what was happening. The *Anton Schmitt* broke in two; the other three ships were smothered with hits and near misses while the British destroyers went about attacking every German merchantman they could identify. Completing their loop, the destroyers joined up for a second run, and now the *Hotspur* and *Hostile* accompanied them. When they had sunk or damaged every German ship they could see, the British flotilla retreated, virtually without a scratch.

The ships had no sooner departed from Narvik harbor than Warburton-Lee spotted three untouched German destroyers coming after him out of nearby Herjangs Fjord. A melee ensued, and in the confusion Warburton-Lee fired off a message incorrectly identifying the bigger newcomers as ''one cruiser, three destroyers,'' and announcing his own withdrawal to the west. Then his secretary, Lieutenant Stan-

ning, identified two more surprises, the destroyers *Georg Thiele* and *Bernd von Arnim,* speeding toward the *Hardy* from dead ahead. Warburton-Lee's luck had run out, and now the Germans got their revenge.

The *Georg Thiele* quickly found the *Hardy's* range, and in a few minutes salvo after salvo struck almost everything above the waterline, including the bridge and the men standing on it. Stanning was knocked out; when he came to, he saw dead and unconscious bodies all around him. He managed to beach the *Hardy* with her last bit of steam, and thus save 140 men. Warburton-Lee was to die of massive injuries, as were several of his men.

The *Hunter* was next in line, and the *Georg Thiele* riddled her too, so that she slued around and came to a dead halt. One hit on the *Hotspur,* next in the column, damaged her steering controls, and she plowed at full speed into the derelict *Hunter.* The ships interlocked, and hit after hit registered on them both before the *Hotspur* reversed engines and wrenched clear, leaving the *Hunter* to sink slowly. The *Havock* and the *Hostile* had raced on by, but now they returned in order to shepherd the *Hotspur* to safety. The German ships were drawing on the last fuel in their tanks, and dared not pursue.

In an engagement in which luck had played a greater role

than good management, the British won the last toss. As the three surviving destroyers limped out of Ofot Fjord they encountered a German ammunition ship, the *Rauenfels*. The *Havock* and the *Hostile* opened fire as the *Rauenfels'* crew fled to their lifeboats. The ship erupted in a 3,000-foot geyser of flame that consumed ammunition and other supplies the Germans ashore were counting on. The first Anglo-German battle of Narvik ended with the British the clear winners at sea. But the Germans held the town.

Now the Admiralty sent a much stronger force to clean out Narvik. Warburton-Lee's mistaken sighting of a cruiser had somehow been amplified to two cruisers plus the destroyers known to have survived the 2nd Destroyer Flotilla's attentions. Hoping to land a haymaker, the Admiralty ordered the 30,600-ton battleship *Warspite*, which was bound for another mission in the Mediterranean, to reverse course and steam north for the narrow fjords. She was joined by nine destroyers. Just past noon on April 13, preceded by a Swordfish floatplane launched from its catapult, the heavily armored *Warspite* and her escort went thundering into the Narvik fjord with Whitworth in command; he had transferred his flag from the thinner-skinned *Renown*. The *Warspite's* 15-inch guns pounded and sank the lurking *Erich Koellner* with six salvos, while the destroyers chased their German opponents up the side fjords.

There Captain Erich Bey, who had succeeded Commodore Bonte as commander of the diminished German flotilla, chose to fight a defensive action. He used even his damaged ships to good effect as anchored batteries, manned only by their gun and torpedo crews. Bey's destroyers, though outnumbered and outgunned, gave a good account of themselves; they blew the bow off the *Eskimo*, badly damaged the *Punjabi* and forced the *Cossack* aground. When they had fired the last of their ammunition, the surviving German destroyers ran themselves aground rather than surrender to the British. The crews scrambled back to Narvik. There General Dietl eventually rounded them up, formed the sailors into ad hoc infantry companies, helped himself to the rifles and ammunition from the arms depot, and dug in to await events. He now had twice the mouths to feed, but twice the force to fight with.

Admiral Whitworth briefly considered landing some of his men to seize the town. But by now German planes had appeared, a number of U-boats remained unaccounted for in the fjords, and he feared to linger with his borrowed flagship in such confined waters. So he gathered his destroyers, including the three cripples, scooped up the *Hardy's* survivors, and headed back out to sea on the morning of April 14. He radioed the Admiralty, estimating the enemy ground force at no more than 2,000 "thoroughly frightened Germans," and he urged the immediate landing of a reconstituted *R4* invasion force.

Admiral Raeder's brainchild, the occupation of Norway's ports, had cost the German Navy and merchant marine dearly. Half of his entire destroyer force lay wrecked at Narvik, and 14 of *Weserübung's* supply ships had been sunk before reaching their destinations. The battle cruiser *Gneisenau* and the cruiser *Lützow* had suffered severe damage, and three first-class cruisers had been lost altogether: the *Blücher* in Oslo Fjord, the light cruiser *Karlsruhe* off Kristiansand, and the cruiser *Königsberg*, sunk at Bergen by Fleet Air Arm bombers—the first major warship ever destroyed in combat by aircraft. But Germany had occupied Denmark, and it had established a foothold in Norway. There would be no more trouble about ore shipments from Sweden. If the initial successes at Bergen and Trondheim could be consolidated, Raeder would have deep-water ports for his surface raiders and submarines, an air base at Stavanger capable of covering the North Sea as far as Scotland, and 1,000 miles of sheltered coastline from which to prey on Allied shipping. Careful planning and audacious execution had made *Weserübung* a triumph of coordinated air-land-sea operations. Now it was up to the Luftwaffe and General Falkenhorst to make the sacrifice of the German Navy worthwhile.

Lone survivor in a nautical graveyard, the German supply ship Jan Wellem (left) lies docked among sunken and half-submerged vessels in Narvik harbor following the British sea raids of April 10 and 13, 1940. The Germans' losses included 10 destroyers and more than 300 sailors.

THE SWIFTEST BLITZ

Danish citizens watch passively as a German machine gunner atop an armored car leads a motorized invasion force through the streets of a Jutland town.

DENMARK'S FALL BEFORE BREAKFAST

Of all the blows the Germans struck in Scandinavia on the fateful morning of April 9, 1940, none was so stunning, swift or effective as their invasion of Denmark. Only the day before, Danish truck drivers who were hauling fresh fish to Hamburg had reported a column of German infantry 30 miles long marching toward the Danish frontier. But the significance of that odd intelligence failed to register with officials in the Danish government, and the invasion came as an utter surprise.

At 4 a.m. German Ambassador Cecil von Renthe-Fink roused Danish Foreign Minister Dr. Peter Munch to present an ultimatum: Accept German occupation, or in an hour beautiful Copenhagen will be bombed. When the Minister tried to telephone King Christian X for advice, he could not. Reports are confused, but evidently no one was operating the telephones at that early hour. Only by hurrying into the street and hailing a taxi to take him to the royal palace was the Minister able to confer with his King. Two and a half hours later, after having concluded that to pit Denmark's lilliputian defense force of fewer than 15,000 men against the mighty Wehrmacht would be to send the nation's youth to slaughter, the King reluctantly directed the Danish people to surrender and to treat their German conquerors with courtesy.

The announcement, made by the War Ministry at 6:20 a.m., was only *pro forma*, for even before the King and his Cabinet had concluded their talks, the German troopship *Hansestadt Danzig* had docked in icy Copenhagen harbor with an invasion force 1,000 strong. By the time most Danes had risen to breakfast, 40,000 German troops were rolling through their land.

Here and there a few Danes objected, contending that the King should have urged his country to resist. But by and large the Danes were too stunned to react belligerently—a condition that bewildered the advancing Germans. ''In Prague they spat at us, in Warsaw they shot at us,'' one German officer noted in amazement. ''Here we are being gaped at like a traveling circus.''

German soldiers paint a swastika on the deck of the Hansestadt Danzig in Copenhagen harbor to warn the Luftwaffe not to bomb her by mistake.

Curious Danish citizens line the harborside in Copenhagen to take a look at the converted merchant vessel that delivered the German invasion troops.

A QUICK PAYOFF
FOR CAREFUL PLANNING

The ultimatum to surrender had scarcely been issued to the Danish Foreign Minister before German troops were surging across Denmark. They came by sea, land and air, and immediately after arrival they deployed for action, heading for strategic Danish defense points by foot, train and truck. The Citadel, the ancient fortress that commanded the harbor at Copenhagen, was swiftly seized by a raiding party of bicyclists who had disembarked from the troopship *Hansestadt Danzig*.

Every detail of the lightning-quick take-over had been carefully prepared in advance, and what the Germans did not bring along with them they procured locally: Only a day before the invasion, one German officer who was dressed in civilian clothes rented a truck from a Danish civilian for the purpose of hauling heavy radio equipment.

So quickly did the invaders establish themselves on Danish soil that by mid-morning German planes were flying from Danish airports to support the simultaneous invasion of Norway.

With a microphone in hand, a German officer announces the fact of Copenhagen's occupation to the public. The Germans insisted that they had come to protect the Danish nation from invasion by Allied forces.

Freshly landed at Korsør on the west coast of Zealand, a company of German Naval men forms up underneath a sign that advertises a brand of Danish margarine. The landing party soon took possession of the port.

Junkers-52 transports fly unopposed over the port of Skagen. Long-range German planes flew out of Denmark for the rest of the War.

German sentries guard the Belt Bridge, which links Jutland and the island of Fyn. The Germans feared—unnecessarily—that the Danes might try to blow it up.

GUARDING AGAINST A COUNTERATTACK

It required more German soldiers to occupy Denmark than it did to conquer it; eventually the Occupation force reached 130,000 troops.

As they settled in, the Germans took no chances. In line with their protestations that the object of their presence was to spare Denmark from invasion by the Allies, they took all military precautions to secure themselves against hostile encounters. They posted guards at bridges, at ports, at airfields and even at park sites; and they came prepared to tend their own wounded (*page 64*).

Entrenched in a Copenhagen park, a German soldier lies ready with carbine and hand grenades while another keeps watch.

German soldiers man a field-radio station, quickly set up in Copenhagen to provide communication among scattered units.

A German ambulance and a staff car lead a motorcycle platoon in tight formation through an occupied Danish town. On the day of the invasion, such motorized units traveled the full 205-mile length of Denmark.

German soldiers unroll banners emblazoned with the swastika on the grounds of The Citadel, Copenhagen's old fortress, to signal its capture. The Luftwaffe was under orders to bomb the site if the Danes resisted.

A hospitable woman proffers hot coffee to Germans in a patrol car. "The people," observed King Christian, "are treating the Germans with great dignity."

A RECEPTION MOSTLY COURTEOUS

At first, most Danes were so dazed by the abrupt arrival of a German army in their midst that they reacted with instinctive politeness *(above)*. The Germans responded by extending friendly gestures to everyone, although the relationship between victor and vanquished was bound to cool.

"The soldiers do everything to make themselves popular," King Christian was soon to write to a friend, "and yet manage to achieve the opposite effect. The Germans simply do not understand that their presence is undesired." Perhaps it was only the youngest Danish citizens who dared to give candid expression to their feelings *(right)*.

An armed German reconnaissance unit pauses to get acquainted with some young Danish women.

A German soldier bestows a friendly pat on a Danish toddler—and gets a dubious frown in return.

THE MILITARY SIDE OF OCCUPATION

The Germans were not always cordial, and their military regimen soon let the Danes know that they were a captive nation. The Germans set up checkpoints at key locations in order to control civilian traffic and routinely stopped pedestrians for questioning. They rounded up Danish military personnel for interrogation and interned some of them.

Danish newspapers were subjected to strict censorship. One outspoken journalist was arrested and sent to Hamburg; when he returned a few weeks later he was in a state of shock and refused even to talk about the treatment he had received at the hands of the Germans.

Armed Germans halt a private automobile on the Belt Bridge between Jutland and Fyn. Civilian movement across the bridge was allowed, but all vehicles

Blindfolded to conceal the details of German headquarters from him, a Danish Naval officer is led to interrogation.

A Danish woman, out on an errand with her son and his dog, is questioned by a trooper at a German strong point.

UNIFORMED TOURISTS IN A FAIRY-TALE LAND

"You Germans have done the incredible again," said King Christian of Denmark in rueful admiration to Brigadier General Kurt Himer, who was chief of staff of the invading task force. "One must admit that it is magnificent work."

Their work accomplished after a single day, the Germans found they could travel unarmed throughout the bucolic kingdom without fear of attack—a condition that prevailed until later in the War, when the passive Danish resistance to occupation turned to active militancy.

Off-duty German soldiers became tourists. They explored shops filled with locally made curios and craftwork, and clothing manufactured in Great Britain. They dined in restaurants that served abundant meats, seafoods and dairy products, which were rationed in the homeland. And of course they took in the many sights for which Denmark was famous.

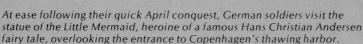

At ease following their quick April conquest, German soldiers visit the statue of the Little Mermaid, heroine of a famous Hans Christian Andersen fairy tale, overlooking the entrance to Copenhagen's thawing harbor.

German soldiers touring Odense listen to a civilian guide as he describes the 19th Century childhood home of Hans Christian Andersen, whose stories were almost as well known in Germany as they were in Denmark.

3

At 7:23 on the morning of April 9, 1940—just three hours after Admiral Kummetz' unsuccessful bid to bring the German heavy cruiser *Blücher* and an invasion fleet of 16 vessels into the port of Oslo—a special train pulled out of the Oslo railroad station. On board was Haakon VII, Norway's widower king, who was fleeing the city together with the Crown Prince and Princess, their three children, members of the Cabinet and Parliament and a coterie of civil servants. The German ships that had escaped the *Blücher's* fate had fallen back about 10 miles and put their troops ashore. At the same time, at an airfield only five miles west of Oslo, German planes had begun landing airborne troops and paratroops. From the early hours of the morning it was clear that the city would be taken.

The Norwegian Cabinet, in a predawn conference, decided that King Haakon and his government should not knuckle under to the invaders. Instead they should leave Oslo, try to reestablish themselves at a safe distance, and from there direct the fight to keep their country free. Haakon's party moved out barely in time; by 5 o'clock in the afternoon a motorcade of German troops under Captain Eberhard Spiller, Air Attaché to the German Embassy, was racing overland in pursuit of the King. Haakon eluded them, and found haven in the small town of Nybergsund, about 120 miles northeast of Oslo.

Norwegian citizens by the hundreds helped their popular King get away. The chief savior was Colonel Otto Ruge, Inspector General of the Norwegia infantry, who formed an impromptu military guard augmented by a number of volunteers from a local rifle club. Together they stopped the German motorcade at a roadblock some 70 miles north of the capital. In a quick fight they mortally wounded Captain Spiller; the rest of the Germans withdrew to Oslo, leaving their dying commander behind.

The King's haven was a temporary one; Haakon and his officials would spend the next 60 days moving from place to place. The King and his entourage finally left Norway altogether in the hope of setting up a government-in-exile in Great Britain. The failure to capture the King came as a surprise to the Germans, and gave them a taste of what lay in store. Having expected Norway to capitulate in the face of their successful landings all along the coast on the morning of the 9th, the invaders found instead that the Norwegians

A FAILED RESCUE

were disposed to put up a fight. The Germans had taken control of five major ports, from Kristiansand in the south to Narvik in the north, but they would now have to force their way inland to link up their dangerously scattered forces. Moreover, they soon would have another enemy to contend with: An Allied expeditionary force would be rushed in to prevent Norway's fall.

Early in his flight, King Haakon made Colonel Ruge a major general, appointed him commander in chief of the Norwegian Army and charged him with directing the resistance to Germany's take-over.

Ruge's task appeared hopeless. In addition to the five ports, German troops occupied every major airfield in Norway; they had disrupted the nation's radio and telephone networks, captured most of its arms depots and were bombing the rest as fast as they could locate them. Such meager forces as Ruge could muster were losing heart. Major General Einar Liljedahl, commanding the Norwegian 3rd Division near Kristiansand, quickly surrendered, and in less than a week after the invasion the area all around that port city was firmly in German hands.

To the east of Oslo the story was much the same. The general who was in command of the Norwegian 1st Division, after fighting three losing battles, lined up his surviving 1,000 men and marched them across the nearby border into Sweden. There they remained, interned, for the duration of the War.

The men of the 4th Division, hastily mobilized under General Wilhelm Steffens, eluded the German troops who landed in Bergen. Hoping to join General Ruge's forces north of Oslo, they withdrew eastward, marching for about two weeks over mountainous country. They beat back repeated infantry assaults while withstanding attacks by Stuka dive bombers. But in the end Steffens' men, too, had to surrender after a fierce two-day battle.

Only a few combat-ready Norwegian troops remained. Among them were some 3,000 men of the 5th Division under Colonel Ole B. Getz in the Trondheim area about 260 miles north of Bergen, and 7,100 men of the 6th Division commanded by General Carl Gustav Fleischer, based 700 miles farther north in the Arctic provinces of Finnmark and Troms. But Getz's men were in sorry straits; their supply de-

pot and almost all of their artillery had been captured by the Germans. And most of Fleischer's troops were stationed along the Finnish frontier, far from the nearest German-occupied port, Narvik.

General Ruge, trying to establish headquarters in the town of Rena, near Oslo, was hard pressed to communicate with his far-flung units. The telephone system was largely in enemy hands and Norway's mountainous terrain played havoc with radio signals. Three of the four divisions located in southern Norway were effectively out of the fighting; the only one that remained was General Jacob Hvinden Haug's 2nd Division—and it was still trying to organize itself under German pressure in the country north of Oslo. In one week's time General Hvinden Haug was able to mobilize some 3,000 men, but they were in no better shape to stop the Germans than their comrades had been. Norway had no tanks or antitank weapons, few antiaircraft guns, and its typical citizen-soldier had been trained for a period of only about eight weeks.

But the 2nd Division was a nucleus, and around it General Ruge began to organize an army—a growing force of reservists, retired officers and civilian volunteers. They arrived on foot, on skis, and in automobiles and trucks—many of them bringing along their own hunting and target rifles. An elderly taxi driver who gave Ruge a ride on the first day of the German invasion stayed on as chauffeur to the new commander in chief. A civilian doctor, leaving the town of Eidsvoll with only a box of aspirin in his pocket, recruited other physicians and nurses and opened a field hospital in the mountains north of Oslo.

The Norwegians improvised. "They gathered around a leader," Ruge recalled later, "and became a 'company'; they met other groups of the same kind and became 'battalions' under the command of some officer. Casually assembled infantrymen, artillerists, sailors and aviators, with cars and chauffeurs collected from God-knows-where, became fighting units."

Ruge also received some badly needed financial help in the form of 11.1 million kroner—almost 4.5 million American dollars—in Norwegian bank notes. The notes had been spirited out of the Bank of Norway in Oslo under the noses of German guards by the driver of the bank's armored truck, Rudolf Sandergren. In a daredevil exploit, Sandergren concealed the money in five potato sacks and smuggled it through German lines and roadblocks to the town of Hamar, where he turned it over to Anders Frihagen, Norway's Minister of Commerce. On the 13th of April, Frihagen appeared at Ruge's headquarters in Rena and presented the money to him, for use in paying the recruits and purchasing food and other supplies.

Help was also on the way from the outside. The British, while sending ships to challenge German Naval forces in the captured Norwegian ports, also dispatched a military attaché, Lieut. Colonel E. J. C. King-Salter, who reached Ruge's headquarters on the 14th of April. From there he besought London for infantry, arms and artillery units to help the Norwegians.

Until such help could arrive, Ruge's task was to contain the Germans. With only 12,000 troops and no armor at his disposal, he realized he could not engage the enemy on the flat, open country directly north of Oslo. He decided that his—and Norway's—best hope lay in the recapture of Trondheim, the port city in central Norway that in medieval times had been the nation's capital. The Germans had but a weak hold on Trondheim, having landed only 1,700 troops there, and no city in Norway was so strategically placed. It had an excellent harbor that could accommodate vessels of deep draft. Moreover, Trondheim lay at the head of two valleys—the Gudbrandsdal and the Osterdal—that led south through the mountains to Oslo, and it was at the foot of the only road and rail link with northern Norway.

Ruge urged the British to make Trondheim the focus of their relief effort. He decided to make his own stand in the rugged mountain country 160 miles south of the city. Here the Norwegians could use the terrain to their advantage. The valley floors were narrow and would be difficult for German tanks to negotiate; the steep sides were heavily forested with birch, pine and spruce that would provide cover for the defenders, as would the deep drifts of snow, which in Norway lingers into May. Ruge deployed his troops at the mouths of both valleys, with orders to ambush German patrols, blow up bridges and tunnels, and block the narrow roads with rockslides and trees as the men fell back. These were only holding tactics and could not drive the Germans out, but they might slow the German effort to link up their Trondheim and Oslo forces. If luck was with the Norwegians, the British might arrive in time to recapture Trondheim for Norway.

The Germans, in the meantime, gave the Norwegians one last opportunity to quit. On the 14th of April, the German commander in Norway, Lieut. General Nikolaus von Falkenhorst, issued a no-nonsense proclamation that was posted all over occupied Norway. "It is my task to protect Norway against attack by the Western powers," it read. "If opposition is offered and the hand of friendship is rejected, I shall be forced to employ the severest and most relentless means to crush such opposition."

A hastily mobilized soldier unloads ammunition from the private car in which he reported to the battle zone. Norway's unreadiness for war prompted the President of its Parliament to warn the rest of the world that "every unsuspicious nation is living under mortal menace."

Receiving no response to this demand for surrender, Falkenhorst opened a campaign to gain control of the roads and railroads connecting the ports the Germans had already seized. While ships and planes continued to pour guns, supplies and as many as 3,000 men per day into Oslo, Falkenhorst sent his 196th Infantry Division, under Lieut. General Richard Pellengahr, toward the Gudbrandsdal and Osterdal valleys. Falkenhorst had motorized much of the division by commandeering trucks, cars and buses in Oslo, and had collected civilian stocks of skis for those German soldiers who knew how to use them.

The advancing troops received neatly coordinated air support from the Luftwaffe's Fifth Air Force, under the command of General Erhard Milch, a veteran of the blitzkrieg in Poland. Milch worked his ground crews tirelessly to refuel and rearm their aircraft, while supply and construction personnel quickly established forward air bases and stocked them with essential matériel and antiaircraft defenses. As the German ground troops advanced, Milch leapfrogged Luftwaffe squadrons forward, thus providing a continuous umbrella of reconnaissance, fighter and bomber support. Within a week, the Germans had taken full control of the coast from Oslo to Bergen.

To Adolf Hitler, who was fretfully following the Norway campaign from the headquarters of the German High Command in Salzburg, the prospects of reaching Trondheim looked grim. Snowstorms and fog closed down all the airfields near the city, preventing the reinforcement by air of the two battalions of mountain troops already there. Then came the news of stunning British Naval victories at Narvik on the 10th and 13th of April *(pages 54-55)*.

Hitler panicked. He fired off frantic and contradictory orders to his headquarters staff for relay to Brigadier General Eduard Dietl, commanding the land forces at Narvik. Dietl should withdraw overland toward Trondheim, said one order, since Narvik could not possibly be held. He should plan to evacuate his men by air, said another. A third suggested that he retreat eastward along the iron-ore railroad leading to the Swedish border. OKW Chief of Operations Brigadier General Alfred Jodl quietly intercepted the orders and managed to calm the Führer: "A thing should be considered lost," he said, "only when it is actually lost." By April 18, Hitler had recovered sufficiently to approve an order instructing Dietl to hold Narvik as long as possible before withdrawing into the interior.

Meanwhile, a Luftwaffe intelligence report provided Hitler with new cause for concern. British ships were in the vicinity of Trondheim, and if they landed forces that took the city before the German reinforcements from Oslo arrived, the entire invasion would be in peril. Colonel Walter Warlimont, OKW Deputy Chief of Operations, recalled seeing the Führer "hunched on a chair in a corner, staring in front of him, a picture of brooding gloom. He appeared," said Warlimont, "to be waiting for some piece of news that would save the situation."

The Germans actually engaged in the fighting were finding the Norwegians not only stubborn but maddeningly elusive. One German foot soldier recalled coming upon a nest of machine gunners hidden in some trees. "They disappeared as if swallowed up by the ground," he wrote. But their disappearance did not mean the end of trouble. "Suddenly, there was a tremendous detonation," said the German, "immediately followed by large masses of rock crashing down. The Norwegians had started a landslide and tons of debris rolled down on the road."

The Germans, however, soon improvised special tactics to deal with the Norwegians. They put one or two tanks and a detachment of motorized engineers at the front of their columns. Behind them came an infantry company with attached heavy weapons, followed at the rear by a platoon of motorized artillery. Overhead, reconnaissance planes darted back and forth, scouting for enemy positions.

When the advance guard hit a roadblock, it opened fire with all available weapons. Machine guns pinned down the defenders, while mortars and infantry howitzers lobbed shells behind the steep hills. The tanks then broke through, and a rush of infantry followed close behind. If the defense was especially stubborn, dive bombers and artillery were called in to soften it up while small assault detachments attacked at several points, probing for a weak spot. Infantrymen on skis frequently worked their way up and across the ridges to outflank the Norwegians. Engineers repaired roads as they advanced, clearing rubble and trees and rebuilding bridges. After a heavy engagement, fresh troops leapfrogged forward to keep up the momentum of the attack.

THE MAN WHOSE NAME SPELLED TRAITOR

One reason why Hitler expected Norway to be an easy conquest was that an ambitious Norwegian politician had assured him that much of the nation was ready to embrace the "Pan-Germanic ideal." The man was Vidkun Quisling, a former defense minister and leader of a tiny political party modeled on the German Nazis.

Early in 1940, Quisling offered the Germans some exciting intelligence. The British, he said, were planning landings at the air bases of Stavanger and Kristiansand; Quisling's pro-Nazi party was ready to seize the bases and turn them over to the Germans. The information won Quisling two audiences with Hitler, who paid him handsomely: 200,000 gold marks.

No sooner had the Germans invaded Norway—without any measurable assistance from Quisling's henchmen—than Quisling appropriated the microphone at an Oslo radio station and announced to his country that he was now Prime Minister. But the Norwegians resented the turncoat bitterly, and within a week the Germans unceremoniously shelved him.

If Quisling's usefulness was marginal, his notoriety was both immediate and enduring. "To writers, the word 'quisling' is a gift from the gods," wrote *The Times* of London. "If they had been ordered to invent a new word for traitor they could hardly have hit upon a more brilliant combination of letters." His name did, in fact, become a synonym for traitor.

Major Vidkun Quisling (right), Germany's puppet in Norway, returns a salute during an Oslo ceremony. At War's end, Quisling was executed by a Norwegian firing squad.

By these means the Germans reached Lake Mjosa, a 65-mile-long body of water at the southern end of the Gudbrandsdal valley. Here General Pellengahr split his division into two columns. He ordered them to advance along both shores of the lake and to converge on the city of Lillehammer at the lake's northern end. The going was slow; the column on the east side was stopped in its tracks at the village of Strandlokka by Norwegian troops under the command of General Hvinden Haug. The Norwegians were able to hold their ground for several days, until Pellengahr sent a battalion of infantry across the still-frozen lake from the west side and surprised the Norwegians from the rear. Simultaneously, another German unit launched a tank attack from the east side, threatening to trap the Norwegian forces in a pincers.

With great haste, Hvinden Haug's forces abandoned their positions on both sides of the lake and fell back toward Lillehammer. They left the town of Hamar undefended and the Germans, making short work of the roadblocks that lay in their path, pressed forward and took it. From Hamar, a battalion crossed into the Osterdal valley on the east, linking up with other advancing German forces at the town of Elverum on April 20.

The German columns were still 190 miles short of Trondheim. But Norwegian resistance was slackening. Ruge's men were worn down by the constant combat; their ammunition supplies were practically exhausted and there were no Norwegian reinforcements available. Only if the British came through with help could Ruge hope to stem the German tide in the Gudbrandsdal.

In London, the British military establishment was moving at a pace unsuited to cope with the blitzkrieg tactics of the German Army. Bitter and long-standing rivalries among the various military services prevented proper coordination of Britain's ground, air and naval forces. Complained First Lord of the Admiralty Winston Churchill: "There are six Chiefs of Staff and three Ministers who have a voice in Norwegian operations. But no one is responsible for the creation of military policy." Churchill himself, however, was part of the problem. He was obsessed with the recapture of Narvik, which he called "my pet, my first love." Half-cajoling, half-driving, he exerted pressure on the British War Cabinet to earmark most of the available troops for that obscure northern port, even though help was more desperately needed at Trondheim.

When at last General Ruge, with the backing of British Attaché King-Salter, had convinced the War Cabinet of the importance of Trondheim, the authorities in London proceeded to launch an expedition that was marred from the start by confusion and inefficiency. Fearing that a direct attack on Trondheim from the sea would be too risky, the British instead sent troops in two groups to less conspicuous ports that were still in Norwegian hands. One group was to land at Namsos, 80 miles north of Trondheim. The other was to go to Andalsnes, 100 miles to the southwest. The two forces, code-named respectively "Mauriceforce" and "Sickleforce," were to converge and envelop Trondheim from the landward side.

The heart of Mauriceforce, the northern arm of the Trondheim pincers, consisted of the British 146th Brigade. Mauriceforce's commander was Major General Sir Adrian Carton de Wiart, a stiff-backed veteran who had left Oxford to enlist in the British Army during the Boer War. He wore a piratical black patch over the empty socket of an eye he had lost in the Middle East, an artificial hand to replace one lost in France during World War I, and a splendid collection of medals that included the Victoria Cross.

Carton de Wiart had arrived at Namsos by flying boat, intending to prepare the way for his troops. He was greeted by a full measure of troubles. The 15-mile fjord leading to the tiny port proved too winding and narrow for bulky troop transports to navigate; the ships would be easy targets for the Luftwaffe. Before entering the fjord, therefore, much of the British brigade had to be transferred to destroyers, which were more maneuverable. In the confusion, equipment was misplaced, and one transport sailed home with 170 tons of weapons, rations and ammunition still aboard, leaving the 146th Brigade with only two days' supplies. Even the brigade commander was missing; he was aboard one of the transports heading for Narvik.

The troops that joined Carton de Wiart in Namsos were an unlikely sight. They had been issued Arctic kits, which included fur-lined boots, heavy woolen sweaters, kapok sleeping bags and coats lined with sheepskin. The clothes were so heavy and bulky that once the men donned them they could hardly move. To their general's skeptical eye they looked "like paralyzed polar bears."

Moving inland 80 miles to the village of Steinkjer, Carton de Wiart's 146th Brigade linked up with Colonel Getz's Norwegian 5th Division. There the British general found trouble of a more serious kind: The Norwegian troops had enough ammunition for only one day's fighting. The British could not even share their meager ammunition supply; their 7.7mm bullets would not fit the 6.5mm rifles that the Norwegians carried.

On April 19 French reinforcements began to arrive: 4,000 mountain ski troops of the 5th Demi-Brigade of Chasseurs Alpins. The French had been dogged by trouble. Their convoy had been bombed by the Luftwaffe; one escorting cruis-

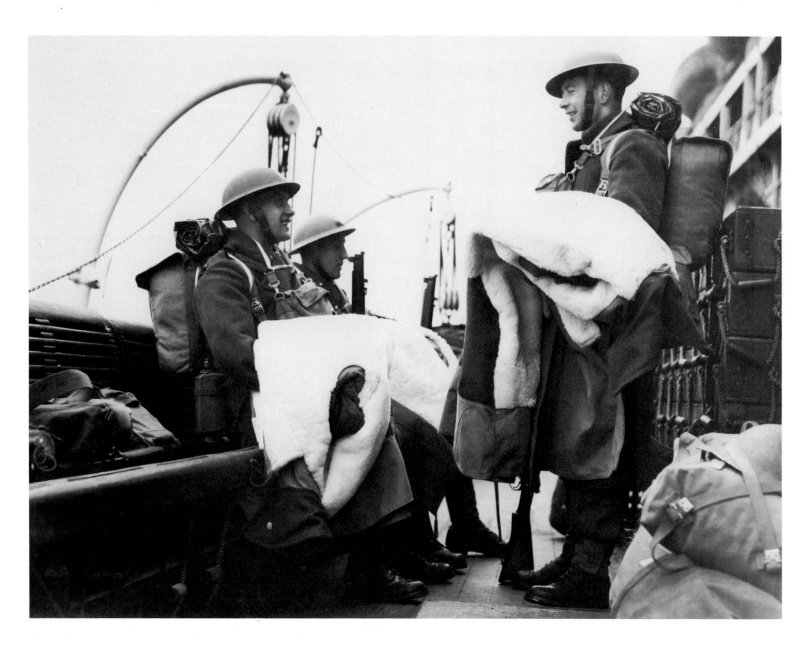

Smiling British soldiers carry sheepskin-lined Arctic coats aboard a tender for the troopship that will take them to Norway. The coats, which weighed 15 pounds, were warm but were difficult to maneuver in.

er was so badly damaged that it had to put back to France. When they reached port and began unloading cargo they discovered that their skis were useless—they had been shipped without bindings.

Sickleforce, the southern arm of the pincers attack on Trondheim, was under the command of Brigadier General Harold de Riemer Morgan. It consisted initially of the British 148th Brigade, which on April 18 sailed directly into Andalsnes. A small fishing port hardly equipped for unloading men and matériel, Andalsnes had been chosen primarily because it was connected by single-track railway to the village of Dombas at the upper end of the Gudbrandsdal valley. From Dombas, the main railway line from Oslo ran due north 240 miles to Trondheim. The 148th Brigade arrived at Andalsnes at night, with maps that proved to be inaccurate, and without radios, mortar ammunition or fire-control equipment for the antiaircraft guns.

Morgan nevertheless loaded his men on trains that carried them the 60 miles inland to Dombas. From Dombas he intended to turn north toward Trondheim, as he had been instructed to do. But General Ruge, who was eagerly awaiting his arrival, had a more pressing need for the British. "My men are near exhaustion," he told Morgan, and he warned that the Norwegian positions to the south were in danger of imminent collapse unless the British general rushed troops to their assistance.

Ruge's appeal, which was seconded by Colonel King-Salter, seemed logical enough to Morgan. If the British advanced northward and the Norwegian positions were overrun, the Germans could readily cut the only supply line from Andalsnes to Dombas. The British would be stranded in unfamiliar terrain, wedged between the German garrison at Trondheim and the advancing spearheads of the German troops from Oslo. Reluctantly abandoning his original mission, Morgan ordered his men to move south 80 miles to Lillehammer and to take up positions on the southern approaches to the city.

The hard-pressed Norwegians were aghast at the unmilitary bearing of their new British allies. Lieut. Colonel Ragnvald Roscher Nielsen, an officer on General Ruge's staff, thought they looked like "untrained steel workers from the Midlands." Roscher Nielsen was not far off the mark. Morgan's men were all Territorials—recently mobilized reservists. They barely knew how to operate their trench mortars, and were less than expert with their Bren guns. Worst of all, they were ill prepared for winter warfare; they did not know how to make camp in the frigid weather, nor had they come equipped with skis.

The British had scarcely settled in at Lillehammer on April 21 when General Pellengahr's men hit them. The Germans quickly outflanked the British position, forcing Morgan's entire line to fall back. That night a German motorized machine-gun battalion made a daring drive through the retreating British and Norwegians and seized Lillehammer. Morgan tried to form a new position the following day, but the Norwegians could not help; they said their ski troops were too weary to provide cover for his flanks. Small parties of Germans on skis worked into Morgan's flanks and rear, and they even managed to raid his brigade headquarters. The British fell back along the east bank of the Lagen River to a bridge at the village of Trettin. The bridge had to be held until the Norwegians and British west of the river could retreat across it.

Around Trettin the valley becomes especially narrow and crooked, offering excellent defensive positions. Nevertheless, the British were unprepared for the sudden attack that came on April 23. Three German tanks charged through Morgan's center, jeopardizing his position. Troops west of the Lagen had to withdraw in haste; those east of the river were cut off. After a further retreat of 45 miles, Morgan could count only nine junior officers and some 300 men out of his original strength of 1,000. The 148th Brigade, routed in its first major engagement, no longer existed as a fighting unit. Morgan sent the badly shaken survivors back to Andalsnes for evacuation.

For several days the hills along the Gudbrandsdal were full of stragglers and detachments that had been cut off. A few men reached Sweden and were interned; some made it to the coast and escaped to Scotland in Norwegian fishing boats. But most were rounded up by the Germans. One isolated party of six officers and 50 men marched through the night. Finding themselves in Lillehammer the next morning, they asked for breakfast at a small hotel. The proprietor would not serve them anything; in hushed tones he told them that a group of German officers had preceded them and taken over his hotel as their headquarters. Hungry and exhausted, the British headed back to the hills and a long overland trek to refuge in Sweden.

From the German point of view, operations were going so well that, on April 24, General von Falkenhorst decided that most of Pellengahr's division could be diverted from Trondheim and sent instead to Andalsnes, to complete the destruction of Morgan's forces. The relief of Trondheim would be the responsibility of Colonel Hermann Fischer, who was pushing up the Osterdal valley with three infantry battalions, two artillery battalions, an engineer battalion and some tanks and motorized units.

As Pellengahr set out for Andalsnes, he encountered a new British force, the 15th Brigade, whose 3,800 men had been hurriedly shipped to the aid of Sickleforce. The brigade's three battalions were regular Army. One of them had served in Palestine until 1939 and was experienced in small-unit hill fighting. In fact, the 15th Brigade was trained and fit to fight anywhere—except in the deep snow of Norway's interminable winter.

Under Major General Sir Bernard G. T. Paget, to whom General Ruge had assigned a few Norwegian ski detachments and some trucks for transport, the 15th Brigade moved forward through Dombas, setting up supply dumps in railroad tunnels as it moved. The going was rough; German air attacks on road and rail movements went on through the increasingly long hours of daylight, taking a toll in casualties and frazzled nerves.

Pellengahr's spearhead made contact with the 15th Brigade early on April 25 at Kvam, 35 miles south of Dombas. The brigade's five French 25mm Hotchkiss antitank guns stopped the first German rush, knocking out two tanks, but the Germans began working around the British left flank. The British held through the day, and that night they reorganized their lines, abandoning two antitank guns in the process. Early next morning Pellengahr attacked again, enveloping both flanks of the new British position and driving hard at its center with artillery and air support. Mortar shells set the woods on fire, eventually forcing the British to retreat three miles to a position at Kjorem.

Paget dug in, but soon found himself threatened from behind and from above. The German advance up the Osterdal valley might turn westward toward Dombas and cut his line of communications, and the Luftwaffe had begun bombing both Andalsnes and its sister port of Molde, on the opposite shore of Romsdal Fjord. A major raid on April 26 set fire to the wooden wharf at Andalsnes and destroyed Paget's reserve stocks of ammunition and rations. The same raid badly damaged Molde, knocking out the town's electric power and temporarily crippling a Norwegian radio transmitter that the British had been using to communicate with London.

The Luftwaffe then extended the raids along the railroad to Dombas, systematically bombing every farmhouse and village in which British soldiers might be sheltering. The British quickly discovered that they were no longer welcome; wherever they stopped, destruction soon rained down on the civilian community. Farmers began pleading with British and even with Norwegian officers to move off their land. "If you fight here," said one plaintively, "we will lose our barns and our homes."

Meanwhile, Pellengahr reached Paget's line at Kjorem on April 27. The British held stubbornly, but once more the Germans circled up over the snowy ridges, outflanked the defenders and inflicted heavy losses; one 700-man British unit suffered nearly 400 casualties. Paget urgently asked London for another brigade of infantry, more antiaircraft artillery and effective air support. Without that, he radioed, he could not hold any position against Pellengahr for more than two days, and he would be lucky to manage a delaying action back to Andalsnes on the coast.

Improved visibility and the unbroken string of German victories in the Gudbrandsdal had meanwhile permitted Falkenhorst to build up his Trondheim forces by airlift to a strength of five and a half battalions. Brigadier General Kurt Woytasch of the 181st Infantry Division took command and prepared to launch an attack on Carton de Wiart's 146th Brigade near Steinkjer. Two German destroyers, which Hitler had insisted on leaving at Trondheim after the port was captured, gave Woytasch complete naval superiority in Trondheims Fjord. Now that the ice was breaking up, Woytasch dispatched a destroyer and a commandeered merchant ship into the lesser fjord that led to Steinkjer, with orders to land troops behind the British and Norwegians.

At the same time, a German column moved overland

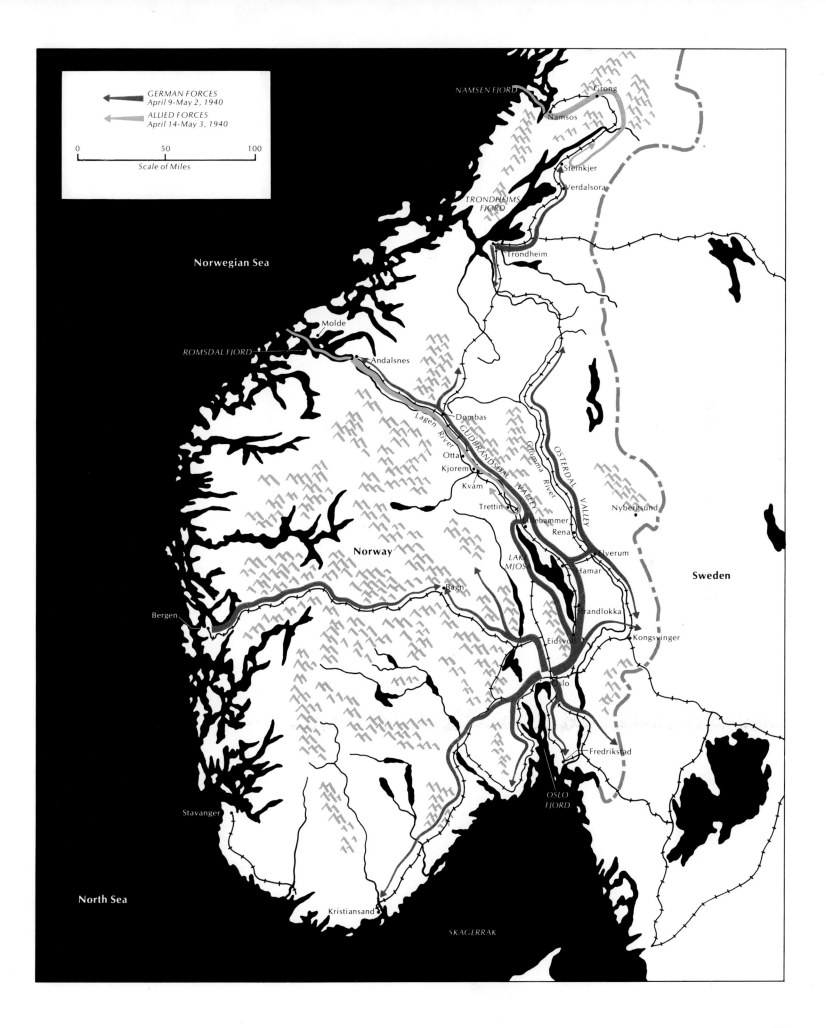

GERMAN FORCES
April 9–May 2, 1940

ALLIED FORCES
April 14–May 3, 1940

0   50   100
Scale of Miles

Norwegian Sea

NAMSEN FJORD

Grong

Namsos

Steinkjer

Verdalsora

TRONDHEIMS FJORD

Trondheim

Molde

ROMSDAL FJORD

Andalsnes

Dombas

Lagen River

GUDBRANDSDAL VALLEY

Otta

Kjorem

Kvam

Glomma River

OSTERDAL VALLEY

Trettin

Nybergsund

Lillehammer

Rena

Norway

Elverum

LAKE MJOSA

Hamar

Bagn

Strandlokka

Sweden

Bergen

Eidsvoll

Kongsvinger

Oslo

Stavanger

Fredrikstad

OSLO FJORD

North Sea

Kristiansand

SKAGERRAK

from Trondheim to Steinkjer by rail and road. These were mountain troops, equipped and trained for snow fighting, and supported by a battery of mountain guns. Carrying their mortars and machine guns forward in motorcycle sidecars, they used minor farm roads to get into position and confronted the Allied defenders on April 21. The weight of the attack hit hardest against the Lincolnshire Battalion, one company of which suffered 25 per cent casualties. As the fighting continued into April 22, the Lincolnshires began to waver. Ordered to retire on Steinkjer, they got out of hand and could not be rallied for a rear-guard stand. That evening, as the German destroyer shelled the village, German troops came ashore and seized the only bridge across the Ogna River, cutting the road north to Namsos.

Those British troops east of Steinkjer were now cut off. But by chance one of their senior officers, a Lieut. Colonel H. B. Hibbert, had spent several boyhood holidays fishing in the nearby mountains. Hibbert dimly remembered an old wooden bridge well to the east of Steinkjer. Thinking that the bridge might provide an escape route, Hibbert dispatched a volunteer Norwegian guide on skis to look for it while he got his battalion ready for a forced march. The guide returned. There was indeed a bridge east of Steinkjer; it was six miles away as the crow flies, but a much longer hike over mountain trails. Hibbert's men loaded their wounded onto sleds and moved out, single file and three yards apart so that if one man fell on the slippery footing he would not bring down the whole line behind him. They covered approximately 82 miles in 67 hours, reaching Mauriceforce's new position north of Namsos without losing a weapon or leaving behind a single straggler.

Steinkjer was now left to the Germans, who halted their drive and turned south to join the columns advancing from Oslo. On April 30 they linked up with Colonel Fischer's advance guard at Berkak, some 35 miles below Trondheim. Overland contact was thus established between Oslo and Trondheim, and both British landing forces were on the run. Southern Norway was firmly in German hands.

By April 28, the government in London had to face the fact that the Trondheim campaign was a failure. Neither Sickleforce nor Mauriceforce had made a single gain. Between them they had suffered 1,559 casualties, and they were in danger of losing the men remaining. The British high command concluded that both forces must be brought home.

Evacuation was not going to be any easier than reaching their present positions had been. Namsen Fjord, the escape route for Mauriceforce, was a narrow stretch of water, difficult for troopships to navigate without colliding with one another while under repeated attacks by the Luftwaffe. For Sickleforce, the perils were even greater: To reach the coast, it had to withdraw 100 miles through a narrow valley with one poor road and a single-track railway, both of which were being heavily bombed.

One British officer recalled how the Luftwaffe pilots, unchallenged by the Royal Air Force, flew up and down that narrow road leading back to Andalsnes. "In relays of two and three," he said, "they would come out to bomb the bridges and crossroads; then, with their bombs spent, they would drop down on their remaining petrol for the sport of shooting up anything left in sight. That first attack either got you or it missed you; and only after it was over would there follow the exhausting process of tumbling out and plowing through snow to the nearest tree or wall, or even the roadside drain, in the few minutes that were left before the next one."

Paget was given the bitter task of telling General Ruge that his allies were abandoning him. The Norwegian commander was at first sardonic. "So Norway must go the way of Czechoslovakia and Poland," he said. But accepting the inevitable, Ruge generously asked what he could do to help the British and French get away. His men located some vehicles to speed the evacuation and a battery of four field guns to hold off the Germans, who were now only 30 miles southeast of Dombas.

Thanks partly to the Norwegians' assistance, Sickleforce covered the 100-mile distance back to Andalsnes in less than 48 hours, and early on April 30 the sea phase of the evacuation began. First a sloop took off 340 men. After darkness fell that evening more than 1,800 British troops, exhausted and hungry, stumbled aboard blacked-out warships and transports.

With daylight on May 1 the Luftwaffe arrived in force, driving out to sea two World War I vintage British cruisers, converted for antiaircraft duty, that had been sent to protect the port. After twilight two more cruisers and five destroyers came in and picked up 1,300 additional men. More troops remained on shore—their number uncounted in the darkness and the confusion. After midnight the last available cruiser edged in, expecting to retrieve a 240-man rear guard—and instead found almost 1,000 soldiers waiting on the dock. All of them crammed aboard, and by 2 a.m. on May 2 the last of Sickleforce's survivors were away. Behind them they left 1,402 men of the 148th and 15th Brigades, either killed, wounded or prisoners of the Germans. That afternoon, when advance elements of the German 196th Division marched wearily into Andalsnes, they found the port ruined by the bombs of their own Luftwaffe—and empty of British troops.

The evacuation of Mauriceforce from Namsos was scheduled for the nights of May 1 and 2, and it escaped annihilation by a hair's breadth. A dense offshore fog settled in on May 1 and most of the French and British relief ships lay to, waiting for it to lift. General Carton de Wiart, unaware of the offshore weather, had all his men out of hiding and waiting down by the battered docks. Morning found them still waiting. There was barely time to get them back under cover before the first German reconnaissance planes arrived at daylight. Not until late the following day did the fog lift and the rescue begin. By early morning of May 3, Mauriceforce was safely off, leaving behind 157 killed, wounded or missing.

That afternoon, a German plane spotted the fleeing convoy. After a long running fight, dive bombers sank the French destroyer *Bison.* The British destroyer *Afridi,* covering the rear, plucked the *Bison's* surviving crewmen out of the water—only to be sunk herself shortly afterward. She carried with her both the British rear guard and the briefly rescued Frenchmen.

Norway was now in German hands as far north as Namsos, and the greater part of the Norwegian Army was out of action. The campaign was not over, however; Churchill all along had refused to take his eye off Narvik. "We ought to take it for granted that the Germans will try to enter the ore field and carry succor to the Narvik garrison by force or favor," he wrote. Possession of the Swedish ore fields, he said, "is the main objective of the whole of the operations in Scandinavia." He added that only two weeks remained for the British to seize Narvik; after that the Baltic ice would break up and permit the Germans to land at Lulea, another transshipment site even closer to the ore fields, and seize them for Germany. So at Churchill's insistence the best troops of Britain's Norwegian expedition had been sent to attack the northernmost port held by the Germans.

The Narvik campaign was no better managed than Trondheim had been. The British not only divided the command of their forces, but the separate commanders received distinctly different orders. The Naval commander, Admiral of the Fleet the Earl of Cork and Orrery—more conveniently known as Lord Cork—had instructions to "turn the enemy out of Narvik at the earliest possible moment." The commander of the ground forces, Major General Pierse J. Mackesy, had been ordered not to land against opposition or to bombard any populated areas.

The commanders' temperaments were as mismatched as their orders. Lord Cork, a short and red-haired man, had a hot temper; he steamed into the Lofoten Islands off Narvik

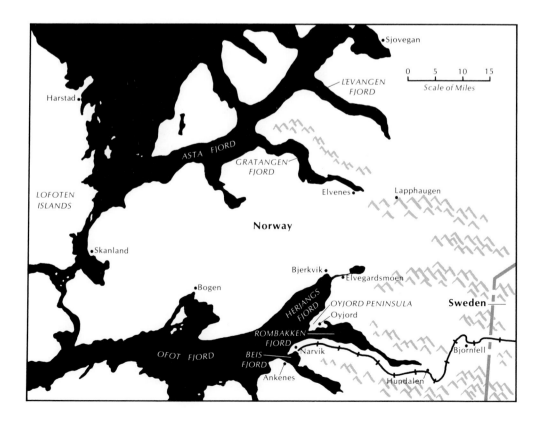

In mid-April of 1940, Allied troops landed at Harstad and nearby ports and joined the Norwegian Army to mount an offensive against the Germans occupying Narvik. During an eight-week campaign, the Allies took Narvik and pushed the Germans east almost to the Swedish border. But then the British government decided Narvik could not be held, and ordered the expeditionary force evacuated.

lusting for immediate action. Mackesy was a more cautious man. While Lord Cork hatched plans to storm the enemy positions in Narvik, Mackesy methodically landed his supplies, organized a base at Harstad, about 50 miles by water to the north, and established contact with General Fleischer's still-intact Norwegian 6th Division.

Mackesy intended that as soon as his troops landed on either side of Narvik, he would launch a double-pronged attack to cut the ore railroad to Sweden, the Germans' only overland supply route. Simultaneously, Lord Cork's warships would seal off the seaward approaches. General Dietl and his 4,600-man German occupation force would be isolated and surrounded, with little choice but to surrender.

On April 14, Mackesy made his first cautious moves. From Harstad he dispatched the three battalions of his 24th Brigade to strategic points on the mainland. He stationed a force of Irish Guards at Bogen on the north shore of Ofot Fjord. Nearby, the South Wales Borderers encamped near the little port of Skanland. Mackesy also posted two companies of the Scots Guards battalion at Sjovegan, 33 miles north of Narvik, where they linked up with the Norwegian 6th Brigade. The Scots were to stand in reserve while the Norwegians attacked Dietl's defenses, which were just to the north of Narvik.

Unfortunately, as the 24th Brigade had neither radios nor motor vehicles, communicating with these scattered units was difficult. Orders had to be hand carried by couriers in boats and on bicycles or by runners on foot. By the time most messages were received, one Scots Guardsman remembered, they "were of historical interest only."

Supplying the units from Harstad was an equally tedious process. The drafts of the Royal Navy ships were too deep for navigating the narrow side fjords. So Mackesy had to hire 120 local fishing boats, which chugged slowly back and forth on single-cylindered diesel engines. The Scots Guards, who had similar vessels at home, promptly gave them the name they knew them by, "puffers."

Mackesy had all his troops in place by April 16—and then he stood pat. He wanted the weather just right before starting his attack, and a series of blizzards was filling the valleys with snowdrifts, some of them eight feet deep. To pass the time, the Guards officers gave ski lessons to their men. When there were not enough skis to go around, some of the men switched to tobogganing. To the Guards, who had never been on toboggans before and might need them now for transport in the strange terrain, tobogganing was serious business. To the local Norwegians, familiar with toboggans from childhood, it seemed that their British allies were merely playing in the snow—while the Germans sat menacingly nearby.

Relations between the Norwegians and the British were becoming strained in other respects as well. By now General Ruge was dubious of his allies' competence. His requests to London for weapons and equipment were given little attention. General Fleischer, moving his 6th Division troops against Dietl's outposts north of Narvik, grew increasingly sour as the British remained motionless.

Churchill, who from his Admiralty offices in London had little idea what the men were facing, ordered Mackesy to make an assault landing in Narvik harbor at once. Mackesy retorted that to bombard Narvik would be a disgrace; it would endanger the lives of innocent civilians. Churchill

French troops sprint across a railroad track in the mountains near Narvik. The French brought a special zest to the war in Norway: "The men love fighting first," said one of their commanders, "and after that, drinking."

then directed that Dietl be notified that he had six hours—an impossibly short time—to get all civilians out of town. He also ordered Lord Cork, in command of the Navy's end of the operation, to proceed against Narvik. At this point even the impetuous Lord Cork was reluctant to move; he was short of supplies, and he badly needed fighter planes for cover. Moreover, he had too little information about Narvik; he had flown over the port, but German camouflage had successfully screened everything except rocks and snow from his view.

Orders were orders, however, and Lord Cork was not a man to flout them. On April 24 he ordered a battleship, three cruisers and a destroyer into the fjord to bombard the hillsides around Narvik for three hours—yielding only to Mackesy's pleas that the town and its civilians be spared. The Irish Guards embarked in light craft from Bogen, ready to run in and land at Narvik if opportunity offered—but it did not. Heavy snow squalls blanked out the entire area, so no German positions could be identified.

On the same day, Fleischer's Norwegian troops launched an attack from the north. One battalion advanced against a commanding hill at Lapphaugen, which was held by approximately 150 Germans; another circled widely toward the village of Gratangen to cut off their retreat. The same storm that blinded the British bombardment stymied the Norwegians, piling up three feet of snow in 24 hours and blinding their artillery observers. The men of the battalion attacking Lapphaugen were expert skiers, but the storm was so severe that they needed 15 hours to advance less than two miles up a 1,300-foot rise—and they reached the top too exhausted to go farther. The other battalion reached Gratangen without trouble and took shelter there for the night. But next morning, before reinforcements could reach them, Germans swooped down on the village, killing or capturing some 278 Norwegians and sending the rest fleeing northward across the snows.

The Germans were having troubles of their own. General Dietl had two thirds of his mountaineers north of Narvik, holding a thin line of machine-gun posts sited as far apart as a half mile. The rest of his infantry were in and around Narvik and its sister town, Ankenes. The sailors in his command were stationed around Herjangs Fjord and along the railway. The German government had pressured Sweden into granting permission to send rations, medical supplies, clothing and ski equipment to Dietl over Swedish railroads. But the Swedes absolutely refused to permit the shipment of ammunition, which consequently had to be air-dropped—when the weather allowed.

Getting supplies to the troops on the line was an even greater problem. Dietl had established his major supply depot at Bjornfell, close to the Swedish frontier. From there the ore railroad could be used to ferry supplies as far as the village of Hundalen, 15 miles east of Narvik; the remaining miles of track were exposed to the fire of British warships. So supplies had to be lugged by backpack over the mountains from Hundalen to Narvik.

Dietl expected the Allied probe on April 24 to develop into a major attack. Although it did not, he tightened his lines, retreating from Lapphaugen and Gratangen in the north and pulling all nonessential troops out of Narvik. He also shifted his own headquarters from the top three floors of the Hotel Royal in Narvik to more primitive accommodations along the railroad.

On April 27, the first elements of a new French force, a light division under the command of Brigadier General Antoine Marie Émile Béthouart, began landing in Gratangen Fjord. Béthouart was an aggressive commander who quickly won the respect of both Norwegians and British. Among other things, he understood mountain warfare, having done a prewar tour of duty as an attaché to the Norwegian Army.

But Béthouart's men did not represent the pick of the French Army. His two demi-brigades of Chasseurs Alpins were short of pack mules and of experienced skiers. His Podhalansha Brigade, made up of Polish expatriates living in France, was eager to take revenge on the Germans, but ill equipped to do so; although the French gave the Poles the grandiose title of Chasseurs de Montagne (Mountain Light Infantry), by their own account few of them had ever seen a mountain before.

Finally, there was the 13th Demi-Brigade of the French Foreign Legion, a potpourri of nationalities, ideologies and temperaments. Its members ranged from a White Russian prince who had served in the Legion since 1924 to a Susan Travers, the only female Legionnaire, who had been recruited as an ambulance driver when the Legion was passing through England. Commanding this military smorgasbord was one Lieut. Colonel Magrin-Verneret, a swashbuckling Frenchman who, like many in the Legion, used a *nom de guerre*, Montclar. The colonel possessed a Gallic wit. When beset by complaints from his officers that they were being committed to a sideshow, he responded disarmingly. "We have to learn to detach ourselves completely from the glamor of glory," he said. "What are my orders? To take Narvik. And why Narvik? For the iron ore, for the anchovies, for the Norwegians? I haven't the faintest idea." It was the right touch to take the edge off his men's grumbling.

General Mackesy, with his forces thus increased to approximately 25,000 men, at last got his offensive moving. On April 26 the South Wales Borderers landed on the south shore of Ofot Fjord and began to advance on Ankenes. The Germans there put up a stiff defense, with frequent small-scale counterattacks. Neither the Welshmen nor the French battalion that relieved them a few days later made much progress. Fleischer's Norwegian 6th Brigade began working south through the mountains toward Bjornfell; his 7th Brigade, reinforced by two French companies, pushed off against Bjerkvik, at the head of Herjangs Fjord. They too found the going slow, with snow up to five feet deep on the level ground. The French were poorly equipped and suffered greatly from frostbite and snow blindness. By May 10 they had gained only five miles.

Churchill had long since lost patience with Mackesy's delays and had relieved him of command of the ground forces at Narvik. To replace him Churchill chose Lieut. General Sir Claude Auchinleck, a career officer who had spent years in India. Auchinleck's orders were just as unrealistic as Cork's and Mackesy's had been: He was to capture Narvik and convert it into a strong Allied base that the Germans would make "repeated, costly and ineffectual efforts to recapture." He also was ordered to repair the railroad, start a flow of iron ore for Allied use, prepare to seize the Swedish mines, and assert the King of Norway's authority.

Auchinleck arrived at Harstad on May 11, in the middle of an air raid, to find an oversupply of troubles. Though the men ashore were desperate for ammunition and equipment, supply-laden ships stood idle in the harbor. Norwegian crewmen were reluctant to unload them for fear of damage to their tenders by the German air raids. Distant events contributed to his woes; on May 10 the Germans had invaded the Netherlands, Belgium and Luxembourg—prompting the British Admiralty to recall all destroyers for the protection of home waters, and depriving Auchinleck of the only ships that could penetrate Norway's broken coastline to deploy his troops.

Auchinleck had no sooner digested this news than he became aware of a new German threat approaching from the south. On May 4, General von Falkenhorst had ordered the German 2nd Mountain Division, then assembling at Trondheim, to move overland through Grong, Mosjoen and Bodo to reinforce Narvik. The straight-line distance from Grong was about 300 miles through a thinly settled, snow-covered region of high mountains. Roads were poor and broken by fjords that required ferry hauls up to 10 miles long. For the last 85 miles there were no roads whatever. But the German commander, Major General Valentin Feurstein, began marching the division northward the next morning, without even waiting for all of his troops to reach Trondheim. In four days the Germans covered almost 90 miles across country that Carton de Wiart's staff officers had reported impassable a few weeks earlier.

Lord Cork already had asked London what might be done to halt such an advance. London had replied that he was responsible; he would be assigned some newly organized volunteer companies, but was not to expect any more planes or ships. Lord Cork, who took little comfort in the prospect of the promised volunteers, decided he would have to shift his 24th Brigade to the ports of Mo and Bodo, where the volunteers would be arriving. He would try to stop the Germans at that point.

There were reasons why London could do no more to help. On May 7, in a speech before the House of Commons, Prime Minister Neville Chamberlain reported the British evacuation from Namsos and Andalsnes—bringing down upon himself a political storm. Barely surviving a two-day debate, he tried to form a new cabinet representing all parties, but he could find no supporters. When Hitler's armies invaded the Low Countries on May 10, Winston Churchill was summoned to Buckingham Palace and appointed Prime Minister in Chamberlain's place—a turn of events that must have seemed unjust to the ousted Prime

Minister, for a large share of the blunderings that had impeded the Norwegian campaign had been the work of Chamberlain's busy First Lord of the Admiralty.

Churchill established his new government with alacrity. He yielded to pressure from the British and French high commands calling on the Allies to evacuate Norway—but he insisted on trying to capture Narvik first, both to destroy the port installations and to cover the evacuation. In that he had plenty of support.

One reason for pressing the attack on Narvik was that even a temporary victory would help Allied morale. Another, expressed by the French General Béthouart, was common decency: The Allies could not in honor abandon Norway without attempting to give the Norwegians time to demobilize and get home. Otherwise they would be herded into German prisoner-of-war camps.

A final attack was planned for May 27. It was to begin with an amphibious assault from Oyjord straight across Rombakken Fjord to a beach north of Narvik, using the 13th Demi-Brigade and a Norwegian battalion. All available Naval vessels and three batteries of field artillery—one Norwegian and two French—would support this attack. The Polish brigade, backed by British artillery, would advance through Ankenes. Two French light tanks were assigned to each force. Farther east the Chasseurs Alpins and the Norwegians would maintain pressure on Dietl's right flank. Royal Air Force patrols, operating from two small airfields established at Bardufoss and Skanland, a short distance to the north of Narvik, would drive off any attempts by the Luftwaffe to break up the attack.

On May 21 the RAF 263rd Squadron, equipped with Gladiator fighter planes, flew off the carrier *Furious* into Bardufoss. The 46th Squadron, a unit with newer Hurricane fighters, took off from the carrier *Glorious* five days later and landed at Skanland.

The landings at Skanland proved to be a series of small disasters. The airfield was not built to handle the heavy, high-speed fighters. Squadron commander Kenneth Cross brought his Hurricane down perfectly—until his wheels bogged and his plane stood on its nose, bending its propeller. Another fighter did a half-somersault when it caught a wheel in chicken wire used to hold the field's sod runways

in place. Clambering out of his plane, Cross stormed over to a graying airfield construction officer and demanded, "What the hell sort of place is this to bring Hurricanes into?" The officer, who had worked himself to exhaustion to get the field ready, burst into tears. The upside-down Hurricane was righted, someone straightened Cross's propeller with a hammer, and the squadron managed to take off for Bardufoss. The Skanland field was abandoned.

On May 27 the first assault wave of Legionnaires and Norwegians embarked well inside Herjangs Fjord, which was concealed from Narvik by high ground behind the town of Oyjord. While every available warship pounded the Narvik-Ankenes area, the first wave swept into and across Rombakken Fjord. Legionnaires poured ashore and cleared a beachhead. The Norwegians passed through them and started up the slopes behind Narvik. A second wave began mustering at Oyjord to cross the fjord. Hurricanes and Gladiators swept overhead, shooting down and driving off German planes as soon as they appeared. By 3:30 a.m., 1,250 men were ashore.

Despite the crashing naval bombardment, a German gunner got the range of the waiting second assault wave and began slamming shells into the boats. The embarkation point had to be shifted back to Herjangs Fjord, and the undertaking threw the attack off schedule. Then, although no one at Narvik knew it, sea fog began rolling in over the airfield at Bardufoss. Planes on the ground could not take off; those in the air had to return hurriedly while they still had a place to land. As if on cue, the Luftwaffe arrived in force to harry the British warships westward down Ofot Fjord. German infantry, which had been hidden in a crease in the bluff above the bridgehead, came howling down the slope behind a shower of "potato masher" hand grenades. They piled the Norwegians into the Legionnaires, and drove both groups back onto the beach.

Lieut. Commander S. H. Balfour, serving as Naval liaison officer to the French, lost his signal lamps and was unable to call for naval gunfire support. Resourcefully, he commandeered a beached landing craft and—while a deadly game of tag stormed along the beach—went after the dodging British ships, finally reaching the destroyer *Beagle*. Coming about amid Luftwaffe attacks, the *Beagle* ran in close to the beach, firing at short range. The Germans returned toward the ridge, rallying on the high ground behind Narvik until their comrades in the town could withdraw.

Driving at Ankenes, the Poles lost both of their tanks to mines, but broke through. Beyond Ankenes, a German counterattack caught them in the flank and threw them back. Rallying, they found the enemy withdrawing and managed to sink the last boatload of Germans escaping across Narvik harbor. The day ended with rear-guard fighting as the Germans extricated themselves, keeping their front intact. The Poles and the Legionnaires linked up at the head of Beis Fjord that evening, then pushed the Germans back. At 5 p.m. on May 27 the Allies entered Narvik, General Béthouart chivalrously putting the Norwegians who had fought with him at the head of the column.

With Narvik occupied, the Allies' first move was to bring in a fleet of "puffers" from the Lofoten Islands and evacuate the civilian population, to save them from vengeance bombing by the Luftwaffe. Totting up their losses, the Allies counted only some 150 casualties. They had taken 300 German prisoners.

Allied attacks on May 29 and 30 beyond Narvik made few gains despite heavy naval gunfire support. Then, in early June, the Norwegians scored a considerable advance near the Swedish border. Dietl wisely shortened the German front, taking some units out of line to form a reserve. Bad weather had halted supply drops, his stores were running low, and his men had little shelter. The Norwegians enthusiastically planned a final attack, hoping to drive Dietl

Behind a German destroyer waiting to pick up survivors, the upended British troopship Orama plunges toward the bottom on June 8, 1940. The Germans were bitterly surprised when they found that the Orama carried 100 German prisoners of war and not evacuating British troops.

over the border into Sweden, and probable internment.

Meanwhile, General Feurstein's 2nd Mountain Division continued its advance toward Narvik. The Germans had routed Lord Cork's 24th Brigade and the newly arrived volunteers at Mo and Bodo, and Lord Cork had been lucky to evacuate the survivors with the help of some Norwegian fishing trawlers. Before Feurstein reached the end of the last road, 85 miles south of Narvik, he had shaken down his division to form three battalions from the pick of his mountaineers—men who could cross the trackless ranges and still be in condition to fight. Supplies would be air-dropped to the battalions as they went; just before they reached Narvik, planes would parachute heavy weapons and ammunition to them. Feurstein named the arduous undertaking Operation *Buffalo.* On June 2 the men were taken by boat to the head of Leir Fjord, and through rain, snow, fog and mud they moved inland.

General Ruge, informed that the Allies intended to hold Narvik only temporarily, pleaded for postponement of the evacuation until the Norwegians could deliver their final attack against Dietl, planned for June 8. He was refused, and the attack never took place. Instead, General Fleischer and some other Norwegian officers left for England to organize an army-in-exile. But there were neither plans nor means for evacuating the Norwegian troops. Ruge remained with his men. Destroyers and other light craft gathered the British and French troops from their various perches around Ofot Fjord and ferried them to Harstad. The weather cooperated; low clouds and mist blinded German aerial reconnaissance for four crucial days. Six big transports with 15,000 men on board left Harstad between June 4 and June 6; seven more carrying 10,000 men sailed during the next two nights, together with a convoy of eight supply ships. The cruiser *Southampton* gathered the last parties at 9 a.m. on June 8.

The next day General von Falkenhorst, belatedly learning of the evacuation, ordered a halt to Operation *Buffalo,* just short of halfway on its difficult march. A lieutenant and 20 men pushed on to Narvik, just to show that it could be done. Ruge and Dietl agreed on a preliminary cease-fire, effective at midnight on June 9. Norwegian troops moved into their demobilization points, without incident, and the Germans consolidated their holdings as far as Tromso, which was occupied by paratroops on June 13.

The conquest of Norway reinforced the military reputation the Germans had won in Poland the previous September. Germany gained air and naval bases flanking the British Isles. Covered by the Luftwaffe, coastal batteries and light Naval units, the once-neutral Leads became a private thoroughfare for German ore ships, blockade runners and raiders. And the Germans had Narvik harbor rebuilt and handling ore shipments in six months—half the time the Allies had estimated they would need.

Considering the intensity of the campaign, casualties were surprisingly low. The Germans reported 1,317 killed, 1,604 wounded and 2,375 missing; most of the missing were the men who drowned when the *Blücher* was sunk off Oslo in the initial assault on April 9. The British lost 1,896 men ashore and more than 2,500 at sea. Norwegian casualties, not counting prisoners, totaled 1,335; the French and Poles approximately 530. The Luftwaffe had lost 242 planes, of which 127 were combat aircraft; the Royal Air Force approximately 112. Warship losses were roughly equal, but the British Navy could better afford to suffer casualties; the German fleet was left with only one heavy cruiser and two light cruisers able to fight—and Hitler was to become obsessive about guarding these. His destroyer force was down to a mere four. Such losses greatly reduced the German capacity for invading Britain—one of the reasons for seeking bases on Norway in the first place.

Hitler's Scandinavian gamble had been a showy success that gave Germany great tactical advantages for the next three years. Even so, senior German officers were not sure that the advantages were decisive. They were now required to maintain a powerful occupation army on Norwegian territory—a burden that would grow increasingly oppressive.

A MASTERPIECE OF MOVEMENT

Straining in the Norwegian mud, German troops emplace a field gun, one of only eight heavy artillery pieces they brought with them in the April 1940 invasion.

CHUTES AND SADDLES FOR A "SAUCY" ATTACK

Hitler boasted that his campaign in Norway was "one of the sauciest undertakings in the history of modern warfare." The claim was fairly made; not in modern times had such a massive strike been hurled from such a distance, nor had any found its targets with such perfect coordination and such attention to fine detail.

German naval and land forces struck with an armada of 370 ships, 107,000 troops, 20,000 vehicles and 109,000 tons of supplies—all of them transported from Germany over a period of no more than 12 days. The ships were of every kind: cruisers, destroyers, minesweepers, submarines and merchantmen. Among the land vehicles were tanks, armored cars, tractors and trucks.

In addition, the Germans used air transports and paratroops to hit the defending Norwegians from behind; during the first three days of the campaign, planes carrying 8,000 men landed on airfields that had been secured by paratroopers. But exploiting new forms of transport did not deter the Germans from using older and more conventional ones: They also brought with them from Germany 20,000 horses.

Not the least of German innovations was the careful prearrangement of supplies. Since the beginnings of organized warfare, armies had moved their gear in bulk—artillery in one load, ammunition in another, food in a third, troops separate from those; and quartermasters had devoted hours on end, sometimes days to sorting out and dispersing the consignments on arrival. Now, someone in the High Command had the idea of distributing supplies among separate transports and assembling them ahead of time in the combinations that would be needed.

This prepackaging was not only novel but often was of great strategic value. If a ship was sunk en route, for instance, the cargo that went down with it existed in duplicate on some other vessel. But a more important advantage was speed: The moment the Germans unloaded a ship at its destination, whether in a Norwegian port or a deserted fjord, supplies and men could be matched up, ready for the drive inland.

A German parachutist descends near Narvik in 1940. This was the first use of paratroops to surprise and capture key points behind enemy lines.

In a scene that is reminiscent of the First World War, two horse-drawn trains hauling German artillery pass on the narrow street of a Norwegian town.

At dockside in Oslo, a German transport is readied for off-loading. The tractor trucks in its hold are already packed with an assortment of ammunition and

In Trondheim, an 88mm antiaircraft gun rises from the hold of a German collier. The ship had sailed from Germany with a layer of coal on deck (foreground) to conceal her real cargo from British aerial reconnaissance.

Ready for combat, a German squad awaits orders after arriving at a captured Norwegian airfield in the Junkers-52 trimotor in the background. The Junkers ferried nearly 30,000 German infantrymen to Norway.

supplies, and the soldiers who will man the trucks are waiting on the pier.

En route from Oslo to Bergen, German soldiers stay alert on a freight car. Within four weeks of invading Norway's coast by sea and air, German troops had moved inland and seized more than 850 miles of rail line.

Moving over the countryside by bicycle and on foot, a German vanguard finds the road blocked by boulders—among the Norwegians' few defenses. German engineers usually made short work of such obstacles.

Under fire from snipers on the wooded mountainside, a German bicycle patrol takes cover in a ditch and behind an escorting two-man Mark I tank. Although outdated by German standards, the Mark I was useful in this campaign: It was capable of maneuvering on mountain roads, and it was impervious to the limited firepower of the Norwegians.

A Heinkel-111 blasts a village in Norway, wiping out a pocket of resistance. The Germans blitzed the country with more than 400 bombers and fighter planes, achieving uncontested control of the skies.

German soldiers race into the smoldering ruins of a town readied for them by a half-hour bombardment. Taking town after town in this manner, the Germans secured 60,000 square miles of southern Norway in 25 days.

Outside a church in Trondheim, German servicemen attend a funeral
for their fallen comrades. The campaign cost the Germans about 4,000
lives on land and at sea—less than 4 per cent of the invasion force.

Gaunt and exhausted at the conclusion of their hard fighting, soldiers
of the Wehrmacht slump on the doorstep of a village bakery. After their
opening onslaught the victorious German troops had little more to do.

SWEDEN ON THE ALERT

In a demonstration of national preparedness in the spring of 1940, three Swedish Air Force bombers fly over a Stockholm park crowded with spectators.

A NATION'S BRISTLING DEFENSE OF NEUTRALITY

That the democratic kingdom of Sweden escaped invasion during World War II was the result of timely alertness, unstinting defense measures and resolute will. As early as 1936, when the Germans were conspicuously rearming, the Swedes took a first step toward preparing themselves by extending mandatory military training from 125 days to 175. They were just as coolheaded about neutrality—although that policy required walking a tenuous tightrope of diplomacy and logic.

In 1940, one seventh of the nation's export income came from iron ore, and Sweden continued to sell ore to Germany despite the fact that the iron became the steel of the German war machine. When Finland called for troops to help expel the Russian invasion, the Swedish government refused to oblige; those Swedes who answered the call (and more than 8,000 of them did) went as volunteers and fought under the Finnish flag, not their own.

Staying neutral did not mean staying inert. Sweden could not hope to win a war against any of the great powers, but it could hope to convince such potential aggressors as Germany and the Soviet Union that war against Sweden would cost more than it was worth, because the 6.5 million Swedes were primed to fight back hard if attacked.

Swedish defense measures began in earnest in 1939, as soon as Germany capped a series of expansive moves by invading Poland—thus planting Wehrmacht armor on the opposite shore of the narrow Baltic Sea, scarcely 300 miles from Stockholm. The Swedish government immediately called up 70,000 reserves. And as the War proceeded, Sweden increased its defense budget so that by 1942 the level of military spending was 10 times higher than it had been five years earlier.

Every diplomatic effort was made to emphasize that the purpose of this beefing up was not to go on the attack, but only, as Foreign Minister Christian Günther declared in 1940, "to make ourselves as indigestible as possible." And as the War raged around it, Sweden remained the most indigestible morsel in Scandinavia.

In the uniform of an Army general, Sweden's Crown Prince Gustaf Adolf returns his officers' salute as he boards a coast guard craft for inspection.

Citizens of Stockholm gather at the window of a newspaper office in September 1939 to read chilling headlines announcing Hitler's bombing of Warsaw.

Concrete pipe sections line a sidewalk in front of Stockholm's historic Adolf Fredrik's Church, in preparation for the construction of an underground bomb shelter across the street from Sweden's Royal Palace.

From a window made more cheerful by a pot of flowers, a Stockholm woman peers through a protective barricade that has been constructed of wooden planks piled high with a small mountain of sandbags.

STACKING THE ODDS ON SURVIVAL

Because the likeliest threat was from the air, Sweden took special pains to protect its citizens from bombardment. A Royal Evacuation Commission arranged housing and stockpiled food in the countryside in case the cities should have to be evacuated. Civilians cooperated with alacrity: Nearly 45,000 of them organized to scan the skies around the clock for enemy aircraft, and some 600,000 volunteered as air-raid wardens should an attack occur.

In a broader sense, the Swedes also observed events occurring abroad, and they drew lessons from the misfortunes of their neighbors. Noting, for example, that the Germans had landed assault troops on unprotected airfields in Norway, they took to parking taxicabs and private automobiles on their own airstrips, when they were not in use, to bar the landing of enemy planes.

Into a sculptured porcupine symbolizing Sweden's forbidding defenses, a woman fits a quill marking the latest purchase of defense bonds. Between April 1940 and September 1942, Swedish citizens bought the equivalent of nearly one billion dollars in such bonds.

PITCHING IN TO PAY FOR BOOTS AND GUNS

Defense cost money, and the government of Sweden found ways to raise it. Between 1938 and 1943, personal income taxes, sales taxes and duties on imported goods rose by a steep 35 per cent. Propaganda posters reinforced these measures, constantly reminding the public of the needs of the nation.

The Swedes themselves accepted the economic burden with humor. Likening their nation to the porcupine—a creature that minds its own business until affronted, and then protects itself with bristling effectiveness—the Swedes did everything they could to sharpen their defenses. They even reached into their pockets for more than the government asked. Various charitable societies sprang up to collect funds for items that the suddenly expanded armed forces desperately needed, and individual citizens gave generously of their time as well as their money.

Carrying a milkcan inscribed "For the Neutrality Watch," two Swedish students collect money for the armed forces. The funds went to buy such items as marching boots, warm sweaters and skis for mountain troops.

"Donate your share for air defense," pleads a fund-raising poster on the side of a city streetcar. Appeals such as this one were common and reflected the Swedes' incessant fear of a surprise attack from the air.

Swedish workers assemble armored cars and light tanks in a converted automotive plant. By the end of the War, Sweden had produced 790 such vehicles.

A factory worker tests the elevating gears of an antiaircraft gun.

CONVERSION TO AN ARSENAL ECONOMY

At the beginning of the War Sweden was importing at least 20 per cent of its armaments from overseas, primarily from Germany, Italy and the United States. But the Swedes were quick to foresee that arms imports would evaporate as the demands of the warring nations intensified, and in 1939 they started converting factories that produced consumer goods into war plants. Manufacturers of automobiles and trucks switched to tanks; makers of hunting rifles upgraded to machine guns; and manufacturers of kitchen matches began to spew out ammunition.

When the Swedes declared that those arms were intended to be used for defense, they meant what they said. In April of 1940, when the Luftwaffe sent war planes to Norway through Swedish air space, the Swedes tried to shoot them down with their antiaircraft guns—and the chastened Germans did not retaliate.

Technicians put finishing touches on the wings of fighter planes bearing the insignia of the Swedish Air Force, which by 1945 boasted nearly 1,000 aircraft.

Young Swedish men line up at a registration desk to enlist in the armed services. The response to the call for national mobilization in 1939 was so enthusiastic that, virtually overnight, the Army doubled in size.

A column of infantrymen in combat dress marches down a street in Malmö, just across the narrow strait that separated Sweden from German-occupied Denmark. The government often used public functions to bolster morale at home and demonstrate Swedish readiness to the world.

A ROBUST SHOW OF READINESS

Sweden's defense preparations were nowhere more evident than in the mobilization of its limited manpower. Between 1939 and 1944 the nation's standing army rose from 100,000 to 600,000—a force that was supplemented by approximately one million auxiliaries, which included a home guard of 100,000 men exempt from the draft and 800,000 women serving in noncombat jobs. Service was required of all able-bodied men between the ages of 20 and 47 (and the nation's health was so robust that fewer than 5 per cent of the men of draft age failed to meet the physical requirements).

"The fault will not be ours if our peace is broken," said Sweden's Minister of Defense in 1943. "But if our country is threatened," he added with confidence, "then we shall defend it." The Swedes never had to. Their bristling defenses had exactly the deterrent effect that Sweden intended.

To the Finnish people, the cessation of the Winter War against the Soviet Union came as a painful surprise. When terms of the peace were made public on March 13, 1940, many citizens wept openly on the streets of Finland's major cities. Newspapers framed details of the punitive agreement with black borders; throughout the country, people lowered Finland's blue-and-white flag to half-mast. "The cease-fire came as a flash from the sky," recalled one Finnish soldier. "All of us, men and officers alike, felt that we had been struck on the head by a club. The whole day passed in a kind of stupor."

Shocked though they were, the Finns were alert enough to place little stock in Soviet Foreign Minister Molotov's assurances that the pact had settled all differences between the two countries and that the Soviet Union sought no economic advantages from Finland. Their concern proved well founded; eventually, after a long period of pressures great and small, this stubborn, pragmatic people were driven into alliance with the Germans, probably the strangest combination of World War II. At the same time, the determination with which the Finns fought when the conflict returned to their soil, and the prickly self-assertion they maintained even while dependent on German favor, won them once again the admiration of the Allied world.

The Soviets had no one but themselves to blame for the renewal of the fighting. They hardly waited for the ink on the 1940 treaty to dry before they unleashed a torrent of new demands on Finland and began waging an economic and psychological war that was as nerve-racking and debilitating as actual combat. The Finns—their frontiers not yet fortified, their armed forces battered, their economy in chaos from the problems of resettling more than 400,000 refugees and rebuilding their foreign trade practically from scratch—could only stiffen their backs and endure.

As the Soviets surged into the territory ceded them by the treaty, they disregarded agreed-upon boundary lines whenever it seemed economically or strategically advantageous. In the Salla area, Red Army surveyors pushed the border westward to place certain dominating heights within Soviet territory. Similarly, they altered the map to give the Soviet Union the town of Enso, a wood-processing center that had yielded important revenues to the Finns. As though that were not enough, the Russians then required the Finns

4

THE NECESSARY ALLIANCE

to furnish free power for the center from the local hydro-electric plants.

The Soviets also made demands on material property in the ceded territories. Many factories had ceased to function during the Winter War, some because they had been damaged by the Soviets, others because the Finns had stripped them. Now they had to be put back in working order and supplied with spare parts and raw materials by the Finns. Railroads had to be equipped with rolling stock, again by the Finns. "It was particularly depressing," noted Marshal Mannerheim, "to see 75 locomotives and 2,000 railway carriages departing over the frontier." The Naval base at Hango had to be restored to its prewar condition. The Soviets did not limit themselves to war matériel; they required the Finns to replace such diverse items as movie projectors, feather beds from hotels, privately owned wood-working equipment—even bathtubs that owners of private homes had taken with them when they were dispossessed.

In June the Soviets added diplomatic pressures. Juho Paasikivi, now Finland's Ambassador to Moscow, was summoned to the Kremlin and told by Molotov that the Finns would either have to demilitarize the Aland Islands, which guarded the entrance to the Gulf of Bothnia—and Finland's western shore—or fortify them together with the Soviet Union. The Finns chose demilitarization, and were told that a Soviet consulate would be established there to oversee the work. Accordingly, 38 Russians arrived on the main island of Aland in the spring of 1940.

In July came a more worrisome demand. The Soviets wanted transit rights for troop trains traveling from Leningrad across southern Finland to Hango. This demand was particularly menacing to the Finns because the railroad to Hango cut across both of the north-south rail lines to Helsinki. Soviet troops moving on the Hango railroad could readily disrupt Finnish rail communications and threaten the capital. Eventually the Finns yielded; they had no choice. They managed to wring from the Soviets a pledge that no more than three trains would run on Finnish territory at any one time, and that soldiers and weapons would be hauled separately. But the Soviets reneged on that promise as they had on so many others. They were soon running as many trains as they pleased.

Once that summer, the pressure turned deadly when Rus-sian fighters shot down a Finnish commercial airliner carrying seven passengers to Helsinki from Tallinn, Estonia, where the Soviet Union had installed a garrison. A nearby Soviet submarine, though it took the trouble to fish a French diplomatic pouch out of the Baltic, made no effort to recover the passengers' bodies. Outraged, but determined to make no protest that might push its already strained relations with the Soviets over the edge, the Finnish government publicly attributed the loss of the aircraft and its passengers to an explosion of "unknown origin."

Inevitably, the mounting pressures told on the Finns. "The consequence of all this," wrote Ambassador Paasikivi, "was that in the summer and autumn of 1940, in our lonely position, feelings of insecurity and fear, and uncertainty of the future, increasingly ruled us Finns. I had the continuous feeling that we were on the brink of a volcano."

During the spring the Finns had raised the possibility of a defense alliance with Sweden and Norway, only to be frightened off by Soviet threats. In mid-September they tried again, this time opening discussions with Sweden for a Swedish-Finnish union under the King of Sweden. The union would have a common foreign policy and united armed forces, possibly commanded by Mannerheim. When Molotov got wind of the proposal, he was so irritated that he had Paasikivi rousted out of bed at 11:30 one night to make it understood that Finland's safety depended on Soviet good will alone. Paasikivi's report of the incident to Helsinki so alarmed the Finns that they broke off all discussions with the Swedes.

These developments were watched with keen interest by the other belligerents—and nowhere more keenly than in Germany. The Germans had honest feelings of sympathy for the Finns, many of whom had fought with the Germans against czarist Russia in World War I. They also had practical concerns. The German arms industry urgently needed Finnish copper, nickel, molybdenum and other minerals. "I do not wish to deliver Finland into the arms of the Russians," Hitler said to his military chiefs, as he watched the Finns yielding to one Russian pressure after another. In August he ordered an increase of German strength in northern Norway from 1,000 troops to about 55,000. He ordered preparations made for the occupation of the Petsamo area by the mountain corps stationed in Norway (the plan was to be called Operation *Reindeer)*, and he decided to court the Finns with weapons.

But because the Germans were still paying lip service to the pact they had made with the Soviet Union the previous summer, negotiations for the arms would have to be conducted secretly. Accordingly, in mid-August, Lieut. Colonel Joseph Veltjens, a crony of Reich Marshal Hermann Göring, began a series of closed-door conferences in Helsinki with Mannerheim. Veltjens informed Mannerheim that Germany would sell Finland modern weapons, and release or replace those en route to Finland that had been held up in Norwegian ports. Germany would also furnish Finland with fuel and foodstuffs. In return, the Germans wanted temporary permission to send troops and equipment across Finland to Kirkenes in northernmost Norway—the shortest and safest route from Germany.

The Finns readily agreed. In late August, the first shipment of German weapons—which would in time total 63 batteries of field artillery, 28 batteries of antiaircraft guns and 150,000 antitank mines—arrived in Finland. A few weeks later, on September 22, German troops began crossing the Baltic in Finnish ships to the ports of Vaasa and Oulu. From there, they traveled in sealed railway cars to the end of the track at Rovaniemi in northern Finland, then they marched up the Arctic Highway to Ivalo and along mountain roads to Kirkenes. Supply depots were set up along the route at Vaasa, Rovaniemi, Ivalo and other points along the highway; eventually they would be manned by about 2,200 housekeeping troops.

The Finns knew that the transit agreement was risky; the sight of German soldiers moving freely across Finland was bound to raise Soviet hackles. "But at the time the agreement was signed," Mannerheim recalled, "it released a sigh of relief from the whole country." The Germans held fewer terrors for the Finns than the Russians, and in the face of the looming Soviet menace the German reputation for invincibility gave the Finns a sense of well-being.

Long before the Finns made their arms deal with the Germans, Soviet demands had so disturbed the Finns that the Finnish government had given Mannerheim a free hand to rebuild his battle-ravaged army. Mannerheim received indirect help in this great task from the Soviets themselves, who, flush with a sense of martial accomplishment, had written no military limitations into the treaty that ended the Winter War. The Finnish forces had been required neither to demobilize nor to return the weapons and armor that they had captured.

The government acted quickly on Mannerheim's recommendations. In December of 1940 it increased the period of compulsory military service from one year to two. The number of Army divisions was raised from nine to 16, and each division was required to have at least one active brigade. Nine of those brigades—about 54,000 men all told—were positioned on the country's southeast frontier. One was placed outside the Soviet base at Hango, three were spread along the northeast border and three were kept on standby in the interior. In case of war, each brigade would hold its position until the remainder of its division—another 8,000 men—could join it.

Two elite light infantry brigades, a motorized cavalry brigade and the beginnings of an armored division (equipped largely with captured Russian vehicles) also were assigned to the reserve. When fully mobilized, the revitalized Finnish Army would be able to put more than 400,000 men in the field, 100,000 more than before the Winter War—and an astonishing 10 per cent of the nation's total population. The increase in strength was made possible by calling up men who had been exempted before 1939 and by using 80,000 members of the Lotta Svärd, the women's auxiliary, in clerical and battle-support jobs.

In the meantime, the Finnish armaments industry was tooled up to turn out modern antitank and antiaircraft guns, 120mm mortars, 105mm fieldpieces, and the shells to supply them.

The Finnish Air Force, which had lost perhaps a third of its strength in the course of the Winter War, also sought to improve its fighting capability—and let no obstacle stand in its way. One escapade by a group of daring Finnish aviators netted 44 new war planes that had seemed destined never to reach Finland. The Finns had been dispatched to an airfield near the west coast of Sweden to take delivery of the planes, surplus Brewster B-239 fighters that the United States was sending Finland via Sweden. By the time the Finns arrived to pick up the planes, however, the Swedes

In the summer of 1941, German and Finnish troops launched attacks on Soviet defenses from the Arctic Ocean to the Gulf of Finland. They struck east and southeast through former Finnish territories (shaded areas) lost to the Soviets the year before, and headed for various points along the vital Murmansk railroad. The offensive ended in December along a stationary front that in places lay 225 miles inside the Soviet Union.

had decided to take the Brewsters to beef up their own Air Force—the Germans having invaded neighboring Norway that very day. For two days the Finns were stymied. But then a Swedish officer told them in jest, "You can take off if you can get the fuel."

The offer seemed harmless enough, for fuel supplies at the airfield were kept under lock and key. But the Finns saw it as an opening. "There and then we decided that he who

laughed last . . ." remembered one of them; he telephoned a local civilian distributor and arranged for him to deliver an order of high-octane fuel to the field at a time when the Swedish guards would be at lunch. The fuel came, and the Finns were soon revving the Brewsters' engines. "Without waiting for a complete warm-up," one pilot recalled, "we took off directly from the concrete apron, circled the field once, pretending not to understand the frantic signals of

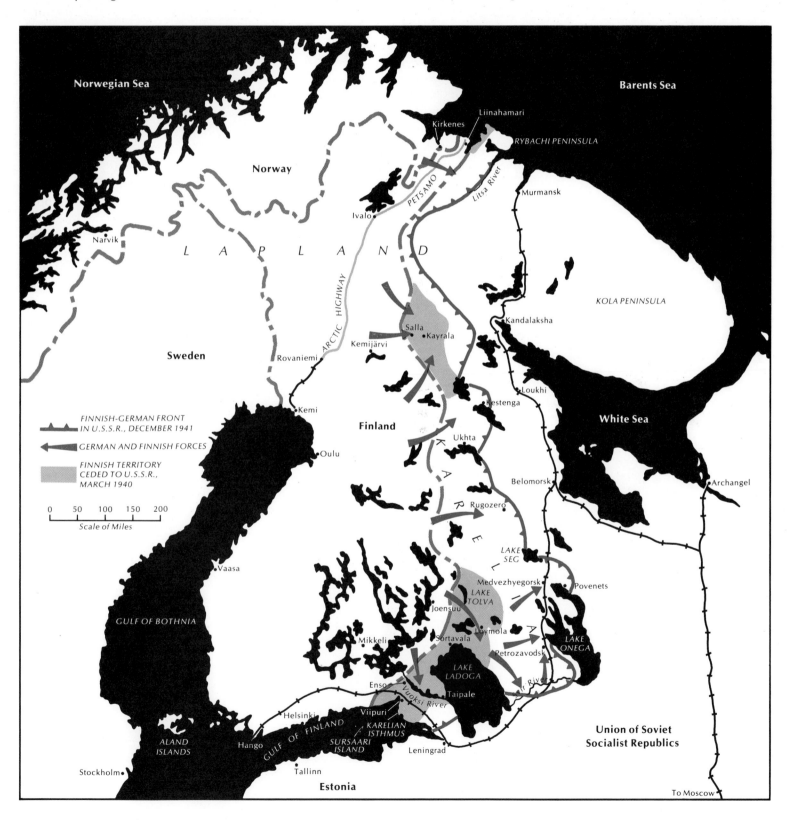

FINNISH-GERMAN FRONT
IN U.S.S.R., DECEMBER 1941

GERMAN AND FINNISH FORCES

FINNISH TERRITORY
CEDED TO U.S.S.R.,
MARCH 1940

0   50   100   150   200
Scale of Miles

the Swedes who were now milling around below us, and were on our way."

To the Soviets, the Finns' military build-up and their open abetment of the Germans was a dead-serious affair. When Molotov arrived in Berlin on the 12th of November, 1940, for talks with Hitler, one of the first topics he brought up was Finland. Did the Germans, he inquired, intend to honor the provision in the 1939 German-Soviet pact that established Finland as part of the Soviet Union's sphere of influence?

Hitler equivocated. He realized that Finland was in Russia's sphere, he said, and thus he would end the transit agreement by which German troops were passing through Finland en route to Norway. On the other hand, Germany had a legitimate interest in the uninterrupted delivery of Finnish nickel and lumber, and wished to avoid the disturbances in the Baltic that a new Russo-Finnish war would bring. Such a conflict, Hitler added ominously, would have "unforeseeable consequences." With that pronouncement, observed one German diplomat, "the Führer held his umbrella over Finland."

Two months later, the British and the Soviets heedlessly drove the Finns even further under that umbrella. In January of 1941, after pointing out to the Finns that permitting German troops to cross their territory was eroding British sympathy, Prime Minister Churchill threatened to deny Finland's ore-laden ships from Petsamo access to the North Sea—their trade route to Germany. Then the Soviets, who had promised to provide the Finns with grain and oil, halted all trade with Finland.

The Finns faced a hungry time. Sweden could supply only a trickle of grain. Germany was the only place to turn. Within a few weeks of the Soviet embargo, Mannerheim noted, "90 per cent of our imports were coming from Germany." But Germany would soon demand a heavy price for that timely support.

On December 18, 1940, Hitler had issued Führer Directive No. 21—an order that was to have somber consequences for the Finns. The culmination of months of planning, the directive was code-named *Barbarossa* (Red Beard) after Frederick I, a red-bearded Germanic ruler of the 12th Century. It was an elaborate scenario for a massive invasion of the Soviet Union by three million German troops along a 1,250-mile front.

The northernmost flank of that front stretched from Arctic Norway across Finland to the northern reaches of Russia, an area known to cartographers as Lapland. The area worried Hitler for two reasons. First, he feared that once his armies were committed inside Russia, the British would invade Norway and seize his bases there, thus severing German land and sea communications with northern Finland. Second, he fretted over the possibility that Stalin would use the 850-mile-long railroad from Leningrad north to Murmansk to position troops for a stab at Petsamo and the Swedish iron mines just east of Narvik.

Those fears were reinforced in early March when a mixed force of British Commandos, Royal Navy engineers and Norwegians raided the Lofoten Islands, a few miles off the coast of Norway. The force destroyed 11 fish-oil and fish-meal factories, petroleum storage tanks containing 950,000 gallons of fuel oil, several merchant ships and an armed trawler. They took 226 German prisoners without suffering a single casualty. To prevent any further coastal incursions by the British, Hitler immediately ordered 160 batteries of artillery rushed to Norway, along with two garrison divisions and SS reinforcements—bringing his troops in Norway to 150,000 men in all. He then informed General von Falkenhorst, commander of the Occupation army, that his primary mission during Operation *Barbarossa* would be the defense of Norway.

With Norway protected, Hitler planned to secure the Petsamo area, advance into Russia, cut the Murmansk railroad and capture the port of Murmansk, Russia's only ice-free port with year-round access to the Atlantic. These moves depended on the connivance, if not the outright participation, of the Finns, whom Hitler had not officially notified of *Barbarossa*. Nevertheless, the Führer had little doubt they would join him; for months, officers of his military staff had been holding secret talks with senior Finnish officers, and had found them eager to provide information on such matters as Soviet defenses along the border. "They are a plucky people," Hitler told his staff, "and they are thirsting for revenge."

To organize the Petsamo-Murmansk operation, Hitler had already chosen one of his favorite generals—Eduard Dietl, the officer who had been lionized in the German press as the "Victor of Narvik" for his take-over of that port a year earlier. Now, in April 1941, Hitler summoned Dietl to the Reich Chancellery in Berlin.

Dietl arrived on the 21st of the month to find Hitler, who had celebrated his 52nd birthday the previous day, in an expansive mood. Wearing his old-fashioned nickel-framed spectacles, Hitler strode to a table map of Scandinavia and northern Russia and placed the index finger of his left hand on Petsamo and that of his right hand on Murmansk. "The distance to the nickel mines is only 60 miles, and from Petsamo to Kirkenes is only another 30," he explained. "To have the Russians in this area would be disastrous. We must eliminate this danger at the very beginning of our Eastern campaign. Not by waiting, but by attacking. You've got to manage those ridiculous 60 miles from Petsamo to Murmansk."

General Dietl was flabbergasted, for although he had been planning his attack in accordance with Hitler's wishes, he knew that those 60 miles were anything but ridiculous. Indeed, he had come to the meeting intending to dissuade Hitler from attacking across the tundra. "My Führer," he replied, "the landscape up there outside Murmansk is just as it was after the Creation. There's not a tree, not a shrub, not a human settlement, nothing but rock and scree. There are countless torrents, lakes and fast-flowing rivers with rapids and waterfalls.

"In the summer, there's swamp—and in winter there's ice, snow and it's 40 to 50 degrees below zero," Dietl continued. "This 60-mile belt of tundra surrounding Murmansk like protective armor is one big wilderness. War has never before been waged there, since the pathless, stony desert is virtually impenetrable for formations."

Dietl's outburst was only a partial summation of the woes that would face any operation across Lapland. The general could have added that Lapland is also the land of the midnight sun and the northern lights. That close to the north magnetic pole, radio signals are easily distorted; radar, magnetic torpedoes and compasses are similarly affected. Mirages haunt the coastlines—distant islands, ordinarily beyond the horizon, are lifted into view. Images expand, blur and shrink; ships and airplanes vanish into the grayish glimmer of Arctic sea and sky. There may be night frosts even in summer, yet July has afternoon temperatures of more than 80° F.—and this heat brings bloodthirsty mosquitoes in clouds. In midwinter, the snow is usually too deep for any but specially qualified ski troops. Spring and autumn are seasons of thaw and storms; roads dissolve, airfields are flooded, and latticed wooden runways must be put down if planes are to land or take off.

Through this wasteland trek only the Lapps, a nomadic people who have herded their reindeer across the barren landscape for thousands of years. For an appropriate reward—useful items like blankets, coffee, brandy and tobacco—they might be persuaded to smuggle a British agent from Norway to Sweden, or to chop wood for the Germans, but otherwise they had no interest in the War except to keep out of its way.

Instead of attacking across such a forsaken place, Dietl urged, why not cut the Murmansk railroad farther south, in territory better suited to military operations? Such a move, he said, would be just as effective in keeping the Soviets away from Petsamo. Dietl's argument made sense, but Hitler believed in his own innate military genius and he was loath to change his mind. "Leave your papers with me," he told Dietl. "I'll think it over."

What emerged two weeks later was a compromise plan that reflected some of Hitler's ideas and some of Dietl's. It called for two operations that would sever the Murmansk railroad at three points. The first operation, dubbed *Polar Fox,* followed Dietl's suggestion. Two divisions launched from the town of Rovaniemi in central Finland would strike the Soviet strong point at Salla, then advance on the railhead at Kandalaksha, 220 miles south of Murmansk. As part of the same operation, another two divisions—both of them Finnish—would simultaneously cross the border to the south, one to help in the attack on Salla, and the other to cut the railroad at Loukhi. The second operation, designated *Platinum Fox,* was pure Hitler: Two more divisions would advance from Petsamo across the tundra that Dietl judged impassable and that Hitler had dismissed as "a ridiculous 60 miles." Their mission was to cut the railroad and capture Murmansk.

To connect this advance with his main offensive into Russia, and to pin down as many Soviet troops as possible while his spearheads dealt with the Red Army concentrated behind the Russian frontier, Hitler would need Finland's assistance. He had been impressed with the Finns' bravura performance in the Winter War and hoped, at the very least, to induce Mannerheim to lend two divisions for the attacks on Salla and Loukhi. As May wore on, Hitler decided it was time to let the Finns in on what he had in store for the Soviet Union—and for Finland. Accordingly, he sent Karl Schnurre, an officer of the German Foreign Ministry, to call on Finnish President Risto Ryti. Schnurre explained that tensions between the Soviet Union and Germany had increased to the point where both countries were making preparations for war. Of course, he added, Germany would never start such a war.

Finland also did not want to be drawn into war with the Soviet Union, Ryti told Schnurre, but would surely fight if attacked. Would Germany, he asked, regard a Soviet attack on Finland as an act of war? Schnurre, who had been waiting for just such a question, replied in the affirmative and asked Ryti to send his generals to the headquarters of the German Armed Forces High Command (OKW) for further consultations.

On the 25th of May, Lieut. General Erik Heinrichs, Mannerheim's chief of staff, arrived with a delegation of Finnish military men at the OKW headquarters in Salzburg, under orders from Mannerheim to "let the Germans talk and explain while you listen." Heinrichs did exactly that, providing an attentive audience for OKW Chief of Operations Alfred Jodl. If war came, General Jodl stated, Germany wanted the Finns initially to mobilize their armed forces in order to tie down as many Soviet troops along their frontier as possible, without actually opening hostilities. Germany

would also want free use of Finnish airfields and the support of Finnish troops in the Petsamo area. In addition, the Germans would expect the Finns to capture Hango, and would provide them air and possibly ground support for that operation.

The next day the Finnish delegates moved on to Berlin, where they met with Army Chief of Staff Franz Halder. He told them that a Finnish offensive to the east or west of Lake Ladoga would also be helpful. Halder was careful to discuss German plans in hypothetical terms, but the Finns were under no illusions about what lay ahead. In any event, the Finns probably could not keep the Germans from occupying Petsamo, and once that happened, the Soviets would surely strike at Finland.

"A war between Germany and Russia may be to the advantage of the entire world," President Ryti reasoned after listening to the delegation's report. "Germany is the only state presently capable of destroying Russian military power, or at least of considerably weakening it; nor would the world greatly suffer should Germany itself be weakened in this process. But weakening Russia to as great an extent as possible is the primary condition for our survival." The Finns were confident of a German victory, and supporting that victory would earn them back the territory they had surrendered to the Russians in 1940, and probably East Karelia as well.

Thus the Finns decided to cast their lot with the Germans. A final series of talks took place in Helsinki during the first week of June, and the Finns and the Germans worked out details for a joint attack on the Soviet Union—still without naming a date. At the conclusion of these talks Halder noted in his diary that "the Finnish high command has squared

A member of the Lotta Svärd, Finland's women's auxiliary, spoon-feeds a wounded German soldier at a field hospital during the Continuation War. About 200,000 Lottas served as volunteer cooks, nurses, radio operators and aircraft spotters—often so close to the front that more than 400 were killed.

its plans with ours and seems to be going at it with every ounce of energy."

For all that, the Finns wanted to preserve the illusion that they had been unavoidably drawn into fighting, so they insisted on the right to limit their role to that of cobelligerent instead of ally. This technicality would allow them to keep most of their troops under Finnish command and—significantly—enable them to determine the extent of their own participation in the War.

The Finnish President and a Cabinet committee approved the plan, and told the Germans so on June 14. By then the Finns were already mobilizing. On the 16th, Germany informed the Finnish government that Operation *Barbarossa* would be launched on June 22.

The movement of more than 48,000 German troops across Finland was carried out under the guise of a major exchange of troops stationed in northern Norway. The general concentration of forces along the Soviet Union's border was screened by Operation *Harpoon,* which simulated preparations for a full-scale invasion of England. Air reconnaissance of Great Britain was intensified, English-German language handbooks for the guidance of invading troops were published, and the Wehrmacht was screened for men who could speak English. Throughout Norway, Denmark, France, Belgium, Holland, Austria and Poland, troops maneuvered as if preparing to head for the English Channel. The deception worried the British and deceived the Soviets.

Barbarossa began on schedule. At approximately 3 a.m. on June 22, masses of German artillery pounded Red Army positions all along the Soviet border from the Baltic to the Black Sea and thousands of panzers burst through the disorganized Russian lines; over the next few hours Luftwaffe strikes knocked out 1,200 Soviet planes. In Finland, during the same hours, Mountain Corps Norway had marched at a leisurely pace into the Petsamo area and occupied it without incident. At the same time, the Finns landed a Naval detachment on the Aland Islands—a move that surprisingly brought no reaction from the Soviets—and began laying mines in Finland's territorial waters.

The world first learned of Germany's audacious invasion of the Soviet Union later that morning, when Hitler announced that "in league with Finnish divisions, our comrades under the Victor of Narvik stand on the shores of the Arctic Ocean." The Finnish government formally declared itself uninvolved in the war between Germany and Russia, but added that Finland would defend itself if attacked.

To the surprise of no one, the Soviets quickly responded. On June 25, large numbers of Russian planes struck at towns and cities across southern Finland. The Finnish Air Force shot down 26 enemy planes, and the Finnish government promptly repeated its intention to fight in self-defense. Because the new conflict had come scarcely 15 months after the cessation of the Winter War, the Finns labeled it the Continuation War. Mannerheim quickly set up headquarters at Mikkeli, the little town from which he had directed the Winter War. There he worked out details of his main offensive, which would ultimately send the Army of Karelia down the isthmus between Lakes Ladoga and Onega.

Of all the operations that thrust into the Soviet Union during the final days of June 1941, the hardest assignment fell to Dietl. In charge of *Platinum Fox,* he had the unenviable task of pushing east from Petsamo to Murmansk—the 60-mile route that Hitler had called ridiculous. The ordeal was to exceed Dietl's worst fears, for to the frustrations provided by nature, the Russians added others—and so did Hitler and the German High Command.

Dietl's offensive began propitiously enough. He launched it at 3 a.m. on June 29, advancing his 2nd and 3rd Mountain Divisions and a Finnish detachment of 600 to 800 men through a heavy morning fog that made air support—and Soviet strafing attacks—impossible. The 2nd Division, the northernmost of his columns, rolled over light Soviet border defenses and progressed about 15 miles into Russia in six days. By July 4, two battalions of the 2nd Division had cut the neck of the Rybachi Peninsula, isolating the Soviet forces on the peninsula and protecting the Germans' northern flank.

The 3rd Division, 10 or 12 miles to the south, had a harder time, thanks to some careless German intelligence. Major General Hans Kreysing, commanding the division, had expected to roll a light-tank battalion along a dirt road into the town of Motovka and on to Murmansk. To his chagrin, there was no road—only impassable terrain. German map analysts had read the double dotted lines on Soviet maps as dirt roads, when in fact the dots denoted telegraph lines and reindeer trails. The 3rd Division thus had to switch routes and move northward through wilderness to link up with the 2nd Division.

After some rough going they made it, and on July 6 the two divisions mounted an attack across the Litsa River, the icy waterway that guards the far western approaches to Murmansk. Paddling across in inflatable dinghies under heavy Soviet shelling, the Germans reached the Litsa's east bank and—within tantalizing sight of the main road to Murmansk—established a bridgehead. It was a tenuous one: Only two artillery batteries had been able to manhandle their guns across the rocks and scree to the bridgehead, and between them they had no more than 40 shells. Nevertheless it was a bridgehead, and for Dietl it represented a gain.

Now distant events conspired to plague the general. German Naval Intelligence notified Hitler that an Allied convoy was in Arctic waters, destination unknown. Hitler leaped to the conclusion that the ships signaled an invasion of Norway. He ordered Dietl to release a battalion of infantry and three artillery batteries and send them back west to strengthen the defenses of Petsamo. The loss of those 1,500 men from his front lines was a crippling blow, particularly because Soviet transports had landed two fresh battalions at a bay on his left flank. Dietl had no choice but to withdraw to the west bank of the Litsa.

Five days later, the German commander recrossed the river and reestablished a bridgehead. But now the Soviets trucked artillery and reinforcements up to the front, positioned infantry atop several 1,000-foot hills overlooking the river, and made a shambles of Dietl's assault. Their guns were too much for an attacking force that lacked artillery, air support and reserves. As German soldiers fell to the Russian fire, a double task fell upon Dietl's service troops; after lugging supplies forward to the front, they had to turn around and carry the wounded to the rear—a distance of some 10 miles. Each trip required two four-man stretcher crews, who often took as long as 10 hours to bear a single casualty across the rugged terrain. The strain of conducting an assault under such conditions was enormous; one of Dietl's divisions reported that even its pack mules were dying of exhaustion. Reluctantly, on July 17, Dietl ordered his men to take the defensive.

Murmansk was only 30 miles away, and again and again throughout July and early August, Dietl reported to headquarters that he could take the port only if he had more men. At length, through the intercession of General von Falkenhorst, who was commanding seven divisions in Norway that had little to do but admire the scenery and wait for an attack that did not come, Hitler yielded grudgingly and approved the transfer of two regiments to Dietl.

On September 8, once the reinforcements arrived, Dietl resumed his assault. To his dismay he found the new regiments of little help. They were green troops with no combat experience. Typically, they would blunder through jumbles of huge boulders, marshy tarns and small, blind valleys—

bypassing cleverly camouflaged Russian positions. They would then be encircled by the Soviets and mauled.

For a week Dietl urged his men on through cold and rain, defying constant counterattacks by three tough Soviet outfits, one of them composed of sailors, labor-camp inmates and convicts. His stocks of ammunition, gasoline and rations were dangerously low, and in the middle of September he received the bad news that they would not soon be increased; Allied ships had sunk six German vessels off northern Norway, and Admiral Raeder had halted all merchant shipping through those waters.

In two and a half months of fighting, Dietl had punched a salient 15 miles into Russian Lapland at a cost of 10,290 casualties. The Soviets were holding firm, and on September 18, Dietl decided he could push no more. In frustration, he ordered the construction of winter fortifications along the Litsa and across the neck of the Rybachi Peninsula. There his troops dug in for the long Arctic winter.

While Dietl was launching *Platinum Fox*, Lieut. General Hans Feige, a career officer with four decades' experience, and Brigadier General Hjalmar Siilasvuo, the Finnish hero of Suomussalmi, had been marshaling their forces for Operation *Polar Fox*. Feige's objective was to capture Salla—now held by a 20,000-man Soviet garrison—then drive on to Kandalaksha, 90 miles beyond, and cut the Murmansk railroad. Siilasvuo, meanwhile, would cover Feige's southern flank while leading a Finnish advance on the railroad at Loukhi, 70 miles inside Soviet territory. Feige had 40,600 German troops for his part of the operation, among them the 36th Corps, consisting of two divisions, and Battle Group North, an 8,000-man SS unit newly formed from police and security units in Germany. He also commanded 12,000 men of the Finnish 6th Division. Siilasvuo commanded the Finnish III Corps, numbering another 12,000 men.

Battle Group North, like all SS combat units, which were Hitler's favorites, was superbly equipped. It had two infantry regiments, a machine-gun battalion, an antitank battalion, an artillery battalion, an engineer company—all completely motorized—and a light-tank battalion.

Unfortunately for the operation, Battle Group North's abundance of up-to-date equipment was neutralized by a lack of training. The officers had received no more than a short course of lectures and demonstrations of combat tactics; the artillery battalion had fired its guns but once; even the infantrymen had scarcely tried their weapons until their commanding general gave them a little target practice en route to the Russian front. Their rawness was to be a terrible handicap.

General Feige planned a four-pronged assault on Salla. One of his German regiments was to advance along the Kandalaksha-Salla road for a direct attack on the garrison there; two more regiments would swing around Salla to hit it from the north, and Battle Group North would attack from the south. Meanwhile, the Finnish 6th Division would cross the Russian front 45 miles south of Salla and try to take the enemy from the rear.

The undertaking got off to a poor start. The only one of Feige's groups that made any progress at all was the northern group, which advanced through the forest and got about three miles into Soviet territory. The frontal attack was stopped 500 yards across the border and thrown back by a Soviet counterattack. And the southern prong fared even worse. At the first sight of the Russians, some of the green troops of Battle Group North lost heart and straggled toward the rear; eventually they fell off in such numbers that the Soviets were able to leave them and concentrate on the other two groups to the north. The resulting three-day battle set the woods aflame, and Feige and his experienced troops had all they could do to hold their ground.

Feige finally got his center regiment moving and broke through the first line of defenses around Salla. But on July 4 the soldiers of Battle Group North bolted once more, and this time their fright led them to stampede. The men poured down the road toward Kemijärvi, shouting that Russian tanks were at their heels. Feige and his staff stationed themselves across the roadway and spent several difficult hours getting as many careering vehicles and panicked men halted and turned around as they could. Some vehicles broke through their roadblock and raced all the way to Kemijärvi, 50 miles to the west. Battle Group North's first taste of combat had cost it 73 killed and 232 wounded. Another 147 were missing. The losses in themselves were comparatively minor. But the flight of the survivors had left Feige with a gap in his forces.

He ordered the SS men back into his line, but because

125

they had proved so untrustworthy, he appealed to Falkenhorst for reinforcements of more reliable troops. Falkenhorst obliged with a motorized machine-gun battalion and a regiment from the 163rd Division. When they reached him, on July 6, Feige resumed his advance on Salla; after two days of hard fighting his column clubbed the Russians out of their stronghold, seizing most of their artillery and knocking out or capturing 50 tanks.

Wherever they fought together, the Germans were astonished by the attitude of their Finnish comrades, who seemed to take the business of war quite nonchalantly. For instance, during a Soviet strafing attack over Salla at 3 a.m. the Germans rushed out of their hillside dugouts fully dressed and wearing steel helmets to man their antiaircraft guns. By contrast, the Finnish troops casually appeared outside their dugout doors, as their lieutenant noted, "in their long white flannel underwear, leisurely contemplating the spectacle." It was a common saying among the German officers that "with half the losses, the Finns will accomplish twice as much as the Germans."

The difference in attitudes did nothing to hamper the undertaking; in fact, the two armies fought well in harness, and German commanders sought to incorporate Finnish units into their forces whenever possible.

Despite their success in wresting Salla from the Soviets,

the invaders had not been able to prevent the Russian troops from escaping 10 miles eastward to the village of Kayrala, which was protected by lakes on its northern and southern sides. There the Soviets rallied and, with the help of 20,000 reinforcements, they entrenched themselves and waited.

The Germans made two stabs at a frontal assault, but were easily rebuffed. Feige decided that if he were to take the town at all, the Germans would have to detour around the northern lake—a time-consuming flanking movement that meant building a road through forested bogs—while the Finnish 6th Division attacked around the southern lake.

The movement seemed to take forever, and on July 23 Falkenhorst paid a visit to Feige's 169th Division in the wilderness to find out why. He was outraged to find soldiers lounging in the sun in hammocks instead of working on the supply road they had been assigned to build. Feige's staff had an explanation: The weather had been unusually hot in the land of the midnight sun; several times the temperature had been above 85° F., and twice it had gone as high as 97° F. The heat—and accompanying clouds of mosquitoes—made it impossible to work during the day; consequently, the men were resting then and working during the sunlit nights, which were cooler and free of insects. Feige's officers added that the odd regimen was beginning to exhaust the men and ruin their morale.

Falkenhorst, who was himself under merciless pressure from Hitler, was unappeased. He told Feige that the men were talking of "stationary warfare" and "defense," and added that if Feige could not stop such talk, Falkenhorst would ask headquarters for a more energetic commander who could. He then ordered Feige to name a day and hour, and prepare to attack.

Feige set the attack for three nights later—July 26 at 11 p.m.—and was ready on schedule. For three days he drove his men on, here and there gaining a mile or so but making no real headway. He asked for more men, but now Hitler refused—he could not drain his army in Norway any further—and abruptly ordered the 36th Corps to halt the attack on July 30.

Feige's men had gone through much, for little gain. In one month, the 36th Corps had advanced little more than 13 miles; it had suffered 5,500 casualties—3,296 of them from a single division. Salla was in German hands, but the drive on the Kandalaksha railhead was now suspended for a few weeks. Then followed another month of fitful fighting, after which the drive was abandoned altogether in late September.

To the south, Siilasvuo's III Corps, heading for Loukhi, had thrust swiftly forward some 40 miles into Soviet territory by July 18, moving across and along lakes and streams in logging boats and timber rafts towed by motor tugboats appropriated from lumber companies. By August 7 they had reached Kestenga, 40 miles short of their objective. Then the Soviets sent in a patchwork group of reserves: 500 forced laborers, 600 men from their Fourteenth Army Headquarters Guard and a replacement battalion from Murmansk. For another three weeks the Russians held on, slowing the Finnish drive. Then came more reinforcements: the 88th Rifle Division from Archangel. By now the Finns were exhausted, and on August 25 General Siilasvuo decided it was time to halt and regroup.

Meanwhile, other Finnish troops were busy on the Karelian Isthmus, which they had lost to the Soviet Union at the close of the Winter War. Mannerheim planned a major offensive that was to open north of Lake Ladoga and head down the isthmus between Ladoga and Lake Onega as far as the Svir River. He assembled a force he called the Army of Karelia, composed of five divisions and three brigades, totaling 100,000 men. Its left flank consisted of the cavalry brigade and the 1st and 2nd Jaeger Brigades, parts of which were mounted on bicycles. The center, which was to make the main thrust of the attack from 25 miles north of Lake Ladoga, was made up of the VI Corps; on its right was the VII Corps. To the west, and poised to move down the isthmus in support of the same drive, were three divisions of the II Corps and four divisions of the IV Corps. The 17th Division and a separate brigade were to contain the Soviet garrison at Hango. At the last moment, part of the German 163rd Infantry Division was stationed at Joensuu, northwest of Lake Ladoga, as a reserve.

All these gave Mannerheim a 3-to-1 superiority, because when Operation *Barbarossa* began the Russians had been forced to pull three or four divisions from the region surrounding Lake Ladoga to meet the German drive on Leningrad, leaving only four divisions on the Karelian Isthmus and three northeast of the lake. The garrison at Hango was left with only two rifle brigades, plus a few fortification and antiaircraft units.

The 1st Jaeger Brigade got off to a good start on July 10. Its bicycles made it so mobile in the country around Lake Ladoga that it could perform the spearhead role of a panzer division—and it lanced right through the Russian 71st Infan-

Finnish infantrymen pass quickly over the snow-mantled tracks of the Murmansk railroad in late 1941. The seizure of sections of this critical rail link between Leningrad and the ice-free port of Murmansk proved to be the high-water mark of Finland's incursion into Russian territory.

try Division at the village of Korpisel'kya. Behind came the VI Corps, which rolled up the Soviet front on both its flanks as it went. The swiftness of the attack sent the Soviets reeling southward. They tried to regroup at the village of Loymola, directly north of the lake, but a Finnish antitank battalion loaded its guns—which usually were pulled by horses—onto trucks that sped them to a hill overlooking the village. The Soviets were so startled that before they could react, the Finns had scored an easy victory. They took Loymola and a nearby railhead with scarcely a casualty.

In six days the Finns had fought their way through 65 miles of forest, and by July 16 they had reached the northeast corner of Lake Ladoga, driving a wedge between the Red Army forces in East Karelia and those on the Karelian Isthmus. Another eight days' fighting brought the Finnish VI Corps down the eastern shore of Lake Ladoga and 15 miles beyond the 1939 border to the Tuulos River. There, Mannerheim ordered a halt.

Brigadier General Paavo Talvela, commander of the VI Corps, later said he thought that the decision to halt was a serious mistake. He had already lost 3,500 men in his advance, but the Russians were in disordered flight, and he was certain that he could cover the last 40 miles to the Svir River quickly, with few additional losses. Talvela had his orders, however, and Mannerheim was determined to wait.

The respite gave the Soviets time to bring up fresh troops to counterattack, and Talvela would lose another 3,500 men before being allowed to retake the offensive six weeks later.

Mannerheim had his own timetable. On the 31st of July, he launched a pincers attack to clear out Russian forces along the northwest shore of Lake Ladoga. The II Corps attacked from the west, while the VII Corps converged from the north. Two weeks later, Sortavala, which had been lost in the Winter War, once more was in Finnish hands, as were large quantities of weapons and equipment that the Russians had to abandon as they fled by light warships and transports across the lake.

With Sortavala secured, Mannerheim was ready on August 10 to steam-roll down the Karelian Isthmus. The main attack was to follow a slanting, southwest course across the isthmus to cut the roads and railroad between Viipuri and Leningrad, while a secondary attack swept down the western shore of Lake Ladoga. Before 1939 the Finnish Army had conducted war games in the area. Officers and men knew the terrain by heart, and thus were able to outflank and outfox the Soviets at every turn. On August 21, scarcely a week after the Finns opened the drive, the three Red Army divisions around Viipuri began blowing up their border fortifications and falling back. One division was to stay behind to make a rear-guard stand at Viipuri, while the other two were to move northward and try to throw the advancing Finns back across the Vuoksi River.

The weight and determination of Mannerheim's offensive, however, astonished the Soviets and swamped virtually all resistance. By August 25, the Finns were able to encircle Viipuri and put a division-sized force ashore south of the city, thus seizing control of roads and rails in the area. Then, as they had done successfully in the Winter War, they chopped the three Soviet divisions into isolated pockets and proceeded to grind them down.

In the dozens of murderous little fights that followed, the Finns gave no quarter—even when the opponents were women who fought alongside the men in the Red Army. Lieutenant Gregorius Ekholm, who had served as a 16-year-old volunteer during the Winter War, had been assigned to comb the woods for Soviet stragglers. Suddenly he discovered that his submachine gun was empty—and at the same

Finnish gunners take on advancing Russian tanks during the Karelia offensive. Because the Finns had so few tanks of their own, they placed great emphasis on knocking out enemy armor, and the government decorated successful gun crews with the coveted Tank-Killer's Badge.

Barely visible in the Karelian woods, four Red Army soldiers raise their hands in surrender to Finnish troops who have flushed them out. A German soldier wrote admiringly of the Finns: "Nothing is heard or seen of them whether resting or marching, even from the closest proximity."

moment he found himself face to face with a Soviet woman soldier brandishing a Nagant revolver. The woman tried to shoot but her weapon misfired. Ekholm drew his pistol and shot her dead—reflecting later that it had been no occasion for chivalry.

By August 29 the last of the stragglers had been killed or rounded up, and Viipuri—the second-largest city in Finland until the Soviets seized it during the Winter War—again belonged to the Finns. The capture of Viipuri prompted Field Marshal Wilhelm Keitel, OKW Chief of Staff, to propose another task for Mannerheim. What Keitel wanted was to have Finnish troops cross the pre-1939 Finnish-Soviet border and threaten Leningrad from the north, while General Wilhelm von Leeb led the German Army Group North in attacking the city from the south.

Mannerheim was reluctant. According to his memoirs he believed a Finnish assault on Leningrad was politically unwise, so long as the War's outcome was still uncertain, in view of the Soviet Union's long-standing claim that an independent Finland was a threat to that city. Consequently Mannerheim and President Ryti agreed that no such offensive should be launched.

The Germans persisted. They sent Alfred Jodl, recently promoted to Lieut. General, to Mannerheim's headquarters at Mikkeli to renew the plea for action. Jodl presented Mannerheim with all three classes of the Iron Cross—one of Germany's most coveted military honors. When Mannerheim still refused to move against Leningrad, Jodl burst out half in exasperation, half in threat, ''Well, do *something* to show cooperation.''

German medals could not budge Mannerheim, but another consideration did. Finland was negotiating with Germany for 15,000 tons of grain, and rather than let his people go hungry, he promised to cross the frontier and make a few stabs at the Soviets' border fortifications.

Mannerheim never kept that promise, although he positioned enough troops near the border to convince the Germans that a thrust was forthcoming—and to assure delivery of the grain. Even if Finnish troops had attacked the Soviet positions, their effort would have been of dubious value to Leeb, whose operation was hamstrung by Hitler himself. By September, Leeb stood on the threshold of Leningrad. Hitler, not wanting to feed its three million inhabitants, ordered him to surround the city but neither to enter it nor to accept its surrender; instead he was to reduce it by starvation and shelling. The historic 29-month siege that followed was to tie up many thousands of troops that the Germans might have used more profitably elsewhere.

In Mannerheim's view the time had come—since operations on the isthmus had gone in the Finns' favor—for

Talvela to renew his offensive east of Lake Ladoga. On the 4th of September, the Finnish VI Corps laid down its heaviest artillery barrage of the War against Soviet forces positioned along the Tuulos River. "There was rarely a lull in the fighting," recalled a young soldier named Väinö Linna—who later would become one of Finland's most honored novelists—in describing the advance. "On and on they struggled for mile after mile, while from the north and south came the incessant thunder of artillery." By mid-September, the VI Corps had gained possession of the entire north bank of the Svir.

The Finns' next target was Petrozavodsk, capital of the Karelo-Finnish Soviet Socialist Republic, on the west bank of Lake Onega. The task of taking the city fell to the VII Corps and the 1st Jaeger Brigade. The Jaegers approached the city from the south, parallel to the Murmansk railway, while the VII Corps attacked from the west. Then Mannerheim transferred the II Corps from the Karelian Isthmus and pressed the attack from the northwest. The city fell on October 1; the Russian forces that had been trying to hold it fled by boat across Lake Onega.

To the soldiers who captured it, Petrozavodsk seemed hardly worth the effort they had expended. Väinö Linna wrote that they "were astonished at the dilapidated look of the town. Amid a motley collection of shanties stood a few whitewashed brick buildings. That was all there was to the town, and the men were hard pressed to hide their disappointment." But they had scored a major victory. With Petrozavodsk went command of a stretch of the Murmansk railway, and with that in Finnish hands all British and American aid flowing south from Murmansk would now have to be detoured at Belomorsk, on the White Sea, onto a 200-mile-long connector line to the already overtaxed Archangel-Moscow railway.

The Finnish successes over the past three months had provoked loud Soviet demands that Britain declare war on Finland. Churchill told Stalin that a declaration of war would only tighten Finland's dependence on Germany; nevertheless, he sent the Finns a series of increasingly stern notes calling on them to stop fighting. On November 28, Churchill warned the Finns that they had to cease active participation in the War by December 5 or he would have no choice but to declare war.

The next day, Churchill passed a private message to Mannerheim through American channels. "I am deeply grieved at what I see coming, namely, that we shall be forced in a few days, out of loyalty to our ally Russia, to declare war upon Finland," he wrote. "Surely your troops have advanced far enough for security during the War and could now halt and give leave. It is not necessary to make any

Driving the family tractor and towing their household goods on sleds, a farm couple and their baby return home to Karelia after Finnish troops recaptured the area in 1941. More than 200,000 Finns had gone into voluntary exile in 1940 when 16,000 square miles of Finnish territory were ceded to the Soviet Union at the end of the Winter War.

public declaration, but simply leave off fighting and cease military operations, for which the severe winter affords every reason, and make a de facto exit from the War."

Mannerheim replied that he could not suspend all his operations until he had secured the Finnish position. He added that such a position would soon be achieved. Churchill could not wait: Stalin was relentlessly pressing Britain for a second front and greater aid. Declaring war on Finland seemed a cheap substitute, and Churchill chose it on December 6, 1941. "We'll have to shave now that we're fighting against gentlemen," the Finns are said to have joked when they heard the British had declared war. The war with Britain would prove to be a bloodless one, however, for British and Finnish forces never met in battle.

Meanwhile, the Finnish II Corps was pressing northeastward through the thinly populated forest country of East Karelia. The retreating Red Army had swept up most of the men of the area, leaving pathetic little groups of refugees—mostly women and children—huddled along the poor roads and in tiny lakeside settlements. On their march, the Finns also passed several abandoned labor camps, whose appearance was made all the grimmer by skulls that gleamed through the dirt of shallow graves dug outside the barbed wire surrounding the camps.

A hard winter, with sub-zero temperatures and several feet of snow, had set in by mid-November, exhausting men and horses alike. A last-gasp push brought the Finns to the town of Medvezhyegorsk, 20 miles south of Lake Seg, which they took on December 5; nearby Povenets, on Lake Onega's northeast shore, fell the next day. The Finns had meanwhile been driving the remaining Soviet troops in the area into several small pockets; on December 8, they wiped out the last of the pockets and cut the Stalin Canal, which linked Lake Onega with the White Sea.

The Finns also snared a Russian convoy of 41 small boats loaded with supplies, machinery and 1,000 infantrymen. Attempting to flee, the soldiers had waited too long and the boats became locked in the ice at the northern end of Lake Onega. Thereafter, using the captured boats, the Finns formed an improvised flotilla that would control much of the lake for the rest of the War. With Povenets and Medvezhyegorsk in hand, the Finns set up a defensive front that stretched 250 miles from Rugozero, 85 miles northwest of Medvezhyegorsk, to the southern shore of Lake Onega.

It had been a masterly campaign. Despite his limited forces, time after time Mannerheim had been able to concentrate superior numbers of men and guns at the decisive points. The flexibility of his tactics and the ability of the Finnish Army to advance swiftly through almost impassable wilderness repeatedly had caught the Soviets by surprise, whipsawed them out of their defenses and herded them into pockets. Except for the Rybachi Peninsula, all the territory lost in the Winter War had been recovered; in addition, the Finns now held East Karelia, a territory to which they had ethnic and linguistic claims. Altogether, the Finns had performed better than the Germans, who had failed to win a quick victory over Russia and had been halted short of their objectives. German troops were now shivering on a defensive line that ran for 1,500 miles from the Gulf of Finland east to the southern shore of Lake Ladoga, and south to the Black Sea.

Nevertheless, the mood in Finland was grim at the close of 1941. And now distant events combined to increase the pressures on Scandinavia. In December the Japanese bombed Pearl Harbor, inducing the United States, whose role in the Scandinavian battles had been limited to selling food and arms to the Soviet Union, to enter the War against the Axis powers—which meant Germany as well as Japan. Great Britain had declared war on Finland. Finnish harvests had been bad, making Finland more than ever dependent on Germany for food. The Finns could only sit out the winter behind their defensive lines and wait for the Soviets to mount a counteroffensive that was certain to be vengeful. Meanwhile, Germany's attention was diverted away from Finland and back to Norwegian waters.

HARD DUTY IN A HARSH LAND

In a 1944 painting by Emil Rizek, a German soldier in Scandinavia shares picket duty on the Russian front with a dog that carries his food and other supplies.

"A TIME OF LONELINESS AND DARKNESS"

For the German soldiers who carried the War into Arctic Scandinavia in 1941, the four long years that followed were a test of their endurance against isolation, monotony and intense physical distress. "We stood watch on the mountains, in narrow valleys and along the fjords," wrote one veteran of the Wehrmacht. "We lay on our machine guns in the snow, the rain and the glowing sun. We fought against raging snowstorms, marched for days over mountains, along the railroad tracks built for carrying ore, over glaciers and slopes of scree and boulders. We dodged avalanches and crossed rushing mountain streams." The German trooper might have added that duty in Scandinavia consisted of long stints of numbing inactivity, which were interrupted only by the hard labor of pushing a modern war machine into a wilderness where signs of any human presence were few.

In time, the Germans adapted to the bleak land and its harsh demands. They learned how to find summer paths through the swampy woods, and in winter grew adept at using the myriad lakes and rivers as "highways built by nature," as one German officer put it. They also mastered the local tools: curved-handled axes for felling trees and boatlike, skidless sleds for transportation. When there came a respite in the work, they shared in the local amusements, whether a friendly game of chess with an ally, or a Scandinavian sauna—which, according to one enthusiastic Wehrmacht veteran, became a relaxing habit "in the time of loneliness and darkness."

One soldier had a special assignment. He was Emil Rizek, an Austrian-born artist who had lived on and off for some years in the United States. During a visit home to Austria with his American wife in 1938, he was drafted into the Wehrmacht. By good fortune, Rizek was assigned duty suited to his talents, in a special painters' unit. Sent to Scandinavia, he was allowed to roam freely and choose his subjects at will. His tempera, oil and watercolor portrayals of the soldiers' hard existence in the northernmost tip of Europe are presented here.

Standing alone atop a watchtower at a divisional command post in the desolate far north, a German lookout surveys the empty horizon.

Passing the time off duty, a fur-hatted Finnish soldier and an Austrian member of the Wehrmacht match wits in a game of chess as a third soldier kibitzes.

Soldiers man an antiaircraft gun overlooking Kirkenes Bay on the Barents Sea, a position the Germans held in the hope of blocking Allied shipments of food and war matériel to the Russian port of Murmansk.

Makeshift huts nestle against a boulder-strewn tract of tundra not far from the Russian border. The Germans considered the Scandinavian terrain ''a directionless wilderness hardly to be imagined at home.''

LANDSCAPES AS BLEAK AS THE WEATHER

''No sound around me, no interruption in this barrenness,'' wrote a German who served at one remote Scandinavian outpost. ''I stare at the land in order to find some differentiation.''

He found little to relieve the depressing visual monotony. Even the rude encampments that the soldiers built for themselves blended dully with the landscape. Shelter typically consisted of a few earthen huts or log cabins, covered with layers of camouflaging sand, stone and moss intended to obscure them from aerial reconnaissance.

The huts were no easier on the constitution than on the eye. The best they offered in the way of heating was a crude stone oven. In winter, artist Rizek reported, ''25 people lay with their feet around the stove, so that their feet fried and everything else froze.'' The warmer months brought another trial, for the spring thaw left the hut floors sodden with pools of water.

MANY USES FOR A HANDY RESOURCE

The Scandinavian wilderness abounded in a simple but precious commodity: wood. The Wehrmacht felled thousands of trees and used the timber for fuel, for building, for heat. The mobile kitchens that brought hot meals to the soldiers depended on wood stoves. The trains carrying men and supplies to the front ran on wood-burning engines. Even the roads through the forests were built of wood, as were the bridges *(pages 140-141)* that spanned the region's ubiquitous lakes and rivers.

At a Wehrmacht camp, great stacks of cut wood await shipment to the front. The sole mission of some camps was to provide wood for use in the treeless

Near a village well, cooperative civilians set up a wood stove on wheels to fix a meal for Germans camped nearby.

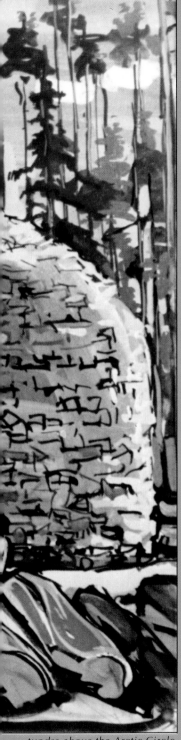

tundra above the Arctic Circle.

Standing on wooden planks that screen out the dampness underfoot, two German soldiers bake bread in the forest.

Watchtowers and German antiaircraft guns safeguard a wooden railroad bridge over the Kemi River near the Finnish provincial capital of Rovaniemi. The railroad was the only one that ran to the Russian front.

Men and horses labor to construct a bridge in the wilderness—part of an undertaking that made it possible to haul Finnish nickel 300 miles overland for transshipment to munitions factories in Germany.

Guided by soldiers, a team of work dogs brought from Germany pulls a wounded man across the Lapland tundra.

A German tries travel by reindeer sled. The reindeer's hoofs adapted to deep snow by expanding to the size of saucers.

A RETURN TO FOUR-LEGGED TRANSPORT

When the German divisions crossed the Arctic Circle into Lapland, they found terrain that defied motorized transport. In order to do the hauling of food, men and munitions that trucks and trains did elsewhere, they turned to primitive beasts of burden. Some divisions brought as many as 7,000 horses and mules from home, as well as dogs broken to harness. They augmented these by drafting an indigenous animal, the reindeer.

Reindeer had several advantages over the other domesticated beasts. Not the least of them was that unlike the horses and mules, which required up to 77 tons of feed per division per day, the reindeer sustained themselves on the lichen and moss that lay beneath the snow. But they were terrifyingly skittish. When riding on a reindeer-drawn sled, Rizek remembered, "I always kept my revolver ready in case the reindeer got frightened and left the path. In that case I'd have had to shoot the poor thing to keep out of the minefield."

Horses lug supplies along a rock-strewn fjord. "Without these untiring helpers," observed one German soldier, "our artillery would have been useless."

SKIRMISHES TO BREAK THE DOLDRUMS

To soldiers chafing under the tedium of duty in the North, combat brought a certain relief. But for some of the German troops, Arctic fighting held unanticipated terrors. The Russians employed guerrilla tactics against them, using snow tunnels and trenches to hide their advance. "The man up front would push the high snow down," wrote a German regimental commander. "Each man would be relieved by another as they worked along. Then some of the guerrillas would post themselves around for security while others attacked our sentries as noiselessly as possible."

With or without the snow tunnels, well-camouflaged troops were all but invisible to unpracticed German eyes. Even their Finnish allies seemed to pop up among them without warning again and again—a habit the Germans found so disconcerting that half in awe, half in irritation, they called the Finns "Snow Devils."

For their part, the Finns at first considered the Germans "quite useless in this murder in the woods." But under Finnish tutelage, the Germans too became able and elusive fighters in the snow.

Camouflaged in white snowsuits, two members of a German patrol—

one of them poised to throw a ''potato masher'' grenade—engage the enemy from a copse of skimpy birch trees while a third stoops to aid a fallen comrade.

5

Anglo-American convoys to succor Russia
"Every German ship not in Norway is in the wrong place"
The terrors of the "Murmansk Run"
If half get through, "the operation is justified"
A week of daylight hunting under the midnight sun
A New Year's triumph denied by bold British tactics
Death warrant—and reprieve—for the Grand Fleet
Last sortie of the gallant "Scharnhorst"

On August 21, 1941, a modest flotilla of eight cargo-laden Allied ships slipped inconspicuously out of Iceland's Reykjavik harbor into the North Atlantic. Joining an armada larger than itself—a heavy guard of two British cruisers, six destroyers and the aircraft carrier *Victorious*—the convoy set a course northeast past Jan Mayen Island, then veered right, entered the Norwegian Sea and sailed past Norway's North Cape. After threading their way through the ice floes of the Barents Sea, the ships swung south into the White Sea and proceeded to Archangel. There they delivered 48 British Hurricane fighter planes and quantities of rubber, wool and tin for the Russian war effort.

The German High Command paid no heed to the successful passage and little suspected what it boded. But the eight-ship flotilla and its escort were the first in a long line of convoys bearing arms and supplies for the beleaguered Soviet Union. The merchantmen and their heavy commitment of British Naval power reflected one of the most pressing Allied concerns of 1941: keeping the Russians fed, supplied and armed in the face of Hitler's Operation *Barbarossa*.

The United States, though not yet a belligerent, clearly favored the Allied cause, and on March 11, 1941, it had passed the Lend-Lease Act, by which the Americans promised to provide Britain and her allies whatever they needed in the way of arms, supplies, clothing and food. The United States arranged to deliver its cargoes, under Naval escort, across the western Atlantic as far as Iceland; from there British warships would escort them past the shores of Scandinavia—perilously close to the naval and air bases that Germany had secured the previous year.

As the autumn months gave way to winter, one convoy followed another as the American arms and shipping industries geared up to keep the promise of Lend-Lease. The British Admiralty, which had hatched the undertaking, designated the eastbound convoys with the letters *PQ*, and numbered them consecutively. By the time PQ-6 docked at Murmansk on the 23rd of December, 52 cargo ships had off-loaded 799 fighter aircraft, 572 tanks, 1,404 armored cars and trucks, and almost 100,000 tons of other matériel. Not one of the ships had been lost, nor had the warships that escorted them suffered any damage.

Such luck was too good to hold—particularly, Winston Churchill noted wryly, since "there was too much jubila-

ORDEAL IN THE CRUELEST SEA

tion'' in the press about the successful passage of supplies to the Red Army. Inevitably, the Germans took notice—and acted to stem the flow. On Christmas Day, 1941, Admiral Raeder ordered a small force of three U-boats to establish a picket line between Bear Island and North Cape. The move paid quick dividends: On January 2, 1942, the British freighter *Waziristan* of PQ-7 became the first convoy casualty. Two weeks later the destroyer *Matabele* went down defending PQ-8 from the U-boats.

From that date onward, the ''Murmansk Run,'' as it became known, was among the most abominated operations of the War. The British Admiralty begrudged the convoys because they took warships from the crucial duty of guarding the Atlantic sea-lanes and the home waters. The men who sailed in them—American and British merchant marine and Navy—hated them because the Arctic seas are among the cruelest in the world. And the Germans detested them for the effect they had on the Führer.

Hitler, by some accounts, had long had visions of making Norway a great northern extension of his empire. ''Norway is the zone of destiny in this war,'' he declared in January 1942. By then he was obsessed with the idea that the British and the Americans—now formally allied—were planning to land in northern Norway, link up with a Soviet thrust through northwestern Finland, and sweep south through Scandinavia toward Germany. A series of British Commando attacks and air raids on Norway's west coast between March and December of 1941 had fed his obsession, and he saw each convoy to Russia as a potential invasion fleet in disguise. To meet the imagined threat, he ordered Admiral Raeder to send the German war fleet north, thundering: ''Every ship that is not stationed in Norway is in the wrong place.''

Raeder dutifully transferred his newest battleship, the *Tirpitz,* to Trondheim on January 16, 1942, and sequestered her there. The heavy cruiser *Admiral Hipper* followed in March with an escort of four destroyers. In May the pocket battleships *Admiral Scheer* and *Lützow* were stationed at Narvik with six destroyers. Later would come the fast battle cruiser *Scharnhorst.* A score of U-boats were assigned to patrol Norwegian waters. In support of the Navy, the Luftwaffe greatly strengthened the air bases along the Norwegian coast with FW-200 Condor long-range reconnais-

sance planes, Junkers-88 dive bombers, and twin-engined Heinkel-111s that had been specially modified to carry torpedoes. Hundreds of artillery batteries were emplaced along the fjords.

Raeder and his fellow German admirals shared neither Hitler's dream of a northern spur to his empire nor his obsession with an Allied invasion of Norway. Some of them complained that the battle for Scandinavia was only a sideshow, that the important action was elsewhere. Others, charged with the maintenance of the German ships, worried about keeping the northern ports properly supplied with fuel oil; it took 4,250 tons of fuel to run the engines of a ship like the *Hipper* for 6,800 miles at a cruising speed of 18 knots—and the Navy had to compete with the Luftwaffe and the Army for its allotment of oil.

Hitler did not concern himself with these particulars. He had a worry of his own—one that practically nullified his order to position Germany's best warships in Norway. Hitler saw the ships as symbols of great power—but they were so outnumbered by the Royal Navy that he concluded he dare not risk them in battle. To preserve them, he decreed that they must never be sent on missions against a potentially superior Allied force—but, to the confusion of his subordinates, he never defined exactly what that meant. Raeder, in sharp contrast, maintained the traditional view that battleships exist to fight, and he chafed under the restrictions Hitler imposed upon him. No sooner had he obliged Hitler by stationing his finest ships in the north than he found that he had to ask the Führer's personal permission to send them out to sea—and as often as not that permission was refused.

Had Hitler but known it, the ships that made up the PQ convoys were no match for his forces. Most were sturdy enough, but many were 20 or 30 years old, and slow. Few could make more than eight knots, and some could manage only six—a turtle's pace against the harelike submarines, which when surfaced could run twice that fast. As defense against German air attack, some of the American merchant ships had only machine guns that were left over from World War I, and their crews had only casual training in firing even these.

The Naval escorts that shepherded the merchantmen between Iceland and the Soviet Union were not much comfort to the convoy crews either. In 1941 and early 1942 they consisted of a few old destroyers, a round-bottomed corvette or two and some coal-fired fishing trawlers enlisted for rescue duty. Most were British, with a scattering of Polish, French and other exile ships. Royal Navy minesweepers based at Murmansk met the convoys in the Barents Sea to protect them as they sailed past the north coast of Norway—the toughest part of the voyage—and to sweep up mines as the vessels entered the channels leading to the Russian ports. Well to the north of each convoy lurked a cruiser screened by a pair of destroyers; they were to engage German surface ships if necessary. This was all the defense the Royal Navy could provide in 1942, and it would prove disastrously inadequate.

Even without the terrors of enemy attack, the convoy run was grim. The distance between the American east coast and Murmansk is some 4,500 miles. North from Iceland in summer the daylight becomes almost constant, with the sun suspended low on the horizon 24 hours a day. Ice packs loosened by the summer warmth drift south to within 80 miles of North Cape, varying from a broken scum on the sea's surface to icebergs as high as a ship's bridge. With the ice, and cloaking it, come thick fogs that can hide the approach of another ship, friend or foe, making navigation difficult and collisions likely.

Autumn brings lengthening dark; winter has 115 days of almost total night, during which convoys had to maintain an absolute blackout for security's sake. Through this darkness course winter storms, their hurricane-force winds building waves from 15 to 70 feet high, wrenching heavy-laden freighters until their rivets pop, heaping them with snow, sleet and freezing spray, draping their upper works with tons of ice that must be chopped away before it capsizes them in the pitching seas.

Crew members had to be tethered by life lines to a hawser that stretched the length of the ship. Even then, to do their work they had to struggle across slippery decks, buffeted by waves that knocked them headlong. A man who fell overboard might live for 10 minutes; the water temperature was below 40° F. Clearing away ice was ceaseless work; so was securing the deck cargo—tanks, locomotives, trucks, crated

aircraft—which frequently shifted with the tossing of the ship and time and again had to be winched back into place and lashed down.

The ferocious weather joined forces with the waiting Germans to torment the convoys. PQ-13, sailing from Reykjavik in March 1942, met a four-day storm with winds up to 100 miles per hour that scattered the 19 merchantmen and nine escort ships over 150 miles of ocean south of Bear Island. A British destroyer and a cruiser tried in vain to reassemble the convoy, but instead encountered Germans and suffered heavy torpedo damage. Five of PQ-13's freighters went down. PQ-14, sailing from Iceland on April 8, collided with rafts of southward-drifting ice floes that sent 16 of its 24 merchantmen and two escorting trawlers limping back to Iceland. And in QP-11 (its letters reversed to indicate the homeward passage from Murmansk) the British sent their own cruiser *Edinburgh* to the bottom; German torpedoes had damaged the *Edinburgh,* and rather than leave her behind for the Germans to claim, the other British escort vessels took off her crew and put a final torpedo in her before running to safety.

When battle was added to the assaults of nature, the strain on the merchant sailors became almost unendurable. The constant alerts, the thudding of gunfire and depth

A surfaced German U-boat refuels a trimotored reconnaissance plane at a rendezvous off the Novaya Zemlya islands in the Arctic Ocean. The slow but sturdy flying boat served chiefly to track Allied convoys approaching Soviet ports, and guide submarines and bombers to the kill.

charges made regular sleep and meals impossible for anyone. It was four hours on watch and four hours off. And the off hours were sometimes broken by emergency orders for "All hands!" Lookouts grew face masks of icicles, and the engine-room crews who served below knew they had little or no chance of escape if their ship was hit. Some men cracked, mentally or physically, and the others did double duty to take up the slack.

The British Admiralty could give little attention to such personal hardships; it had concerns of its own. As long as Germany's battleships lurked in the fjords, an equal or larger force of Allied battleships had to be deployed close to the Norwegian Sea. And the German U-boat and air bases around Norway's northern rim focused potentially overwhelming force against the long last leg of the convoy route from Bear Island to Murmansk. In early April, 1942, First Sea Lord Admiral Sir Dudley Pound warned the British Defense Committee that the convoys would soon be suffering greater losses than the Allies could afford. To his American colleague Admiral Ernest J. King, Pound wrote that "the whole thing is a most unsound operation, with the dice loaded against us in every direction."

Pound and his fellow officers at the Admiralty pleaded with Churchill to suspend the convoys, at least until the return of Arctic winter again cloaked them in darkness. But President Franklin D. Roosevelt and Premier Stalin were bombarding Churchill with urgent pleas for the continued dispatch of arms consignments for the Soviet Union. Stalin pointed out reproachfully that "some 90 steamers loaded with various important war materials for the U.S.S.R. are bottled up at present or in the approaches from America" awaiting British escorts. With reluctance, Churchill asked the Admiralty to send another convoy past Norway; "the operation," he said ominously, "is justified if a half gets through."

And so PQ-16 sailed from Reykjavik on May 21 in the full Arctic daylight. The largest convoy yet, it consisted of 35 ships formed into nine columns and covering a rectangle of ocean five miles wide and two miles deep. Five destroyers, four corvettes, an antiaircraft ship, a minesweeper and four trawlers formed the escort. A battleship task force and submarine patrols cruised between the convoy and the Norwe-

gian coast. Another four cruisers and three destroyers joined the convoy en route.

But all that escort could not keep the Germans at bay. On May 25 a German reconnaissance plane flying out of Norway located the convoy heading for the Barents Sea, and soon air attacks began and submarines closed in. One of the British freighters, the *Empire Lawrence,* carried a single-seat Hurricane fighter plane of prewar vintage and a catapult from which to launch it. The pilot had the daunting mission of attacking the first concentration of German planes to arrive—shooting down as many of them as possible, then crash-landing on the sea near a rescue vessel. The pilot did his best, shooting down one Heinkel-111 torpedo bomber and damaging another before he was shot down himself— by merchant-seamen gunners who mistook him for the enemy. The rest of the torpedo-bearing Heinkels were skimming in from all directions, just above the waves, confusing the inexperienced gunners. To add to the chaos, Junkers-88s attacked from on high, diving almost vertically to drop their 500-pound bombs.

For 16 hours the barrage went on; ships went down and men took to the lifeboats—and the German planes strafed one of these. In turn, the seamen of one Allied ship, passing a German pilot standing on a wingtip of his ditched plane

In a cartoon decorating the conning tower of U-boat 481, Josef Stalin suffers a blow at the hand of a German Naval officer. By 1942 Germany had two Norwegian-based submarine flotillas, each with about a dozen boats, that hammered ceaselessly at Allied convoys to Russia.

and signaling to be picked up, blasted him with their machine guns. In the end, eight ships of PQ-16 failed to reach their destination, and another five were badly damaged.

The worst convoy disaster of all was still to come; its fate hung on wrong guesses prompted by fear on both sides. On June 28, the German High Command was alerted by spies in Iceland and by intercepted radio traffic to the sailing of Convoy PQ-17 from Reykjavik. Three days later a Condor reconnaissance plane ranging far from its base at Trondheim found the convoy—34 merchant steamers and 21 warships massed some 200 miles west of Bear Island.

At this time of year there were no sunsets in the waters well above the Arctic Circle, and throughout Norway, German aviators, ship captains and U-boat commanders made ready for a week of daylight hunting. Admiral Raeder ordered the battleship *Tirpitz*, the cruiser *Hipper*, six destroyers and two torpedo boats north from Trondheim to Alta Fjord, from which they could make an easy exit either to the Norwegian Sea or to the Barents Sea, and asked Hitler for permission to unleash this battle group against what promised to be a veritable shooting gallery of Allied ships. Submarines began tracking the convoy as it edged through the drifting ice closer to Bear Island, and Fifth Air Force Commander Hans-Juergen Stumpff alerted his entire force for action. At his call were 130 Junkers-88 bombers, 15 old Heinkel-115 torpedo-carrying floatplanes, and 42 fast Heinkel-111 torpedo planes.

The following day, July 2, the Germans were ready for their first sortie. Four submarines attacked, followed by a squadron of the Heinkel-115s. That day the convoy was lucky; its close escort of six destroyers, four corvettes, seven minesweepers and trawlers, two antiaircraft auxiliaries and two submarines combined to drive the Germans off without loss to the convoy. The next day their luck held; a low-hanging cloud bank shielded the convoy from the Germans' aerial searchers. But the day after that, July 4, a floatplane dropped through a hole in the clouds and launched its torpedo, which tore into the American freighter *Christopher Newport* and wrecked her engine room. Late the same day, 25 Heinkel-111s arrived from the base at Bardufoss, Norway. Attacking from all directions, they sank one freighter, crippled another and holed a Russian tanker with their torpedoes.

The Allies at this time knew nothing of Hitler's fear of committing his battleships. They did know, through their own reconnaissance, that the *Tirpitz* had been moved. That worried the British Admiralty. At last, just as the convoy reached a point due north of North Cape—still 800 miles from Archangel, its destination—the Admiralty directed the ships of PQ-17 to scatter. The order was meant to save the Navy's cruisers from the *Tirpitz'* battle group and to make the individual merchant ships harder to find. Ironically, unbeknownst to the Allies, the dreaded *Tirpitz* was heading back to her anchorage; Hitler had withheld permission for her sortie. *Tirpitz* or no, the Admiralty's order placed the merchant ships in great danger: It deprived them of the protection that the convoy system was intended to provide.

In the endless summer sunlight, the Germans made the most of the scattered vessels' vulnerability. Torpedo planes, dive bombers and U-boats hunted down the slow freighters and the three rescue ships that stuck with them, sinking all but 11 of the original 34. Almost 100,000 tons of cargo and 430 tanks, 3,350 armored cars and trucks, and 210 aircraft went down with them.

A Heinkel-111 bomber, which is visible above the stern of the ship in the foreground, has penetrated the heart of Convoy PQ-17 in the Barents Sea in July 1942 and is about to loose its torpedoes at a ship in the distance. German bombers and U-boats that were based in occupied Norway sank 22 of the luckless convoy's 36 cargo ships, which were carrying planes, tanks and other vehicles to Russia.

No matter who bore responsibility for the loss of all those ships, there was no question that the Germans were out in force, and the Admiralty now insisted that no more convoys be run until the darkness of winter could provide some natural protection against German aircraft. Churchill concurred, and glumly conveyed that decision to Stalin on July 17.

The Soviet dictator was in no mood to be understanding. He was trying to stem a crushing German land offensive, and his reply to Churchill was curt: "Our Naval experts consider the reasons put forward by the British Naval experts to justify the cessation of convoys to the northern ports of the U.S.S.R. wholly unconvincing." To underline his scorn he ordered two Russian cargo ships awaiting escort by the Allies from Iceland to steam home independently. They made it unscathed.

For seamen who survived the dangers of the convoy run, Murmansk and Archangel were not very appealing ports of arrival. Both were rubble-strewn targets on a barren coast. The Luftwaffe bombed them every clear day and often on foggy ones as well. Their gray harbor waters were studded with wrecks, among which German planes occasionally scattered mines that detonated on the approach of a ship's magnetic field. Every so often a ship blew up as it maneuvered into a berth to unload. A sailor was almost as likely to get killed at Murmansk and Archangel as on the way there, and the cold, the storms, the discomfort and boredom were as pervasive as on shipboard.

By seamen's standards, both ports were poorly managed. Murmansk had only 12 berths for seagoing vessels, and few heavy-duty derricks capable of unloading tanks or other hefty cargo. There were few professional stevedores; much of the unloading was done by women, by wounded soldiers and by political prisoners from Stalin's slave-labor camps. The petty officials in charge were suspicious and uncooperative; if an Allied merchant captain made even a simple request—for special medical help for an injured seaman, for example—the request had to be referred to Moscow, and ships and men then had to wait for a decision.

In August of 1942 Churchill went to Moscow to confer with Stalin. He came away convinced that everything possible must be done to aid the Soviet Union; otherwise its defenses might crumble before winter. Within a month came grim supporting evidence: An all-out German offensive broke through to the Volga River, and German tanks and artillery began pounding Stalingrad into a bloody rubble. On September 6, Churchill cabled Stalin: "Convoy PQ-18, with 40 ships, has started. We are providing a powerful destroyer striking force which will be used against the enemy's surface ships if they attack us. We are also including in the convoy escort, to assist in protecting it against air attack, an auxiliary aircraft carrier just completed."

The gesture was a costly one. As it turned out, PQ-18's covering force did not have to deal with the big German surface ships. Raeder moved the ships to Alta Fjord, but Hitler again refused to grant permission for a sortie. Instead the Germans deployed 12 U-boats and more than 100 torpedo planes and bombers against PQ-18. On one day alone, September 13, while the aircraft carrier Avenger's Hurricane fighters were aloft trying to chase off the German bombers, 40 German torpedo planes swept in abreast, 150 feet above the water, against the convoy's starboard wing. They sank eight merchant ships in as many minutes. U-boats sank another three. The German air and submarine attacks continued all the way into the White Sea, in the teeth of a full gale.

In the end, Convoy PQ-18 got through with 27 of the 40 ships that had left Iceland. But the Royal Navy could not soon again afford to escort a convoy so heavily, for the Allies were preparing to invade North Africa, and both cargo ships and antiaircraft escorts would be needed there. The last of the PQ convoys had completed its mission, fulfilling Churchill's pledge to Stalin and partially erasing the stain of PQ-17. When the convoys resumed in the winter, they would have a new series of numbers—and a new set of woes to contend with.

German officers were no better satisfied than the British with the results of the convoy war. The assaults on PQ-18 had cost the Luftwaffe more than 20 planes. Now German air strength was being further taxed by the demands of the war in the Mediterranean and on the Eastern Front, where the shipments of American tanks, planes and ammunition had helped stiffen the Russian effort.

Admiral Raeder therefore hoped to have a freer hand from Hitler, and again he moved the Lützow and the Hipper to Alta Fjord. His chances increased in mid-November with the news that a homebound convoy of empty ships had eluded the Luftwaffe, and again on Christmas Day, when it was learned that a 16-ship convoy carrying 100,000 tons of supplies had traveled from Scotland to Murmansk untouched. A week later a second large convoy was spotted trailing the first, and Raeder pleaded with Hitler to be allowed to unleash his big surface raiders against it. The convoy appeared to be accompanied by fewer than a dozen small escort vessels. A terrible storm was raging, making an air attack all but impossible. But the *Lützow* and the *Hipper*, Raeder thought, should be able to deal with the convoy. He proposed that they be sent out to engage it on New Year's Eve, when the convoy should have ap-

proached within about 200 miles north of North Cape.

This time, to Raeder's surprise, Hitler was amenable. He was in fact more eager for naval action than he revealed to Raeder. He badly needed a victory somewhere to offset the news from Stalingrad, where German armies under General Friedrich von Paulus were now encircled by Soviet troops. If Hitler was to have any good news with which to cheer his people at the start of the New Year, the Navy would have to supply it.

The man on whom Hitler's hopes hung was Vice Admiral Kummetz, the fleet commander who had led the assault on Oslo in 1940 and who had lost the heavy cruiser *Blücher* to the torpedoes of Oscarsborg Fortress in the first hours

From the deck of the British escort carrier Avenger, crewmen watch helplessly as merchant ships in their convoy, PQ-18, disappear in pillars of smoke. The convoy, fighting its way to Archangel in September of 1942, endured seven days of attacks by German torpedo bombers in swarms so thick that one witness called them "nightmare locusts."

of the battle for Norway. Since then, Kummetz' fortunes had changed for the better. Once the Germans had secured Oslo, he had been freed from his few hours of captivity and restored to active duty; now, aboard the *Hipper*—sister ship of the sunken *Blücher*—he had command of a new battle group.

Kummetz, like most German commanders, had great respect for the Royal Navy. For generations, the British had been the best sea fighters in the world, and now they had a technological edge as well. British radar was far more sensitive than anything the Germans had in use; even in conditions of poor visibility it afforded British commanders accurate information on the location, course and speed of opposing forces. Kummetz, by contrast, knew that once the destroyers of both sides threw up their smoke screens, he would be for all practical purposes blind—and his ships would be vulnerable to close-range torpedo attacks by even the smallest British ships.

Kummetz reasoned that his best chance to conquer such formidable enemies was to divide them. He devised a plan to lure the vessels escorting the convoy on a wild-goose chase that would leave the merchant ships unprotected. He would send the *Lützow* and three destroyers ranging to the east and the south—ahead and to starboard of the convoy's reported track. Kummetz himself would follow in the *Hipper* with three more destroyers, and sneak up on the convoy from abaft. At dawn he would attack, hoping to draw off the destroyers while driving the merchantmen—now unprotected—into the guns of the *Lützow*. Between them, the *Hipper* and the *Lützow* should be able to annihilate the convoy and escape before any heavier British ships could be called to the rescue.

But Hitler's concern for the preservation of his big ships continued to hamper the Navy. As Kummetz trailed the convoy in the early hours of New Year's Day, 1943, he received a radio message from Admiral Raeder relaying an order from Hitler: USE CAUTION EVEN AGAINST ENEMY OF EQUAL STRENGTH; IT IS UNDESIRABLE FOR THE CRUISERS TO TAKE ANY GREAT RISKS. In the snow squalls and darkness of North Cape, an enemy of "equal strength" need be no more than three radar-equipped British destroyers.

Kummetz saw the contradiction inherent in his orders.

"Only speed of action," he wrote in his notebook before closing in on the convoy, "can solve the problem of the danger of torpedo attacks from destroyers, which have to be considered in the light of my directive not to take any serious risks."

As he mused on his predicament, Kummetz suddenly saw two British destroyers dashing forward out of the fog, while a third laid down a smoke screen beyond which the masts of the ponderous freighters of the convoy could dimly be seen. The *Hipper's* lookouts peered anxiously for the tracks signaling that torpedoes had been launched. Once that happened the *Hipper*, to avoid being hit, would have to turn quickly and steam parallel to the tracks. The German gun controllers, trying to bear equally on the madly zigzagging destroyers and the smoke-shrouded merchantmen in the distance, failed to hit either.

Kummetz' Royal Navy opponent—Captain Robert St. V. Sherbrooke, aboard the destroyer *Onslow*—was as bold as the German admirals were cautious. Sherbrooke commanded an escort of five destroyers, two corvettes, two trawlers and a minesweeper surrounding the 13 merchantmen of the Allied convoy, designated JW-51B. He had anticipated just such a ploy as Kummetz was about to execute and resolved to counter it with some well-calculated bravado. He believed that the mere threat of torpedo attacks by his destroyers would be enough to keep the German ships away from his convoy. At the first hint on his radar that German ships were approaching, Sherbrooke had ordered the destroyer *Achates* to lay a constant smoke screen between the convoy and the enemy ships.

By now the *Hipper* was in full sight and firing. Sherbrooke maneuvered his own ship, the *Onslow*, and another, the *Orwell*, dodging and weaving through the mighty shell splashes of the *Hipper's* 8-inch guns. The two destroyers charged from one angle and then another, each time forcing the *Hipper* to pull out of broadside position and turn away. Neither the *Onslow* nor the *Orwell* fired a single torpedo, but for Kummetz, aboard the *Hipper*, the effect was bewildering. Four times he tried and failed to break through the destroyer screen. The convoy was drawing away all the time, and though he was sure the *Lützow* and her destroyers would be waiting to deal with it, he would have to dispose of the escorts before he could get at the cargo ships himself.

He ordered the *Hipper* and her three destroyers, which were now trailing behind, to concentrate their fire on the *Onslow* and the *Orwell*. Salvo after salvo burst among the storm-driven waves, and the erupting water further obscured the targets ahead of him.

On the crowded bridge of the *Onslow,* all hands ducked instinctively as a shell from the *Hipper* hit somewhere aft of the bridge and four near misses curtained the ship in spray laced with flying steel splinters. Captain Sherbrooke maintained a calm and rapid flow of orders to the helmsman and the gunners. At his elbow, officers peered left, right and forward for glimpses of the enemy. Several minutes elapsed before one of the officers noticed that blood was drenching his sleeve and, looking up, found that the blood was issuing from Sherbrooke. The left side of the captain's face had been hit by flying steel; an eyeball dangled on a splintered cheek bone. At that moment two more shells burst forward of the bridge, wrecking both forward guns and igniting their ready ammunition. Sherbrooke, giving no sign of personal anguish, and speaking in the same flat voice, ordered a turn to starboard and then a smoke screen to conceal his ship's damage from the Germans.

His men urged him to let the ship's doctor attend him, but Sherbrooke refused. Standing by his post, he headed his stricken ship back toward the convoy, radioing his position to the two British cruisers he knew were pounding southward in response to his earlier sighting report. Only then did he go below to be patched up by the surgeon.

At this point, with the *Onslow* hidden from him and the *Orwell* preparing for another attack, Kummetz ordered the *Hipper* and her destroyers to turn away from the British ships, and to make a speed of 31 knots. "I was hoping," he carefully noted, "after maintaining a heavy fire on the destroyers to find one or more gaps in the defense through which I could attack the merchant ships."

Actually, there was no chance of doing that. But Kummetz had succeeded better than he knew in drawing the escorts away from their charges. The *Lützow* was even now steaming across the exposed front of the convoy while Captain Rudolf Stange and his lookouts tried to sort out the silhouettes of the freighters from those of the German ships they believed were engaging them. Snow squalls driving ahead of the convoy made this difficult, and Stange decided

to let the ships pass while he turned out of the wind to get a better look. The visibility was no better as he drew parallel to the convoy, and finally he noted in his log: "Owing to the persistent lack of visibility, I decided to turn west to bring under my fire the enemy engaged with the *Hipper* to the north." But a few minutes later he encountered British destroyers and cracked on 24 knots to elude them, deciding that "due to darkness and extremely poor light" he must abandon the engagement before it could start.

Admiral Kummetz, believing the merchantmen to be under the *Lützow's* guns, turned back again toward the escorts that were guarding the convoy's rear. This time his 8-inch shells demolished the bridge of the destroyer *Achates* as she continued to weave her smoke screen across the wake of the convoy. She sank in moments. But now additional British destroyers converged on the *Hipper* as she again tried to come broadside to the fleeing convoy for a salvo, and three slim shapes raced toward her, firing 4-inch shells as they sought to reach torpedo range. For the sixth time Kummetz turned away from the torpedo threat—and into a terrifying hail of 6-inch shells from two new antagonists.

Captain Sherbrooke's sacrifice had not been in vain. His hornet-like attacks had kept the *Hipper* away from the convoy for two hours—long enough for the light cruisers *Jamaica* and *Sheffield* to charge down from 60 miles north of the convoy and bracket the *Hipper* with a salvo at eight miles' range. As the range closed, three hits slowed the German cruiser and started fires on her deck. Now, clearly, the *Hipper* and the *Lützow* were at risk. Reluctantly, Kummetz saw he would have to give up the fight. Cloaking his withdrawal in smoke and his conscience in the words of his orders to avoid "any great risks," he turned his entire force south and headed back to Alta Fjord. He made the decision none too soon. One of his destroyers had already succumbed to the British cruisers' fire. But he got the *Hipper*, the *Lützow* and the remaining destroyers safely back to port.

The episode clearly demonstrated that the Germans' fears for their own ships had crippled them in a battle against diminutive opponents that they should have trounced.

To Hitler, who had spent New Year's Eve in Berlin with high hopes, none of this was known. Early word of Kummetz' engagement had been vague and confusing. One account said that "only a red glow could be seen in the Arctic twilight." He had also received a verbatim report of the terse order from Kummetz to the *Lützow* and the destroyers: "Break off engagement and retire westward." Hitler had taken this scant news as encouraging for the German side, and had gone to bed confident that as a New Year's present to the German people he would be able to report that an entire Allied convoy had been destroyed.

Instead, the Führer awakened to a British news flash trumpeting the safe escape of the convoy from an engagement with German warships. Hitler went into a frenzy—not least because of his inability to get news direct from his own people. By chance, the Teletype from Norway was out of order, and not for another 24 hours would the Naval staff be in a position to deliver its account of the action. When at last Raeder appeared before him, Hitler erupted in a volcanic rage.

For 90 minutes Raeder endured an almost uninterrupted tirade about the sins of German seafarers, from their first encounter with a Danish fleet in 1864 to the moment when the *Hipper* and the *Lützow* had turned away without honorably "fighting to the end." Unlike the Army, snarled Hitler, "the Navy has always been careful to consider the number of its own ships and men before entering an engagement"—an implication of cowardice that ignored his own frequent insistence that ships must never be risked against a superior force. Now, contradicting himself, he shouted: "I demand that once forces have been committed to action the battle be fought to a decision!"

The big ships were useless, the Führer raged; they had spent most of their time running away from the British. Instead, the Luftwaffe, the U-boats and the smaller ships would have to defend Norway; all that the cruisers and battleships did was divert these units from their rightful work. Finally, Hitler thundered that the heavy ships were a needless drain on men and materials, and should be paid off and reduced to scrap.

To Raeder, who in 10 years had built the Navy from virtually nothing, Hitler's announcement was an affront. Sadly he wrote a note to Hitler saying that scrapping the ships would "give our enemies a victory without any effort on their part." He resigned.

Hitler's decision did not quite spell the end of the German Grand Fleet. Hitler appointed Admiral Karl Dönitz, until now commander of the U-boat fleet, to succeed Raeder as commander in chief. Dönitz persuaded the Führer that scrapping the ships would be a waste. Hitler's temper had cooled somewhat, and when Dönitz proposed a modification of Hitler's order, the Führer agreed to it. The Dönitz plan was to scrap the *Hipper* and two old battleships; to station the *Lützow*, the *Admiral Scheer* and the *Prinz Eugen* in the Baltic and use them as training ships while awaiting an Allied invasion; and to send the *Scharnhorst* north to join the *Tirpitz* in a Norwegian fjord. At the very least, their big guns could provide a flexible coastal defense for Norway.

The compromise had merit. Lying together in the Alta Fjord—which, though it provided easy exit for the Germans, was so heavily guarded it was inaccessible to the Allies—the *Scharnhorst* and the *Tirpitz* actually constituted the biggest threat yet posed to the Atlantic and Arctic convoys. As far away as Portland, Maine, battleships were alerted against a possible breakout of the Germans into the high seas. The summer convoys to the Soviet Union were again suspended, and the British Home Fleet laid plans to provide at least three cruisers to accompany the winter convoys when they were resumed in the fall of 1943, and to establish a battleship-led "distant cover force" to be on call for the defense of any convoy at sea.

Meanwhile, the Allies made every possible effort to sink the battleship *Tirpitz* at her anchorage (pages 160-175). When on September 22 they succeeded in disabling her, the Allies considerably reduced the surface threat to their northern convoys. On the 1st of November the crews of 13 empty merchant ships that had languished at Archangel since spring gratefully brought the vessels back safely to Britain through a thick fog. By the middle of December eight Allied convoys—four each way—had slipped unmolested around North Cape. Foul weather and stronger British escorts combined to keep Dönitz' U-boats and the Luftwaffe at a distance.

By now Hitler was seeing a connection—real or imagined—between the convoy shipment of arms and supplies to the Soviet Union and the reverses of his own army there. On December 19, 1943, he suddenly—and perversely—wanted to know what Admiral Dönitz' precious surface ships were going to do about helping the German Army, whose very survival in Russia might depend on stopping the Murmansk convoys.

The question took the fleet officers in Norway by surprise, but for Dönitz it offered a welcome chance to put the Navy into action. He was quick to promise a sortie against the next convoy by the *Scharnhorst* and her escort of five destroyers "if a successful operation can be assured."

On December 22 he got his chance. A German reconnaissance plane caught sight of a flotilla of Allied ships two days out of Scotland. It was Allied Convoy JW-55B, but the German pilot who saw it, excitedly radioed that 40 "troop transports" were headed for Norway with a powerful escort. Was Hitler's long-nursed fear of an invasion of Norway at last about to materialize? To Dönitz and his fellow officers at headquarters, it seemed possible. Every available U-boat was dispatched to Vest Fjord, and a general alert went out to Norwegian ports.

A day later a second sighting identified the ships as a routine Arctic convoy and disclosed that it appeared to be covered by only a few cruisers and destroyers. Dönitz promptly ordered Admiral Otto Schniewind, commander of Naval Group North in Norway, to prepare the *Scharnhorst* and her

destroyers for sea. Reflecting Hitler's determination that there be no repeat of last year's aborted battle with the *Hipper* and the *Lützow*, the orders read: "Tactical situation to be exploited skillfully and boldly; engagement not to be broken off until full success achieved."

Schniewind was a 56-year-old officer who had spent most of his Navy career ashore. Now, as he contemplated the orders given him, he had great misgivings. Admiral Kummetz' misadventure of a year earlier had proved that even in the hands of an expert a big ship at sea was at a distinct disadvantage among hostile destroyers in the storm and darkness of the Arctic winter. And Schniewind was shorthanded; he had been so sure that only destroyers and U-boats would be called out after November that he had been liberal with Christmas leave, and had sent many of his officers—Kummetz among them—home for an extended holiday. The battle group was left under the temporary command of the leader of its destroyers, Rear Admiral Erich Bey.

The weather was deteriorating miserably. Snow squalls and gale-driven waves were rolling 30 feet high and sweeping northwest into the Barents Sea. The weather was so bad that Schniewind distrusted the latest reconnaissance reports

Deceptively painted, the German battle cruiser Scharnhorst looks—from a distance—no larger than a light cruiser. Actually the Scharnhorst, commissioned in 1936, was 770 feet long and displaced 31,800 tons.

describing the convoy and its escorts. Putting his doubts into a message to Dönitz, he urged that the sortie be postponed. Dönitz overruled him; the need to halt supplies to the Red Army was urgent. Schniewind thereupon ordered Admiral Bey to intercept the convoy.

Erich Bey had come a long way since the day in April 1940 when he succeeded to the command of the Narvik destroyer squadron and fought superior British forces to a draw; his successful effort to protect the German landing during that campaign had helped win him the broad gold stripe of a rear admiral and command of all the destroyers in northern Norway. Now, as temporary commander of the *Scharnhorst* and her escort, he would have the unexpected honor of leading a force in battle.

The honor was a hollow one. His fleet consisted only of the 39,000-ton *Scharnhorst* and five destroyers. No other major ships were available to fight; the *Lützow* was in dry dock in the Baltic and the *Tirpitz* was in Kaa Fjord, being repaired for damage inflicted by the latest Allied air attack. The weather was awful and getting worse. Bey doubted that the *Scharnhorst* and the destroyers together stood a chance against a winter convoy. Bey himself had never commanded any ship larger than a destroyer; indeed, the last time he had been on board a capital ship was as a sea cadet.

The *Scharnhorst* slipped her moorings as ordered at 9 p.m. on Christmas night, and in the darkness cranked up her anchor chain. At 17 knots the battle cruiser swept clear of the harbor and down the fjord to the open sea, accelerating to 25 knots as she cleared the harbor's last set of antisubmarine nets.

The five destroyers were stationed ahead, abeam and astern, pitching and tossing as they met the heavy seas. It was terrible destroyer weather; the little ships would have a struggle to keep from foundering and would be unable to aim and fire their guns and torpedoes with any accuracy. At midnight Bey broke radio silence to point this out to Dönitz, who replied: IF DESTROYERS CANNOT KEEP SEA CONSIDER USING *SCHARNHORST* ALONE. The decision was back in Bey's lap; he kept the destroyers with him, and pressed on.

The fact is that the Allied convoy, which appeared to be only lightly protected, was bait in a cunningly contrived trap, and the Germans were obligingly snapping up that bait. Admiral Sir Bruce Fraser, convinced that the passage of four convoys unmolested would at last lure the German battle squadron out of its lair, had provided the 19 ships of Convoy JW-55B with one of the biggest covering forces yet: 37 ships in all. The escort was scattered over a 175-mile radius—so far-flung that German intelligence could not correctly assess it. Immediately surrounding the convoy was an escort of 14 destroyers and three corvettes and trawlers. Loitering secretly some distance due north of Murmansk was a three-cruiser task force, commanded by Rear Admiral Robert L. Burnett. The 35,000-ton battleship *Duke of York,* with Fraser aboard, was trailing the convoy at 200 miles, accompanied by the light cruiser *Jamaica* and four destroyers. So sure was Fraser that the German Navy would come out that as soon as German reconnaissance planes had been spotted

Her 11-inch guns coated with ice, the Scharnhorst bucks the North Sea in January of 1943. The ship took so much water over her forecastle that the range finders in her forward turrets were frequently disabled.

on December 22 he had issued a number of commands calculated to close the gaps between the convoy and its escorts. He ordered the three cruisers north of Murmansk to steam southwest toward the convoy, his own trailing battle group to continue northeast toward it, and the convoy itself to steam in a circle, marking time while the two escort forces approached.

At midnight on the 25th the *Scharnhorst's* mission and position were confirmed by the interception of Bey's message. Fraser had on a chart before him a firm picture of where the British units were. If, as Fraser believed, the *Scharnhorst* was steering a course north from North Cape, Burnett's cruiser squadron would be the first to encounter her. And the encounter, he hoped, would drive the German battle cruiser south to be penned by the destroyers and speared by the *Duke of York's* 14-inch shells.

As Bey made his first pass northeast across the presumed path of the convoy, he had no inkling of the massive ambush being set for him. At 7:30 a.m. on December 26 he sent his destroyer captains plunging head-on into the gale in a southwesterly search while he took the *Scharnhorst,* unescorted, north through the gray-black seas.

Incredibly, neither Admiral Bey nor the *Scharnhorst's* captain was aware that the *Scharnhorst* herself was virtually blind as she went. Her radar antenna, perched high above the bridge, had not been switched on. In operation the radar device emitted a telltale signal that could alert the enemy, so the crew had standing orders not to switch it on until ordered to by the commander. Now they waited below for an order from the bridge, but none came.

They paid in flesh and blood for the oversight. Before anyone on the *Scharnhorst* knew it, Admiral Burnett's cruisers had closed in undetected, and the battle was joined. The first shell from the British cruiser *Norfolk,* fired at 9:30, shattered the *Scharnhorst's* radar mast, tore a leg off the rangefinding officer and wounded three radarmen and lookouts.

In the circumstances, Bey did the best he could. He maneuvered the battle cruiser as deftly as though it were one of the destroyers he was accustomed to. He twisted quickly out of gun range of the three cruisers and, turning south at 32 knots, easily ran away from them. After half an hour Bey assumed that he was safe, and circled north to look for the convoy.

The cruisers did not try to follow. Seeing on his radar that Bey was beginning to double back in the direction of the convoy, Admiral Burnett simply turned in a shorter arc to the northwest and raced ahead toward the convoy himself. He lost contact with the *Scharnhorst,* but three hours later his radar screen again picked up the German ship, approaching the convoy as expected.

It was now high noon, and for a brief moment there was light. At the same instant that Burnett spotted Bey by radar, Bey—who no longer had the benefit of radar at all—saw Burnett's British ships against the horizon. The light lasted just long enough to give the gun crews of the *Scharnhorst* some good shooting, and they hit the *Sheffield* and the *Norfolk* repeatedly before darkness returned and left them blind again. But it was clear to Bey that he could not hope to break through the British cruiser formation to find his elusive quarry, and without his five destroyers, which might have run interference, he could not risk another encounter with the British.

Desperately, Bey set a southwesterly course intended to take him at full speed away from Admiral Burnett's cruisers and home to Alta Fjord. He was too late. The *Duke of York* and the cruiser *Jamaica* with their four destroyers were heading directly toward him, and they and Burnett's trailing cruisers held the *Scharnhorst's* image firmly on their radar screens. Admiral Fraser had plenty of time to sight in the powerful guns of the *Duke of York* and the *Jamaica* on the radar image of the *Scharnhorst,* and he signaled his destroyer captains, who were impatient to get into the fight, to withhold their torpedoes in order not to drive the *Scharnhorst* off target.

Temporarily idle, an officer in the gun-control tower of

the destroyer *Scorpion* had a box seat for what followed. "When the starshell first illuminated the *Scharnhorst*," he wrote, "I could see her so clearly that I noticed her turrets were fore-and-aft, and what a lovely sight she was at full speed. She was almost at once obliterated by a wall of water from the *Duke of York's* first salvo. When she reappeared her turrets wore a different aspect."

Like a stag surprised, the great gray *Scharnhorst* leaped violently aside, jinking toward the north. But Fraser knew—as Bey did not—that Burnett's cruisers were waiting in that direction to drive him eastward, and the *Duke of York* leveled out due east so that her full broadside could bear instantly when Bey was forced to turn again.

As the cruisers under Burnett closed in from the north, Bey's superior speed was pulling him steadily ahead of the converging pack. Soon he had left the cruisers behind; the *Duke of York,* too, gradually lost range after gashing the *Scharnhorst's* flanks and wrecking one three-gun main turret. Suddenly the *Scharnhorst* herself began to lose speed, and the four fast destroyers of Fraser's force, which had been nipping all the time at the *Scharnhorst's* heels, drew abreast. Two on each side, they closed to a range of about 3,000 yards. The right-hand pair launched their torpedoes, and one hit. Violently swerving away from them to the south, the *Scharnhorst* turned into a spread of 12 torpedoes from the other two destroyers; at least three struck with crippling effect.

The *Scharnhorst* had savaged several of her opponents during the chase, but now she was all but defenseless as she blundered back into their midst. The battleship, cruisers and newly arrived destroyers lashed at the dying vessel, which was now glowing a bloody red with fires and explosions, and circling blindly at five knots. "Finish her off with torpedoes," Fraser signaled the cruisers and destroyers. They shot their missiles into a pall of smoke, and after 15 minutes only floating wreckage remained. The British vessels halted their fire and combed the icy waters for survivors, but in an hour found only 36. The remainder of the *Scharnhorst's* company of 2,000—including all the officers—had perished with the ship.

The evening after the battle Admiral Fraser called his officers together and pronounced the mighty cruiser's epitaph. "Gentlemen," he said, "the battle against the *Scharnhorst* has ended in victory for us. I hope that if any of you are ever called upon to lead a ship into action against an opponent many times superior, you will command your ship as gallantly as the *Scharnhorst* was commanded today."

Through the dangerous waters off the Scandinavian coast, Britain and the United States delivered a grand total of 3,964,231 long tons of freight to the Soviet Union, a considerable part of it during 1941 and 1942, when such aid was vital to Russia's survival. They did so at a cost to themselves of 100 merchant ships and 18 warships. German losses also were heavy: three destroyers, 32 U-boats, the *Scharnhorst*. And these were assets that could not be replaced.

The principal reason for the success of the northern convoy system, by general agreement among Allied Naval officers, was less the Allied Naval effort than what one British Naval officer called the "hysterical prohibitions" from Hitler that kept five mighty ships and their escorts from taking necessary risks. Captain Donald Macintyre, a senior Royal Naval officer who commanded escort forces in the North Atlantic, later wrote: "Admiralty opinion was that, were the positions reversed, they could guarantee that not a single ship of a convoy would be allowed to reach Russia."

As the year 1944 began, the fixed star of Hitler's ambitions in Scandinavia was in eclipse. Of the eight major warships assembled by Admiral Raeder to guard the Third Reich's northern approaches, only the *Tirpitz* remained—and she was out of service. The Fifth Air Force, its squadrons drained away to support the collapsing German efforts in the Mediterranean and on the Russian front, had become little more than a static defense force. And Finland, lying between Norway and the Soviet Union, was beginning to have second thoughts about its alliance with Germany.

A BATTLE QUEEN IN EXILE

THE CURBED CAREER OF A SYMBOL OF SEA POWER

The career of the German battleship *Tirpitz* was perhaps the strangest of any capital ship in the War. From the gala day of her launching in 1939, the *Tirpitz* was considered one of the most fearsome seagoing weapons in the world. Her 42,500-ton displacement was greater than that of any British or American ship afloat. Turbines capable of 163,000 horsepower could drive her through the water at 31.1 knots—almost two knots faster than the newest British battleships. Her four main turrets housed eight long-barreled 15-inch guns, whose 1,760-pound shells could penetrate 13 inches of armor plate from a distance of almost 22 miles.

The *Tirpitz* was the only battleship to carry torpedoes, ideal for her intended use as a roving raider against Allied supply convoys. Her defenses, too, were formidable. She bristled with 112 antiaircraft guns, and her heavy deck and hull armor, some of it 15 inches thick, made her invulnerable to all but the heaviest shells.

Yet this ferocious ship was to play an almost passive role. A few months before the *Tirpitz* completed sea trials in 1941, her sister ship, the *Bismarck*, was sunk by the Royal Navy after one of history's greatest ocean chases. Adolf Hitler, in a protective frenzy, decreed that henceforth no German warship might put to sea without his consent; he sent the *Tirpitz* to relatively safe Norwegian waters to protect his northwestern flank. She was to spend most of the War there dodging from one fjord to another, finding anchorages so isolated that the Norwegians dubbed her, with a tinge of compassion, "the lonely queen."

Even in exile, however, the *Tirpitz* was a terror to contend with. The British Admiralty kept three modern battleships in home waters in case she broke out—although these vessels were badly needed elsewhere. "The whole strategy of the War turns at this period on this ship," wrote Prime Minister Churchill in January 1942. Destroying the *Tirpitz*, he stated, must take priority: "No other target is comparable to it."

The *Tirpitz*' band members, their instruments decorated with the ensign of the German Navy and the vessel's coat of arms, stand prepared to perform.

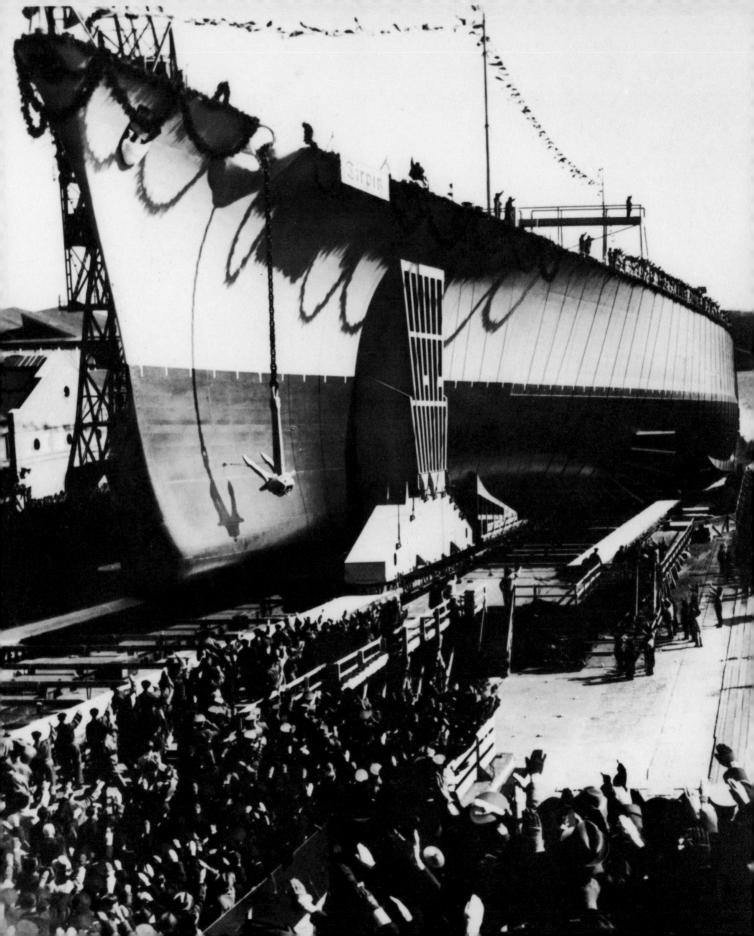

A 21-inch torpedo leaps from one of the Tirpitz' eight tubes during a drill as officers watch from an outboard platform

Bundled against the January cold, German aircraft spotters on board the Tirpitz scan the skies off the coast of Norway in 1942.

The Tirpitz noses cautiously toward the ship's first Norwegian anchorage—at the head of desolate Foetten Fjord, a secluded arm of the 50-mile-long fjord leading to Trondheim.

A THREAT
RARELY EXECUTED

Though sequestered in Norway soon after her sea trials were completed, the *Tirpitz* emerged from her lair several times. The most notable sortie occurred in July of 1942, when she led seven German warships out of Trondheim to intercept an Allied convoy named PQ-17: three dozen ships bound for the Russian port of Archangel under a heavy British escort.

When aerial reconnaissance photos revealed the ominous intelligence that the *Tirpitz* was missing from her anchorage, the British Admiralty made a calamitous mistake: It withdrew the escort and ordered the convoy to scatter. Stripped of its protection, PQ-17 was soon beset by swarms of U-boats and Luftwaffe bombers. They sank all but 11 of the convoy's 36 cargo ships.

Ironically, the *Tirpitz* never came within 300 miles of the action. The German High Command had second thoughts about her engaging the British, and ordered the ship to slip back inside another fjord. There the *Tirpitz* took cover beneath an elaborate cloak of camouflage *(overleaf)*.

Heading for open sea in July 1942, the *Tirpitz* leads a force of German warships to attack a convoy bound for Russia. Before contact was made, the mission was aborted.

Stretching camouflage netting over the Tirpitz, one team of crewmen hides a forward gun battery (right) while another begins the task of concealing the great ship's hull (below).

ELABORATE ATTEMPTS
TO SHROUD A PRESENCE

On the foredeck, rows of small fir trees stand among the guardrails
and anchor cable to disguise the Tirpitz as part of the Norwegian forest.
Tarpaulins shroud the main guns and the looming superstructure.

A fresh snowfall—delineating the telltale outline of the ship's hull and
the torpedo nets surrounding it—defeats the Germans' efforts at
camouflage, as this British aerial reconnaissance photograph shows.

A RELENTLESS CAMPAIGN TO FIND AND DESTROY

Beginning in 1942, the British made 20 attempts to knock out the *Tirpitz*. The Germans simply kept moving the battleship deeper inside Norway's heavily guarded fjords, where the Royal Navy's surface craft and submarines could not penetrate.

The first breaks for the British came with advances in technology. In September of 1943, two new four-man midget submarines eluded the Germans and made their way to Kaa Fjord, an inland finger of the larger Alta Fjord on Norway's northernmost coast, where the *Tirpitz* lay. The sub-

marines attacked, damaging the *Tirpitz* steering gear and propeller shafts, but the Germans soon made repairs on the scene.

The next successful attack came from the Fleet Air Arm of the Royal Navy, which had swift, newly fitted aircraft carriers, and planes armed with 500-pound high-explosive bombs, as well as American-made armor-piercing bombs. In April of 1944 the *Tirpitz* was surprised in her hideout by 42 Barracuda dive bombers that executed two perfectly coordinated attacks. The double onslaught caused heavy casualties and blasted holes in the ship's armor. Altogether the planes scored 14 sure hits that left the *Tirpitz* a shambles, but with her vitals still intact *(pages 172-173)*.

Pointing out the Tirpitz' position on a relief map, the operations officer of the British carrier Furious prepares dive-bomber crews for a mission against the German ship in April 1944.

Aboard the Furious, a sailor chalks a hopeful message on the side of a 1,600-pound armor-piercing bomb loaded on a dive bomber.

Flying at 3,000 feet to clear the coastal mountains, Barracuda dive bombers from the Furious head inland to strike at the Tirpitz.

Smoke billows from both the bridge and the funnel of the stricken
Tirpitz as a British bomb strikes home. The surprise bombing and strafing
attack stunned the crew and left 436 of them dead or wounded.

A reconnaissance photograph taken in July 1944 —three months after
the Royal Navy's air attack —shows the Tirpitz still surrounded by leaking
oil. The boats and scaffolding alongside indicate repairs under way.

Tirpitz' wounds at Kaa Fjord in September of 1944 when the Royal Air Force unleashed a long-range attack by 28 Lancasters—four-engined planes carrying six-ton bombs known as "tallboys." One tallboy scored a direct hit, tearing a gash 48 feet long and 32 feet deep in the ship's hull.

pitz, towing her to a berth near Tromso in hopes of salvaging her. They hoped in vain. On November 12, 1944, another 32 Lancasters flew in for the kill. After eluding the Allies for nearly three years, the Tirpitz came to a swift end: She capsized only 11 minutes after the first bomb struck.

tallboy bomb detonates on Haaköy Island, missing the bow of the already smoking Tirpitz.

Everywhere in the north, by February of 1943, Hitler's forces were beset. In Denmark, university students were publishing a twice-weekly newspaper with an underground circulation of 50,000, dedicated to stimulating resistance against the German Occupation. In Norway, saboteurs damaged a hydroelectric plant where the Germans were conducting high-priority experiments in nuclear research—the kind of research that would elsewhere lead to development of the atomic bomb. In Russia, a Red Army assault punched open a six-mile-wide corridor to Leningrad, breaking the Germans' 17-month stranglehold on the city. And in Finland, the only place in Scandinavia where the Germans had allies they thought they could count on, those allies had turned uncontrollably skittish with the changing military climate.

On February 3, Finnish President Ryti and several Cabinet ministers met at general headquarters in Mikkeli with Marshal Mannerheim. "The War could be regarded as having reached a definite turning point," Mannerheim recalled in his memoirs. The leaders agreed that "Finland must use the first opportunity to get out."

Getting out would not be easy. Three corps of General Dietl's Twentieth Mountain Army—170,000 troops—were dug in along the northern half of Finland's eastern frontier, from Petsamo in the north to Suomussalmi in the south. At some forward points, the Germans were 50 to 60 miles inside the Soviet Union. If Finland tried to leave the War, there was no guarantee that these troops would docilely pack up and leave Soviet territory. If the German troops did not leave, the Soviets would probably drive them back across the border into Finland—and the Russians might stay on permanently in Finnish territory once the job was done. Even if the Germans did agree to depart, it was doubtful that Hitler would continue to provide the German grain and other foodstuffs on which Finland had come to depend. So as not to appear to bite the hand that fed them, the Finns would have to disengage with care.

By summer, Mannerheim was taking the first steps toward ending his country's role in the War. He disbanded a crack Finnish battalion when its enlistment term was up, rather than allow the men to continue serving under the aegis of the German SS in Russia. He also demanded the return of

6

RETREAT IN THE NORTH

five Finnish battalions serving with Dietl's Twentieth Mountain Army on the frontier. Dietl objected, for the forest-wise Finns were invaluable for reconnaissance and screening missions. But the German High Command, anxious to stay on good terms with the Finns, ordered Dietl to return four of the battalions. Finally—and most unsettling of all to the Germans—Mannerheim told the OKW he wanted to build reserve defensive positions behind the German lines for Finnish troops to occupy in case the Germans had to shift their forces to another theater. The existing lines—what remained of the Mannerheim Line, and another defensive position known as the VT line, built in 1942 and stretching from Vammelsu on the Gulf of Finland to Taipale on Lake Ladoga—were unlikely to stand up against a strong Russian offensive.

While the Germans pondered Mannerheim's request, news from elsewhere in the north gave them further cause for worry. By early October, Soviet attacks in the Leningrad area posed an increasing threat to Germany's Army Group North, which was battling desperately to avoid a forced retreat. If Army Group North could not hold on, the Soviets could advance with overwhelming force up the Karelian Isthmus and into the heart of Finland.

Still, the Germans tried to reassure the Finns that there was nothing to worry about. OKW Chief of Operations Alfred Jodl flew to Helsinki on October 14 to give Mannerheim a strategic pep talk. Italy's recent capitulation, he declared, was of little concern to Germany, since Mussolini's military contributions had been negligible. As for second-front prospects, General Jodl went on, the Germans looked forward to an Anglo-American invasion of Western Europe as an opportunity to inflict a decisive defeat on the Allies and thus free more troops for the Eastern Front. In the interim, Army Group North would hold on around Leningrad as long as possible.

Jodl told Mannerheim that Germany was aware of Finland's desire to get out of the War. "No one," he conceded, "has the right to demand that one nation shall go to its death for another." But he pointed out that the Finns had few options open to them. They could conclude a separate peace with the Soviet Union, but they would then risk being swallowed up as the Baltic republics had been. Or they could fight against Germany in alliance with the Soviets, there-

by gaining advantages from Stalin that peace negotiations alone were unlikely to provide. Such a turnaround, Jodl suggested, would be incompatible with Finnish concepts of loyalty and honor. He concluded that Finland's best option was to continue as Germany's ally.

In spite of Jodl's arguments, Mannerheim held fast to his belief that the sooner Finland got out of the War the better. And on November 18, as the German position in Russia continued to weaken, he ordered the construction of the defensive positions he had proposed. The Germans made no effort to stop him.

The new defenses were intended to contain the Red Army, should it come, within the isthmus of Karelia. The first new string of fortifications, known as the VKT line, stretched from Viipuri through the town of Kuparsaari and along the Vuoksi River to Taipale on Lake Ladoga; Mannerheim expected it to provide the Finns with a fallback position on the northern Karelian Isthmus. The second, called the U line, followed the course of the Uksu River northeast from Lake Ladoga and then swung northwest past the eastern shore of Lake Tolva. It was designed to block any Soviet thrust into central Finland.

The VKT and U lines were still under construction when the Germans suffered another stunning reversal. On January 14, 1944, the Soviets opened their final offensive against the German forces still besieging Leningrad; within five days they had broken through and liberated the city. By the end of January the Soviets had driven Army Group North back into Estonia, across the Gulf of Finland from Viipuri.

The Soviet success posed a double threat to Mannerheim's positions on the Karelian Isthmus. The Russians could attack overland up the isthmus toward Viipuri, where Finnish troops were working frantically on the VKT line. And they might supplement such an attack with an amphibious assault across the gulf to outflank Finland's existing lines of defense.

Pressures on the Finnish government seemed to build from every side. The American Chargé d'Affaires in Helsinki passed a note from Washington warning that the longer Finland stayed in the War, the harsher the Soviets' final terms were likely to be; it urged the Finns to sue for peace immediately. The Germans, discovering that peace talks were under consideration, sent the Finns a note demanding that they pledge not to conclude a separate peace. Meanwhile, the Red Air Force launched mass bombing raids against key Finnish cities. On the night of the 6th of February, 200 Soviet planes bombed Helsinki, killing 40 persons and injuring several hundred. Four nights later, 150 Soviet bombers hit the port of Kotka on the Gulf of Finland, knocking out the railway station, the telegraph building and a cellulose factory. The Finns decided that the time had finally come to open talks with the Russians.

On February 12, Finland sent veteran diplomat Juho Paasikivi to Stockholm to confer with Madame Alexandra Kollontay, the Soviet Ambassador to Sweden. Once the Stockholm talks established that the Finns were serious, Paasikivi flew to Moscow in late March to try to forge an agreement with Soviet Foreign Minister Molotov.

Paasikivi found the Russian in no mood for compromise. "I cannot understand why we should make concessions to you," Molotov told him. "Germany has already lost the War, and as Germany's ally you are in the position of a defeated country."

The Soviet terms were tough. Before Molotov would agree to an armistice, the Finns had to return all Soviet prisoners of war and withdraw to the boundaries established in 1940 at the close of the Winter War. They would have to intern the German Twentieth Army (with Soviet help, if necessary), demobilize their own armed forces, cede the mineral-rich Petsamo area to the Soviet Union and pay $600 million in reparations.

As much as they wanted peace, the Finns could not agree to these terms—and Finnish Prime Minister Edwin Linkomies went before the Parliament on April 12 to say so publicly. "The government has not surrendered to any illusions that a turn in world politics favorable to Finland will soon occur," he said. Nevertheless, the Soviet demands would put Finland's independence in jeopardy and rob the people of their freedom. After listening to Linkomies' sober speech, the Parliament unanimously affirmed his rejection of the Soviet terms.

"The feeling in Finland," recalled Mannerheim, "was one of depression. Our peace effort had failed, and our relations with Germany had obviously deteriorated." Indeed, Hitler was not mollified by the Finns' rejection of Stalin's harsh terms. The very fact that they had negotiated with the Russians outraged him, and he retaliated fast. On April 13 the Germans halted their grain exports to Finland; a week later they stopped all deliveries of arms and ammunition.

Stalin's next move after the Finns' rebuff was even more brutal. On June 10, he hurled two Soviet armies across the border. The Finns were a "stubborn" people, Stalin told

U.S. Ambassador W. Averell Harriman. ''Sense must be hammered into them.''

Stalin's assault made clear that he intended to knock his stubborn neighbors out of the War for good. The Soviets had concentrated approximately 450,000 men, 10,000 guns and heavy mortars, 800 tanks and 1,547 aircraft between Lake Seg, in the north, and the Karelian Isthmus. On the isthmus they massed 13 infantry divisions, the equivalent of three tank divisions, and enough artillery to position 500 to 600 guns per mile, wheel to wheel, along the front. Against these forces, the Finns could muster only 74,000 men. They were not only hopelessly outnumbered, but outclassed. Except for an occasional skirmish, the Finnish troops had seen little action over the past two and a half years, and in Mannerheim's opinion they had ''lost the habit of war.'' Even training had been cut back so that the soldiers could build fortifications and help Finland's hard-pressed farmers plant and harvest crops.

The Soviets opened their offensive with the heaviest air and ground bombardment the Finns had yet experienced. The air assault, a carpet bombing on the Karelian Isthmus by more than 1,000 planes, created craters for miles around. The first artillery barrage fell most heavily on the Finnish 10th Division, which occupied a two-mile sector along the western end of the isthmus. According to Mannerheim, the thunder of the Russian guns was clearly heard in Helsinki, 170 miles away. Two Soviet armies, the Twenty-first and the Twenty-third, then attacked up the isthmus, with the Twenty-first Army making the main drive toward Viipuri and Helsinki. The onslaught was fierce; in a few hours it pulverized the Finnish defenses and thrust the defenders back six miles. The Finnish 10th Division could not even tow its artillery away; many of its tractors had long since been sent to the rear to assist on the farms.

Mannerheim rushed his reserve armored force into the battle, intending to fight a delaying action until he could bring up troops from East Karelia and Lapland, which were still relatively quiet. The reinforcements from Lapland had to be funneled along a single rail line through Kemijärvi, a bottleneck in the best of circumstances. One member of the Finnish 3rd Brigade left a harrowing account of the journey. Near Salla, he wrote, strafing fighter planes killed the brigade's commander and wrecked the train's engine. The

replacement locomotive was a small switch engine that lacked power to get the train moving. Everyone, including nurses, got out to push while a detail threw sand on the rails for traction. Finally, the engineer built up enough pressure in the boiler to move the train in five- to 10-yard spurts; gathering momentum, it rolled slowly toward the front.

By June 15, the 3rd Brigade had arrived on the isthmus—just in time to fight a delaying action while the Finns' battered Karelian forces scurried to get behind the VKT line. Fortunately for the retreating Finns, the Russians concentrated on reaching Viipuri and overlooked the strategic importance of a 17-mile gap between Viipuri and the Vuoksi River. Had the Red Army plugged that gap, the Finns would have been forced to squeeze across a single bridge over the river. As it was, the Finns worked their way back to the VKT line only after four days of heavy fighting.

The Finnish 20th Brigade, belatedly assigned to the defense of Viipuri, arrived from East Karelia on June 19 to find the city ablaze from air and artillery bombardments. The streets were blocked by retreating troops, and stragglers were spreading panic by crying that enemy tanks were on the way. As the brigade tried to get into position the next morning the Russians attacked, their tanks moving relentlessly into the city's southern suburbs. The 20th Brigade col-

The Soviet embassy in Helsinki burns (far left) after being attacked by Russian night bombers on February 6, 1944. At near left, Finnish civilians gather the next morning to view the gutted building. The Finns relished the irony of the Russian blunder until, under the provisions of the peace agreement, they were forced to build the Soviets a new embassy.

Madame Alexandra Mikhailovna Kollontay, Soviet Ambassador to Sweden, boards an airplane for home on the 1st of March, 1944, after delivering harsh Soviet peace terms to the Finns in Stockholm. Madame Kollontay, at age 71, was the world's first woman ambassador.

lapsed. Many of its men ran to hide in nearby woods—"joining the Pine-Cone Guards," the Finns called such desertion. The remaining Finns, however, managed to block a Russian attempt west of Viipuri to seize the road to Helsinki.

Temporarily halted, the Russians turned their attention from Viipuri to the northeast, driving through relatively open country into the VKT line. Ten days of attacks and counterattacks, with the Soviets feeding in fresh forces day and night, inexorably ground the Finns down. The Russians hacked a three-mile salient through the VKT line and were almost into the countryside beyond it before the last-gasp effort of a few Finnish infantry battalions stopped them at Ihantala, five miles from Viipuri.

The breaching of the VKT line and the impending loss of Viipuri so rocked the Finns that they had second thoughts about giving up their German alliance. On June 19, Lieut. General Erik Heinrichs, Army Chief of Staff, asked the Germans for men to help hold the East Karelian front.

In spite of the recent coolness, the Germans were receptive. Hitler feared that at any moment a Russian offensive might overwhelm the entire Eastern Front. The Germans' plight made it crucial for them to keep the Finns on their side, no matter what the cost: They told Heinrichs that if the Finns really intended to hold what remained of the VKT line, they would send help.

On June 19, German torpedo boats raced into Finnish harbors to deliver 9,000 antitank grenade launchers called *Panzerfausts*. Next came fighter planes, dive bombers and troops—the 303rd Self-propelled Assault Gun Brigade and the 122nd Infantry Division. German air transports also delivered 5,000 *Panzerschrecks*, 88mm versions of the American bazooka.

In lifting his embargo on arms and aid, Hitler had not asked for any commitment on the part of the Finns—but both parties knew there would be a price. On June 22 German Foreign Minister Joachim von Ribbentrop arrived in Helsinki to present the bill: Finland must agree not to conclude a separate peace. At the same time Hitler threatened to stop all aid once more unless Finland made a public pronouncement of its position. The Finns refused to be backed into a corner, however. The best that Ribbentrop could manage was a letter signed by President Ryti stating that he personally would

neither seek peace with the Soviet Union nor permit anyone else to conduct negotiations without German agreement.

The German help came too late to save Viipuri—which fell on June 21—but it won the Finns time to improve their positions elsewhere before readdressing the question of how to get out of the War. Mannerheim hastily organized a new defensive line behind the breaches in the VKT line and threw in every spare soldier he had to hold it. The Finnish infantrymen quickly learned to operate the new grenade launchers and bazookas—which could blow open the heaviest Russian tank at respective ranges of 30 and 150 yards. The weapons were light and ensured the Finns a mobility that suited their talent for ambush. One Finnish officer, Lieutenant Gregorius Ekholm of the 3rd Brigade, destroyed seven Russian tanks with his German-made bazooka in a single afternoon—an achievement that revived the spirits of his comrades.

With their new weapons the Finns were able to slow the onrushing Soviets, but they could not stop them. By the second week in July, the Russians had driven the Finns out of a bridgehead south of the Vuoksi River, forded the river and established their own bridgehead on the north bank. The Finns contained the offensive with help from troops that had withdrawn from Viipuri, but they could not force the Russians back across the river.

In East Karelia, the Soviets—who outnumbered the Finns there nearly 3 to 1—had landed two marine brigades near Tuloksa on Lake Ladoga's eastern shore, setting up a roadblock that threatened to cut the Finns' route of retreat along the lake. By July 10, the Finns had been pushed back to the partially completed U line, but there they held.

In mid-July, after five weeks of hard fighting, the Finns sensed that the Soviets were winding down their offensive. A long-range Finnish patrol scouting the Viipuri-Leningrad railway reported Soviet tanks being shipped south. And new Russian troops on the isthmus appeared to be second-line units. The reason was not hard to find: On June 6 the British and Americans had landed in Normandy. They were now about to break out of their beachhead and sweep across France. Stalin wanted to pull the best of his forces out of his unexpectedly costly Scandinavian offensive and vie for the spoils of Eastern and Central Europe—which would be his for the taking as Germany pulled back.

The break in the fighting provided a desperately welcome breather for the Finns, who had suffered 60,000 casualties during the summer. Such losses were staggering to a country the size of Finland—they represented 1.3 per cent of its population—and increased the pressures on the government to get out of the War. To do that, however, the Finns would have to find a way around President Ryti's pledge to Ribbentrop that he would not negotiate a separate peace.

A Cabinet minister came up with a solution that saved face all around. The promise to Ribbentrop had been signed only by Ryti. If Ryti were to resign, the agreement would not be binding on his successor. Ryti agreed to step down, and he persuaded Mannerheim, Finland's venerable warrior, to take his place. The Finnish Parliament passed legislation enabling Mannerheim, at the age of 77, to assume the presidency without an election. The stage was finally set for a break with Germany.

Ryti's resignation took the Germans by surprise. They realized that Mannerheim was likely to assume the role of peacemaker, and on August 17 Field Marshal Keitel, OKW Chief of Staff, arrived in Finland to try to dissuade him. ''Hitler's intent was clearly to prevent us from acting inde-

Their weapons held aloft in triumph, Soviet troops stand atop a Finnish pillbox that crumbled under artillery fire in early summer, 1944. In its first three weeks, the Soviet offensive cost Finland some 18,000 casualties.

pendently, even in the eleventh hour," noted Mannerheim. He informed Keitel that Finland simply could not afford any more casualties. He also said that Ryti's resignation had removed any obstacle to a separate peace.

A week later Mannerheim approached Madame Kollontay, the Soviet Ambassador in Stockholm, to arrange for a resumption of peace talks. The Soviets agreed to receive a Finnish peace delegation in Moscow—but only if they met two conditions. First, Finland must announce to the world that it had broken off relations with Germany. Second, the Finns must demand that all German troops leave their territory by September 15 or face internment as prisoners of war. If the Finns did not accept these terms by the 2nd of September, the Red Army would immediately occupy the country.

The Finns had no alternatives. The Finnish Army had men and munitions for only three more months of fighting. The Continuation War was over.

After 33 months in the trenches, Finnish soldiers had trouble believing that the conflict had really ended. Erkki Holkeri, a soldier stationed in central Finland, was awakened by a messenger early on September 4 with an order to cease all firing. "We had heard all kinds of rumors," Holkeri recalled, "but that was the way it had been throughout the War, and we had learned not to take them too seriously. But this time it was in writing; I even had to sign for it. We had talked about peace many times, what we would do, how we would jump up and down for joy. Well, we had peace, but I did not feel like jumping. The peace terms were not the kind that make you jump for joy."

Indeed, the Soviets conducted the final peace negotiations in a manner designed to humiliate the Finns. Finnish delegates who arrived in Moscow on September 7 were ignored for a week. When the talks finally began, Molotov dictated the Soviets' terms, leaving no room for argument.

They were essentially the same terms the Finns had rejected five months before. Finland would have to revert to its 1940 frontiers and surrender the Petsamo area. It could keep Hango but would have to give Russia a 50-year lease on a naval base at Porkkala, within artillery range of Helsinki. The Soviets reduced their reparations demand from $600 million to $300 million—but required payment in the equivalent of 1938 gold dollars, which with wartime infla-

tion brought the price up to $450 million. The Finns also were to reduce their armed forces to 41,500 men, and allow the Soviets unrestricted use of all Finnish merchant ships, port facilities and airfields for the duration of the War. Quietly, the Finns accepted.

Finland was finally at peace with the Soviet Union, but there remained the thorny problem of how to deal with the Germans. Promising to oust them was one thing; delivering on that promise was quite another.

As it turned out, the Germans were already considering withdrawal. The previous February, when Russian bombs were falling on Helsinki, Hitler had ordered General Dietl's Twentieth Mountain Army staff to develop a contingency plan for the German evacuation of southern and central Finland. The plan that Dietl worked out, code-named Operation *Birch*, called for the Twentieth Mountain Army to retain control of Lapland and the essential nickel mines near Petsamo—though a number of German officers favored abandoning Finland altogether, and perhaps Norway as well. General Jodl, for one, compared the German Army to a snake that had lost its mobility from swallowing too large a prey, and argued that Germany must shorten its battle lines. But Hitler still considered Scandinavia one of the most important fronts in Europe, and it was not until October, a month after Finland had agreed to a separate peace, that he ordered the limited withdrawal that had been outlined by General Dietl.

By that time Dietl himself had been killed in a plane crash, and it fell to his successor to carry out Operation *Birch*. General Lothar Rendulic was a humorless Austrian and dedicated Nazi who had been leading German forces against insurgents in Yugoslavia. He struck even the austere Mannerheim, at their first meeting, as "courteous and correct but apparently hard and somewhat unapproachable." Rendulic told Mannerheim that he admired the fighting abilities of Finnish soldiers. But the Germans, he asserted, were equally fearless and could be just as ruthless. His army would withdraw, Rendulic said, but it would do so at its own pace. He ended the conversation on an ominous note: A clash between Finns and Germans would be bloody and cruel, since the best soldiers in the world would be fighting each other. "If they come to blows, 90 per cent will be killed.'' Mannerheim said nothing. For the moment, he was satisfied that a silent accord had been reached to avoid unnecessary bloodshed.

From his headquarters at Rovaniemi, Rendulic put Operation *Birch* in motion. Logistically, the challenge was to swing the 200,000 men of his three mountain corps—presently aligned on a 350-mile-long north-south axis from Petsamo to central Finland—onto an east-west axis from Ivalo, about 120 miles south of Petsamo, to the Swedish border. The 19th Mountain Corps would stay in Petsamo to guard the nickel mines and act as the pivot for the withdrawal. The

36th Mountain Corps would retreat westward 100 miles by road and rail from Salla to Rovaniemi, then swing northward another 120 miles along the Arctic Highway to take up new defensive positions south of Ivalo. The 18th Mountain Corps, the southernmost of Rendulic's units, would withdraw some 200 miles westward to Rovaniemi, then move 170 miles northwest to form a new defensive line opposite the Swedish border town of Karesuando.

It would be a tricky operation, greatly complicated by the political and military uncertainties surrounding it. Rendulic had to guard against a sudden westward thrust by Soviet

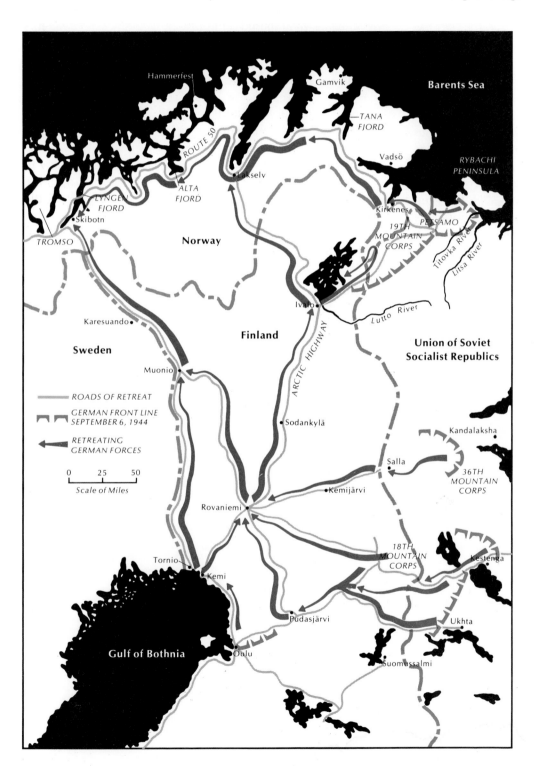

After the Finns signed a separate peace in September of 1944 with the Soviet Union, the German armies left Finland—a logistical feat that required 200,000 troops to withdraw from four scattered fronts, pivot to the north along the Swedish border and the Arctic Highway, then retreat westward along Route 50 in German-occupied Norway.

183

forces that outnumbered his army by more than 2 to 1. Simultaneously, he had to guard his southern flank against the Finns, who might turn their guns against their former allies if the Soviets pressed them. He also had to avoid provoking the increasingly anti-German government of Sweden, which had stationed troops along its eastern borders and had made clear it would not tolerate the movement of any German troops across Swedish territory.

In order to guard his southern flank, Rendulic stationed regimental-sized rear guards near Suomussalmi and at the port of Oulu on the Gulf of Bothnia. Covered by those forces, the Germans began withdrawing on September 6. The first to move was the 18th Corps, which evacuated the Kestenga area without serious incident. Then the 36th Corps began pulling back from its forward positions toward Salla, only to discover that Soviet troops had outflanked it and severed the road. The Germans, however, had cut an alternate track through the forests to the south of the main road. Quickly shifting to this route, they outflanked the Soviets in turn, cleared the main road and continued their withdrawal in good order.

As the retreat began, relations between the Germans and Finns remained cordial and cooperative. Trains evacuating Finnish civilians from Lapland to the south also carried 60 cars of German supplies a day. Finnish and German ships evacuated German wounded from the ports of Oulu and Kemi. Finnish and German soldiers, some of whom had served together for three years, held farewell parties, and an officer of a German supply depot made the gallant gesture of distributing horses to local Finnish war widows.

By September 15—the deadline the Soviets had set for the Finns to expel the Germans from Finland—Rendulic was still conducting a leisurely retreat toward Rovaniemi. For the Soviets the move was not proceeding fast enough, and they began to pressure the Finns for stronger measures to evict the Germans. At the end of the month, Soviet troops began edging over the Finnish frontier at Suomussalmi. The harassed Mannerheim responded by dispatching some of his aides to meet with Rendulic's staff.

Rendulic suspected that the Soviets were planning to move in as soon as the Germans left, and he was in no hurry to abandon his last outlets to the Gulf of Bothnia. Nor—for all his earlier threats—was he anxious to fight the Finns. His aides worked out a plan with Mannerheim's men to deceive the Soviets: The Germans would continue their carefully phased withdrawal, while the Finns followed closely behind—pretending pursuit but avoiding actual combat and serving as a buffer between the Germans and the Russians. Meanwhile, the Finns would send regular reports of their gains to the Russians.

Mannerheim ordered General Hjalmar Siilasvuo, hero of the Winter War, to follow the retreating Germans with three

divisions, headquartered at Oulu. In the spirit of the agreement, Siilasvuo kept his infantry out of rifle range of the Germans and sent his armored division forward on the slowest route available—the Oulu-Kemi road, which was obstructed by a number of river crossings. The Germans evacuated Oulu and methodically moved north, giving the Finns two days' advance notice before each move. Rendulic feared that the Soviets would soon come after him and so, with Finnish consent, he ordered his troops to blow up bridges behind them, sink ferry boats and block roads with minefields. Siilasvuo's soldiers promptly dug up the mines and rebuilt the bridges—taking care that they were not strong enough to hold even the lightest Soviet tank.

The first rupture in this mutual accommodation occurred far to the south of Rendulic's withdrawal, on a Finnish-held island near Helsinki. The German High Command, hoping to maintain control of the Gulf of Finland—and believing that the Finns would not resist—ordered an amphibious landing on the island on September 15. But the Finns fought back, and the Russians intervened with air strikes against the landing forces. The Germans were forced to retreat after suffering heavy losses.

The charade soon ended in the north as well. Goaded by Russian innuendoes of bad faith and by direct threats of invasion, General Siilasvuo's Finnish troops fired on a German rear guard at Pudasjärvi, 50 miles northeast of Oulu.

Rendulic authorized his men to fire back and dispatched an ultimatum to Siilasvuo: Either observe the agreement he had made with Mannerheim or suffer the consequences of war "without restraint."

The Finns rejected Rendulic's warning, using the same kind of legal nicety that they had invoked to nullify Ryti's agreement with Ribbentrop. Any agreement contrary to the Finnish-Soviet armistice, they said, was not binding on Finland. Rendulic, realizing that the Finns could no longer be counted on to withstand Soviet pressure, set about making good on his earlier threat. "As of now," he ordered, "all cover, installations and objects that can be used by an enemy are to be destroyed." With that, the Germans opened a scorched-earth campaign that would turn most of northern Finland's towns and villages into smoldering heaps of rubble (pages 190-201).

Already, German troops in the ports of Tornio and Kemi, at the head of the Gulf of Bothnia, were fighting with Finnish troops guarding industrial plants there. Siilasvuo decided to seize the ports before the Germans could get the upper hand. And reinforcements were on the way; a regiment of the 3rd Division, under the command of Colonel Wolf Halsti, had sailed north from Oulu on the 1st of October in a fleet of transports.

Siilasvuo had planned the operation carefully. The local

A team of eight sturdy work horses hauls a field howitzer camouflaged as a load of hay during the German retreat from Lapland in northern Finland in the early autumn of 1944.

Snaking through the Norwegian barrens, a wooden snow tunnel forms part of Route 50, the 400-mile-long road the German Army built from Narvik to Kirkenes. The tunnel enabled men and supplies to move when snow would otherwise have closed the road.

forces in Tornio, alerted to Halsti's arrival, had a train waiting at the harbor. Hustling his men aboard, Halsti quickly got his regiment into commanding positions around the sprawling German supply base. The Germans fought back fiercely, aware that under the terms of the Finnish-Soviet armistice they would be turned over to the Russians if taken prisoner. But bad weather prevented the Luftwaffe from providing sufficient air support, and after a day's fighting the Germans pulled back.

When Halsti's men took over the supply base they discovered an adversary in some ways more potent than the departed Germans: gallons and gallons of schnapps provided by the German Army for its lonely troops. The Finns, who during the long war had counted themselves lucky to distill the local equivalent of moonshine, made straight for the store of good liquor. In little more time than it took to uncork the bottles, one third of Halsti's men were drunk and his offensive had come to a halt. The imbibing turned into a full-scale bacchanal as the other regiments of the 3rd Division arrived in Tornio. By the time Halsti and other officers restored order, some of the more enterprising men had launched an international bootleg operation, smuggling liquor across the nearby border to equally thirsty Swedes.

Rendulic, meanwhile, had organized his rear guard and an oddment of spare units for a counterattack. The Germans hit Finnish positions around Tornio from the north and east, forcing the Finns back. One gun-shy Finnish battalion fled at its first sight of two German tanks, which on closer inspection turned out to be abandoned derelicts. Fortunately, Siilasvuo had already dispatched his armored division up the coast to reinforce the 3rd Division. The possibility of confronting the Finnish armor prompted Rendulic to break off his attack and withdraw to the north. The Finnish 11th Division then made an amphibious assault on Kemi, and by October 8 had cleared out the remaining Germans.

Siilasvuo's timely action had saved Tornio and Kemi from the destruction visited on most other towns in Finnish Lapland; only 5 per cent of Kemi's buildings had been destroyed, and 1 per cent of Tornio's. Equally important, the attacks on the twin ports had demonstrated that the Finns would tolerate no further delays by the Germans—and thus greatly reduced the risk of a new Soviet invasion.

As Hitler followed the slow retreat of the Twentieth Mountain Army into northern Finland, he became increasingly uneasy. Finnish troops were still tailing Rendulic's men

from the south. To the west, Swedish troops were posted on their side of the border, closely watching events in Finland. In the east, Soviet troops had reached the 1940 border and were poised to push beyond it. And along the Norwegian coast, Rendulic's supply routes were now exposed to a new danger. After breaking out of Normandy, Allied forces had captured key German submarine bases at Brest and Lorient. This action freed powerful British air and naval units, formerly committed to bombarding the bases in France, to move north against Hitler's submarine bases at Trondheim and Narvik. British sea raiders, relieved of the submarine threat, became a menace to coastal shipping; it would be impossible to supply or evacuate the Twentieth Mountain Army without heavy losses.

The German staff had to consider a drastic move: abandoning all of Finland, Lapland included, in favor of the more urgent defense of Norway. Accordingly, Hitler ordered the Twentieth Mountain Army, which was still moving into its new defensive positions in Finnish Lapland, to withdraw all the way to the Tromso region of Norway, some 200 miles north of the Arctic Circle. The operation, codenamed *Northern Light,* presented Rendulic with what may have been one of the most difficult logistical challenges in military history: He would have to move his 200,000 men and eight months' worth of accumulated supplies through 300 miles of Arctic terrain over primitive roads, under constant threat of enemy attack and winter storms.

Rendulic immediately began to evacuate supplies and equipment by sea through Petsamo and Kirkenes, using every available vessel. Timetables had to be worked out so that his three corps could withdraw simultaneously, along specified routes to prevent congestion and to minimize the danger of being outflanked by a pursuing enemy.

The 18th Corps, already advancing north of Rovaniemi toward the Swedish border, would have the shortest route to Norway. Once inside Norway, the corps would continue northward, taking care not to provoke the Swedes. Near Skibotn, its path would join Route 50, the road that ran from Narvik to Kirkenes and was protected from the elements along much of its length by snow fences and snow tunnels. There the 18th Corps would set up new defensive positions at the head of Lyngen Fjord. Meanwhile, the 36th Corps would move north over an all-weather road from Ivalo, then swing west onto Route 50 toward Skibotn and Lyngen Fjord.

The 53,000 men of the 19th Corps—which still held strong defensive positions along the Litsa River, 45 miles inside Russia, and across the neck of the Rybachi Peninsula near Petsamo—faced the most difficult withdrawal. They had been selected to protect the rear of the evacuating forces; nevertheless they would have to reach Lakselv, some 160 miles to the west, by November 15. After that their escape route—a portion of Route 50 that had not been fully protected with snow fences or tunnels—would almost certainly be covered with several feet of snow.

The withdrawal of the first two corps began at a measured pace in late October, much as Rendulic had planned. The 19th Corps was not so fortunate. On October 7, it had been attacked by the Soviet Fourteenth Army, 97,000 strong, under Field Marshal Kirill Meretskov, a veteran of the Winter War. Meretskov's five corps had been specially trained for Arctic warfare, and two were equipped with packhorses and reindeer that enabled them to operate cross-country. Off the coast, ships of the Soviet Northern Fleet were standing by, ready to provide fire support or to land troops behind the German lines.

The Soviet attack hit the German line at its weakest point, a juncture between the 6th Mountain Division along the Litsa River and the 2nd Mountain Division to the west. Backed by air, armored and artillery support, Soviet infantrymen swept over the German positions, rapidly opening a gap between the two divisions. The German strong points—built during the Wehrmacht's three-year Occupation—proved no sturdier than the Finns' ill-fated defensive lines. Many quickly crumbled under the massive assault.

"Our artillery had done its job well," noted Meretskov after he visited the site of the breakthrough. "All around were crippled guns and mortars, and there were gaping holes in the smashed gun emplacements and shelters. There were numerous corpses in dirty green greatcoats with tin edelweiss on their caps."

Russian reinforcements pressed forward through the gap and turned to the north and west, threatening to encircle the entire German corps. Meanwhile, a Soviet Naval brigade made an amphibious landing just west of the Rybachi Peninsula, outflanking German troops guarding the narrow

On the 10th of October, 1944, Soviet marines hit the gravelly beaches of Petsamo. The brigade routed the western flank of the German division that blocked the land route into Finland from the Rybachi Peninsula.

neck of the peninsula north of Petsamo. Within a week, the Soviet assault shattered defenses the Germans had spent three years building. Rendulic, his lines in disarray and facing the possibility that the Soviets might close the circle on his forces, ordered the 19th Corps to abandon Petsamo and fall back into Norway, blowing up the nickel-processing complex at Kolosjoki as it retreated. Meretskov's army pressed hard on the heels of the Germans, following them across the Norwegian border.

Reaching Kirkenes, 35 miles west of Petsamo, the Germans stopped; they would try to hold off the Soviets until a remaining 135,000 tons of supplies could be shipped to safety. Rendulic had already asked the OKW for permission to withdraw before all the supplies had been moved, if nec-

essary, to avoid a needless sacrifice of troops. But the OKW turned him down. The supplies—which included rations and ammunition—were ''rare commodities'' that could not be replaced.

To keep the Soviets at bay as long as possible, the Germans mined the approaches to Kirkenes, blew up the suspension bridge across Jar Fjord, and set the town on fire. Then they withdrew, with only 45,000 tons of the valuable supplies safely loaded. When Meretskov reached Kirkenes on October 25, he found a desolate picture. ''Pulling out,'' he later wrote, ''the Germans had blown up all port installations, offices and residential areas. Only a few small houses on the outskirts of town miraculously remained standing.''

The destruction visited on Kirkenes was destined to be re-

Norwegians emerge from a railway tunnel to greet the Soviet troops who liberated Kirkenes from the Germans on October 25, 1944. ''We got a warm welcome,'' said the Soviet commander. ''The girls looked after our wounded and the young men helped them to the hospitals.''

peated as the Germans fled westward through the northern Norwegian province of Finnmark. Hitler, determined to present nothing of value to the Russians, had told Rendulic to leave behind a landscape devoid of people, shelter or supplies. Rendulic had no qualms about following this order.

Bringing up the rear of the German retreat were special demolition squads that burned and leveled homes and factories, destroyed food supplies and shot livestock. The ruins of Finnmark's ports and villages were grim evidence of the squads' efficiency. In Vadsö, four buildings in five were destroyed. In Gamvik, a fishing village of some 500 people, not a single house remained upright. Hammerfest, once a whaling center, had become a dead city. Complying with a German order to evacuate immediately, 43,000 terrified civilians fled the wasted area.

Ironically, most of this apocalyptic destruction served little purpose. By the time Meretskov reached Kirkenes, he had gone almost as far as he could; the Soviets wanted no charges that they had designs on Norwegian territory. At Tana Fjord, 70 miles northwest of Kirkenes, Meretskov called a halt.

While the 19th Corps struggled westward along Route 50, the Twentieth Mountain Army's other two corps had conducted a routine withdrawal, cleaning out their supply depots and scorching the earth behind as they departed. In all, the movement required three arduous months, but by the end of January 1945 the main body of all three corps had reached the defensive line running south from Lyngen Fjord to the Swedish border. Finland was a battlefield no more.

In London, where King Haakon and his entourage had fled in 1940, the exiled Norwegian government was anxious to reassert its authority in Finnmark now that the Germans had departed. Stalin was eager to help the Norwegians occupy the province. In November, 281 Norwegian soldiers under Colonel Arne Dahl sailed with a convoy from Scapa Flow to Murmansk, and from there to Liinahamari on the Finnish coast. Red Army trucks waited to take them westward and over the Norwegian border near Kirkenes.

The Russians, reported Dahl, seemed bemused by the idea of a relative handful of untested Norwegian infantrymen reclaiming 48,000 square miles of territory. But at least one Soviet truck driver—despite the language barrier—understood the mission's symbolic importance. "I was in a truck," recalled one of Dahl's contingent, "sitting next to the fur-clad driver and trying to make conversation. My knowledge of Russian was limited to three words: 'friend,' 'enemy' and 'house.' So I kept saying, 'Russia, America, England, Norway—friends. Germany—enemy.' The Russian laughed heartily and thought this was wonderful.

"Suddenly we were crossing a bridge. The Russian became very excited and pointed to a small cottage that was standing on the other bank. 'Norveski dom,' he said. 'A Norwegian home.' "

With that, the detachment crossed into Finnmark and a small part of Norway was once again Norwegian. In the rest of the country, 400,000 German troops—including those who had recently arrived from Finland—would spend the remaining months of the War in idleness, on the alert for Allied attacks that never came.

In Denmark, Occupation had long since become a trial for the Germans. The Danes had organized a campaign of resistance—calling general strikes, blowing up ammunition depots, sabotaging shipyards—that prompted the Germans to declare martial law in the summer of 1943. King Christian and his Cabinet retaliated with a strike of their own that brought the government's functions to a halt. The strike compelled the Germans to abandon at last the fiction that Denmark was still an independent country. They disarmed the small remaining units of the Danish Army and Navy and increased their own strength from four to six divisions. But even those troops were unable to quench the flame of civilian opposition, which had been kindled by the university students with their underground newspaper.

In Finland, the northern provinces were a shambles—and the Soviet troops occupying the Petsamo region were there to stay. Some 480,000 refugees who had been displaced from areas all over Finland, from Petsamo to Karelia, were flooding into a country reduced in size and ill prepared for the arduous tasks of resettling and rebuilding. Nevertheless, the Finns would emerge from the War with their independence intact, a better fate than befell much of Eastern Europe. "A high price had been paid for freedom," noted Mannerheim, adding up the human cost of the War. "Fifty-five thousand white wooden crosses in our churchyards bear witness to that."

RETURN TO DESOLATION

Their children and sparse belongings in hand, refugees return home to the ruins of Rovaniemi, the capital of Lapland, in the wake of the German Army's retreat.

THE BITTER FRUITS OF A SUNDERED ALLIANCE

"I was washing milk cans," wrote 14-year-old Tuulikki Soini, "when somebody shouted at the door: 'Finland is burning!' I ran out to see. To the south, the land was red, not like a sunset, but burning red."

Young Tuulikki was one of 104,000 civilians who had fled from the Lapland region of northern Finland to wait out the retreat of the German Army in September 1944. The fiery scene that the girl witnessed from across the Tornio River in neutral Sweden was only an inkling of the extraordinary desolation that awaited her and her countrymen when they returned to their homes. "The Germans had been very thorough in their destruction," another Finn remembered bitterly of his arrival in the provincial capital of Rovaniemi. "There was nothing left except some chimneys and smoke and ashes."

Like any retreating army, the Germans had destroyed everything they could of military value, blowing up bridges, harbors, railways, airstrips, highways, mines and power stations. But the Germans evacuating Finland did not confine themselves to military installations. Nursing a spirit of revenge because the Finns had ended their three-year alliance and signed a separate peace with the Soviet Union, the Germans put whole villages to the torch—and in a land where nearly everything was built of wood, nearly everything burned. Altogether more than 41,000 buildings were destroyed—among them five orphanages, four hospitals, four poorhouses, more than 100 schools, and countless homes and farmsteads. As though scorching the earth were not enough, the Germans sowed the soil with mines that during the next three years killed or wounded more than 200 unsuspecting Finnish civilians.

Not surprisingly, the bitterness of the departing troops was returned in full measure by the Finns. "I never liked the Germans," said one Finnish woman whose harsh feelings were echoed widely. "Now I hate them." All told, the damages totaled some $300 million, and although the Finns began to rebuild at once, it took them more than five years to restore their land.

Homeward bound through the town of Muonio, Finns pass a German sign that reads sarcastically: "Thanks for nothing, comrades-in-arms!"

Retreating west from Finland into Occupied Norway, German Army troopers attach explosive charges to a bridge spanning the Anar River.

WATCHING
THE HOMELAND BURN

From the Swedish side of the River Tornio,
Finns see their village burn. "We stood there on
the riverbank watching the flames on the
Finnish side as if it were a movie," wrote
one refugee. "At least," another tartly noted,
"they haven't burned down the woods."

A RAILHEAD LEFT IN SPLINTERS

Remnants of blasted track, timber and machinery clutter the railroad yard at Kemi, Lapland's largest town and major port of entry from the Baltic Sea.

SIFTING THE WRECKAGE FOR ANYTHING WHOLE

Kemi's city hall, its lower floors gutted by German-set bombs, triumphantly flies the Finnish flag after the Finns reclaimed the town. Nearly 500 state-owned buildings in Lapland were destroyed by the Germans.

Standing in the bombed-out observatory of the village of Sodankylä, a Finn retrieves a stray scrap of paper. The observatory, established in 1913, was one of the first in the world used for studying the geophysics of the Arctic.

At an abandoned supply depot in Kemi, Finns sift through rubble for shoes and canned goods that the Germans might have missed.

Setting about rebuilding, a Laplander muscles a log onto a sled as a reindeer waits to haul the load away. The Germans slaughtered more than 38,000 head of cattle, but they had overlooked the reindeer.

Log by log, a wall is erected on a Lapland farm. More than 30 per cent of the buildings in the region and 30,000 pieces of farm machinery were ruined and had to be replaced.

BIBLIOGRAPHY

Adamson, Hans Christian, and Per Klem, *Blood on the Midnight Sun*. W. W. Norton, 1964.

Andersson, Ingvar, *A History of Sweden*. Frederick A. Praeger, 1957.

Aschan, Lars J., and John R. Elting, personal correspondence, February 19, 1977, to May 6, 1980. Unpublished.

Ash, Bernard, *Norway: 1940*. London: Cassell, 1964.

Bekker, Cajus:
The German Navy: 1939-1945. Dial Press, 1974.
The Luftwaffe War Diaries. Transl. and ed. by Frank Ziegler. Ballantine Books, 1966.

Böttger, Gerd, *Narvik im Bild*. Berlin: Gerhard Stalling Verlag, 1941.

Brown, David, *Tirpitz: The Floating Fortress*. Naval Institute Press, 1977.

Buckley, Christopher, *The Second World War, 1939-1945: Norway, The Commandos, Dieppe*. London: His Majesty's Stationery Office, 1951.

Busch, Fritz-Otto, *The Drama of the Scharnhorst: A Factual Account from the German Viewpoint*. Transl. by Eleanor Brockett and Anton Ehrenzweig. London: Robert Hale, 1956.

Campbell, Ian, and Donald Macintyre, *The Kola Run: A Record of Arctic Convoys, 1941-1945*. London: Futura Publications, 1975.

Carell, Paul, *Hitler's War on Russia*. Transl. by Ewald Osers. London: Corgi Books, 1966.

Carlgren, W. M., *Swedish Foreign Policy during the Second World War*. Transl. by Arthur Spencer. St. Martin's Press, 1977.

Carse, Robert, *A Cold Corner of Hell: The Story of the Murmansk Convoys, 1941-1945*. Doubleday, 1969.

Chew, Allen F., *The White Death: The Epic of the Soviet-Finnish Winter War*. Michigan State University Press, 1971.

Churchill, Winston S., *The Second World War*:
Vol. 1, *The Gathering Storm*. Houghton Mifflin, 1948.
Vol. 3, *The Grand Alliance*. Houghton Mifflin, 1950.
Vol. 4, *The Hinge of Fate*. Houghton Mifflin, 1950.

Cooper, Matthew, *The German Army, 1933-1945: Its Political and Military Failure*. London: Macdonald and Jane's, 1978.

Derry, T. K.:
The Campaign in Norway (History of the Second World War: United Kingdom Military Series). London: Her Majesty's Stationery Office, 1952.
A History of Scandinavia: Norway, Sweden, Denmark, Finland and Iceland. University of Minnesota Press, 1979.

Dickens, Peter, *Narvik: Battles in the Fjords (Sea Battles in Close-Up, Vol. 9)*. Naval Institute Press, 1974.

Esposito, Vincent J., ed., *The West Point Atlas of American Wars, Vol. 2, 1900-1953*. Frederick A. Praeger, 1959.

Etto, Toimittanut Jorma, *Evakkotaival: Kuvia ja Muisteluksia Lapin Evakosta, 1944-1945*. Lapland: Lapin Maakuntaliitto, 1975.

Finland's Ministry for Foreign Affairs, *Finland Reveals Her Secret Documents on Soviet Policy, March 1940-June 1941*. Wilfred Funk, 1941.

Firsoff, V. A., *Ski Track on the Battlefield*. A. S. Barnes, 1943.

Flower, Desmond, and James Reeves, eds., *The Taste of Courage: The War, 1939-1945*. Harper & Row, 1960.

Fox, Annette Baker, *The Power of Small States: Diplomacy in World War II*. The University of Chicago Press, 1959.

Frere-Cook, Gervis, *The Attacks on the Tirpitz (Sea Battles in Close-Up, Vol. 8)*. London: Ian Allan, 1973.

Garrett, Richard, *Scharnhorst and Gneisenau: The Elusive Sisters*. Hippocrene Books, 1978.

Getz, O. B., *Fra Krigen i Nord-Trøndelag 1940*. Oslo: Forlagt Av H. Aschehoug, 1940.

Gudme, Sten, *Denmark: Hitler's "Model Protectorate."* Transl. by Jan Noble. London: Victor Gollancz, 1942.

Halsti, Wolf H., *Suomen Sota 1939-1944*. 3 vols. Helsinki: Otava, 1957.

Hambro, C. J., *I Saw It Happen in Norway*. D. Appleton-Century, 1943.

Harriman, W. Averell and Elie Abel, *Special Envoy to Churchill and Stalin: 1941-1946*. Random House, 1975.

Hayes, Paul M., *Quisling: The Career and Political Ideas of Vidkun Quisling, 1887-1945*. Indiana University Press, 1972.

Hewins, Ralph, *Quisling: Prophet without Honour*. London: W. H. Allen, 1965.

Hölter, Hermann, *Armee in der Arktis*. Munich: Schild Verlag, 1977.

Hubatsch, Walther, *"Weserübung": Die Deutsche Besetzung von Dänemark und Norwegen, 1940*. Berlin: Musterschmidt-Verlag-Gottingen, 1960.

Hyyryläinen, Eino, *"Ryhmänjohtajan sotaa Suomussalmella." Kansa Taisteli—Miehet Kertovat*, Helsinki: Sotamuistoyhdistys, December 15, 1977.

Irving, David, *Hitler's War*. Viking Press, 1977.

Jakobson, Max, *The Diplomacy of the Winter War: An Account of the Russo-Finnish War, 1939-1940*. Harvard University Press, 1961.

Johnson, Amanda, *Norway: Her Invasion and Occupation*. Bowen Press, 1948.

Kallas, Hiller, and Sylvie Nickels, eds., *Finland: Creation and Construction*. Praeger, 1968.

Khrushchev, Nikita S., *Khrushchev Remembers*. Ed. and transl. by Strobe Talbott. Little, Brown, 1970.

Kirby, D. G., *Finland in the Twentieth Century*. University of Minnesota Press, 1979.

Krosby, H. Peter:
Finland, Germany and the Soviet Union, 1940-1941: The Petsamo Dispute. The University of Wisconsin Press, 1968.
Suomen Valinta, 1941. Helsinki: Kirjayhtymä, 1967.

Lapie, Pierre O., *With the Foreign Legion at Narvik*. London: John Murray, 1941.

Lehmkuhl, Dik, *Journey to London: The Story of the Norwegian Government at War*. London: Hutchinson, no date.

Lehmkuhl, Herman K., *Hitler Attacks Norway*. London: The Royal Norwegian Government Information Office, 1943.

Lenton, H. T., *German Warships of the Second World War*. London: Macdonald and Jane's, 1975.

Liddel-Hart, Basil, *The Red Army*. Harcourt, Brace & World, 1968.

Linna, Väinö, *The Unknown Soldier*. Helsinki: Werner Söderström Osakeyhtiö, 1957.

Loewenheim, Francis L., Harold D. Langley and Manfred Jonas, eds., *Roosevelt and Churchill: Their Secret Wartime Correspondence*. Saturday Review Press, 1975.

Lohmann, Walter, and Hans H. Hildebrand, *Die Deutsche Kriegsmarine: 1939-1945*. Bad Nauheim, Germany: Verlag Hans-Henning Podzun, 1956.

Luckett, Richard, *The White Generals*. Viking Press, 1971.

Lundin, C. Leonard, *Finland in the Second World War*. Indiana University Press, 1957.

Luukkanen, Eino, *Fighter over Finland: The Memoirs of a Fighter Pilot*. London: Macdonald, 1963.

Macintyre, Donald, *Narvik*. W. W. Norton, 1960.

Mannerheim, Carl Gustaf, *The Memoirs of Marshal Mannerheim*. Transl. by Eric Lewenhaupt. E. P. Dutton, 1954.

Martienssen, Anthony, *Hitler and His Admirals*. E. P. Dutton, 1949.

Mason, Herbert Molloy, Jr., *The Rise of the Luftwaffe: Forging the Secret German Air Weapon, 1918-1940*. The Dial Press, 1973.

Mercer, Charles, *Legion of Strangers: The Vivid History of a Unique Military Tradition—The French Foreign Legion*. Holt, Rinehart and Winston, 1964.

Meretskov, K. A., *Serving the People*. Moscow: Progress Publishers, 1971.

Mitchell, Donald W., *A History of Russian and Soviet Sea Power*. Macmillan, 1974.

Moulton, J. L.:
The Conquest of Norway (History of the Second World War, Vol. 1, No. 6.). London: Purnell & Sons, 1966.
Hitler Strikes North (History of the Second World War, Vol. 1, No. 6.). London: Purnell & Sons, 1966.
The Norwegian Campaign of 1940. London: Eyre & Spottiswoode, 1966.

Outze, Børge, ed., *Denmark during the German Occupation*. Copenhagen: The Scandinavian Publishing Co., 1946.

Peillard, Léonce, *Sink the Tirpitz!* Transl. by Oliver Coburn. G. P. Putnam's Sons, 1968.

Petrow, Richard, *The Bitter Years: The Invasion and Occupation of Denmark and Norway, April 1940-May 1945*. William Morrow, 1974.

Pope, Dudley, *Battle of Barents Sea (History of the Second World War, Vol. 3, No. 14.)*. London: Purnell & Sons, 1967.

Raeder, Erich, *Struggle for the Sea*. London: William Kimber, 1959.

Rauschning, Hermann, *The Voice of Destruction*. Putnam, 1940.

Reynaud, Paul, *In the Thick of the Fight: 1930-1945*. Transl. by James D. Lambert. Simon and Schuster, 1955.

Rintala, Marvin, *Four Finns*. University of California Press, 1969.

Rohwer, J., and G. Hummelchen, *Chronology of the War at Sea: 1939-1945, Vol. 1, 1939-1942*. Transl. by Derek Masters. Arco Publishing, 1973.

Roskill, S. W., *The War at Sea, 1939-1945*:
Vol. 1, *The Defensive*. London: Her Majesty's Stationery Office, 1954.
Vol. 2, *The Period of Balance*. London: Her Majesty's Stationery Office, 1956.

Ruppert, A., *Front on the Arctic Circle. Book of a Lapland Corps: German Soldiers in the Finnish Wilderness*. Berlin: Wilhelm Verlag, 1943.

Savolainen, Heikki, *"Konekiväärin Piippu Suli." Kansa Taisteli—Miehet Kertovat*, Helsinki: Sotamuistoyhdistys, March 15, 1978.

Schreiber, Franz, *Kampf unter dem Nordlicht: Deutsch-finnische Waffenbruderschaft am Polarkreis*. Osnabrück, Germany: Munin Verlag, 1969.

Seppä, Tauno, *"Viimeiseen Mieheen." Kansa Taisteli—Miehet Kertovat*, Helsinki: Sotamuistoyhdistys, March 15, 1978.

Shtemenko, S. M., *The Last Six Months: Russia's Final Battles with Hitler's Armies in World War II*. Transl. by Guy Daniels. Doubleday, 1977.

Speer, Albert, *Inside the Third Reich*. Macmillan, 1970.

Stein, George H., *The Waffen-SS: Hitler's Elite Guard at War, 1939-1945*. Cornell University Press, 1966.

Sweden: A Wartime Survey. Ed. and pub. in Sweden with the assistance of public authorities. The American-Swedish News Exchange, New York, 1943.

Tanner, Väinö, *The Winter War: Finland against Russia, 1939-1940*. Stanford University Press, 1957.

Taylor, Telford, *The March of Conquest: The German Victories in Western Europe, 1940*. Simon and Schuster, 1958.

Terkelsen, T. M., *Denmark: Fight Follows Surrender*. London: The Information Office of the Danish Council, 1942.

Thomas, John Oram, *The Giant-Killers: The Story of the Danish Resistance Movement, 1940-1945*. Taplinger, 1975.

Thursfield, H. G., ed., *Brassey's Naval Annual: 1948*. Macmillan, 1948.

Toynbee, Arnold and Veronica, eds., *The War and the Neutrals*. Oxford University Press, 1956.

Tuompo, W. E., and V. A. M. Karikoski, eds., *Ära—Fädernesland: Kriget mellan Finland och Sovjetunionen, 1939-1940*. Helsinki: Nordiska Förlagsaktiebolaget, 1942.

United States Army:
Small Unit Actions during the German Campaign in Russia. Department of the Army Pamphlet No. 20-269, July 1953.

Warfare in the Far North. Department of the Army Pamphlet No. 20-292, October 1951.

Upton, Anthony F.:
  Finland: 1939-1940. London: Davis-Poynter, 1974.
  Finland in Crisis, 1940-1941: A Study in Small-Power Politics. Cornell University Press, 1965.
  The Winter War: Finland, October 5, 1939/March 13, 1940. (History of the Second World War, Vol. 1, No. 5.). London: Purnell & Sons, 1966.

Volkischer Beobachter (Nazi Party newspaper), April 2, 1939.

Von der Porten, Edward P.:
  The German Navy in World War II. Galahad Books, 1969.
  Pictorial History of the German Navy in World War II. Thomas Y. Crowell, 1976.

Waage, Johan, The Narvik Campaign. Transl. by Ewan Butler. London: George G. Harrap, 1964.

Warlimont, Walter, Inside Hitler's Headquarters: 1939-1945. Transl. by R. H. Barry. Frederick A. Praeger, 1964.

Woodward, David, The Tirpitz and the Battle for the North Atlantic. Berkley Publishing, 1953.

Zentner, Kurt, Der Widerstand. Munich: Sudwest Verlag, 1966.

Ziemke, Earl F.:
  The German Northern Theater of Operations, 1940-1945. Department of the Army Pamphlet No. 20-271, 1959.
  Stalingrad to Berlin: The German Defeat in the East. Office of the Chief of Military History, United States Army, 1968.

PICTURE CREDITS

Credits from left to right are separated by semicolons, from top to bottom by dashes.

COVER and page 1: Popperfoto, London. 2, 3: Map by Tarijy Elsab.

A MODEL SCANDINAVIAN HERO—8, 9: National Archives No. 306-NT-1325-14. 10: The Mannerheim Museum, Helsinki. 11: B. L. Davis Collection, London. 12, 13: The Mannerheim Museum, Helsinki. 14, 15: The Mannerheim Museum, Helsinki; Bundesarchiv, Koblenz. 16, 17: The Mannerheim Museum, Helsinki. 18, 19: Pictures, Incorporated; Reportagebild, Stockholm.

A WAR THAT WINTER BROUGHT—22: UPI. 23, 24: WSOY, Helsinki. 27: UPI. 30: Novosti Press Agency, London. 32: WSOY, Helsinki.

SPOILS FOR GHOST SOLDIERS—34, 35: UPI. 36: Otava, Helsinki. 37: UPI. 38, 39: Popperfoto, London; AB Text & Bilder, Malmo, Sweden. 40, 41: Popperfoto, London, except bottom right, UPI. 42, 43: UPI.

THE GRAB FOR NORWAY—46, 49: Bundesarchiv, Koblenz. 51: Foto-Drüppel, Wilhelmshaven, Federal Republic of Germany—Bundesarchiv, Koblenz. 52: Ullstein Bilderdienst, Berlin (West). 53: Map by Tarijy Elsab. 54: Bundesarchiv, Koblenz.

THE SWIFTEST BLITZ—56, 57: ADN-Zentralbild, Berlin, DDR. 58-61: Bundesarchiv, Koblenz. 62, 63: Bundesarchiv, Koblenz, except bottom right, Bildarchiv Preussischer Kulturbesitz, Berlin (West). 64, 65: Bundesarchiv, Koblenz. 66, 67: Ullstein Bilderdienst, Berlin (West), except bottom right, Bundesarchiv, Koblenz. 68, 69: Bundesarchiv, Koblenz. 70, 71: ADN-Zentralbild, Berlin, DDR; Bundesarchiv, Koblenz.

A FAILED RESCUE—74: AB Text & Bilder, Malmo, Sweden. 76: National Archives No. 208-N-39871. 78: Imperial War Museum, London. 81, 83: Maps by Tarijy Elsab. 84: E. C. P. Armées, Paris. 88: Bekker-Archiv, Pinneberg, Federal Republic of Germany.

A MASTERPIECE OF MOVEMENT—90, 91: Keystone Press, London. 92: Süddeutscher Verlag, Bilderdienst, Munich. 93: Dever from Black Star. 94, 95: UPI, except bottom right, Wide World. 96, 97: Ullstein Bilderdienst, Berlin (West); National Archives No. 131-NO-7-97. 98, 99: Interphoto. 100, 101: Ullstein Bilderdienst, Berlin (West). 102, 103: Bundesarchiv, Koblenz; B. L. Davis Collection, London.

SWEDEN ON THE ALERT—104-107: AB Text & Bilder, Malmo, Sweden. 108, 109: Pressens Bild AB, Stockholm; K. W. Gullers, Stockholm. 110: AB Text & Bilder, Malmo, Sweden. 111: Pressens Bild AB, Stockholm—AB Text & Bilder, Malmo, Sweden. 112: Scandia Photo Press AB, Malmo, Sweden—Pictures, Incorporated. 113: K. W. Gullers, Stockholm. 114, 115: AB Text & Bilder, Malmo, Sweden; Scandia Photo Press AB, Malmo, Sweden.

THE NECESSARY ALLIANCE—119: Map by Tarijy Elsab. 122: Ullstein Bilderdienst, Berlin (West). 124-128: WSOY, Helsinki. 129: Movietone News. 130: UPI.

HARD DUTY IN A HARSH LAND—132-145: Paintings by Emil Rizek, Vienna, Austria, courtesy U.S. Army.

ORDEAL IN THE CRUELEST SEA—148: Bundesarchiv, Koblenz. 149: Courtesy Karl-Wilhelm Grützemacher, Munich. 150: Frank Scherschel for Life. 152: UPI. 156: Foto-Drüppel, Wilhelmshaven, Federal Republic of Germany. 157: ADN-Zentralbild, Berlin, DDR.

A BATTLE QUEEN IN EXILE—160, 161: Foto-Drüppel, Wilhelmshaven, Federal Republic of Germany. 162: Imperial War Museum, London. 163: British Crown Copyright Reserved, Tirpitz Collection, London. 164, 165: Imperial War Museum, London; British Crown Copyright Reserved, Tirpitz Collection, London (2). 166, 167: British Crown Copyright Reserved, Tirpitz Collection, London. 168-173: Imperial War Museum, London. 174, 175: Imperial War Museum, London—Popperfoto, London; National Archives No. 306-NT-1290A-17.

RETREAT IN THE NORTH—178: Photo Center of the Finnish Defense Forces, Helsinki. 179: Keystone Press, London. 181: Yakov Ryumkin, Moscow. 183: Map by Tarijy Elsab. 184: ADN-Zentralbild, Berlin, DDR. 185: Courtesy Earl F. Ziemke. 186: Yevgeni Khaldei, Moscow. 188: Novosti Press Agency, London.

RETURN TO DESOLATION—190, 191: Lapland Rural Commune Archive, Rovaniemi, Finland. 192: Photo Center of the Finnish Defense Forces, Helsinki. 193: ADN-Zentralbild, Berlin, DDR. 194, 195: Lapland National Archive, Rovaniemi, Finland. 196-198: WSOY, Helsinki. 199: Photo Center of the Finnish Defense Forces, Helsinki. 200, 201: Lapland Rural Commune Archive, Rovaniemi, Finland; WSOY, Helsinki.

ACKNOWLEDGMENTS

For help given in the preparation of this book, the editors wish to express their gratitude to Hans Becker, ADN-Zentralbild, Berlin, DDR; Claude Bellarbre, Musée de la Marine, Paris; Dr. Klaus-Richard Böhme, Associate Professor, Royal Staff College of the Armed Forces, Stockholm; Jacques Chantriot, Musée de la Marine, Paris; Colonel Eero Erasaari, Finnish Army (Ret.), Chief Editor, *Kansa Taisteli— Miehet Kertovat*, Helsinki; Jma Etto, Rovaniemi City Library, Finland; Christine Flowers, Langley, Virginia; Fotokhronika-TASS, Moscow; Karl-Wilhelm Grützemacher, Munich; Professor Vilho Lukkarinen, Nummela, Finland; The Mannerheim Museum, Helsinki; Marjolaine Mathikine, Director for Historical Studies, Musée de la Marine, Paris; Françoise Mercier, Institut d'Histoire du Temps Présent, Paris; Brün Meyer, Bundesarchiv/Militärarchiv, Freiburg, West Germany; Timothy P. Mulligan, National Archives, Washington, D.C.; The Museum of Denmark's Fight for Freedom 1940-1945, Copenhagen; Meinrad Nilges, Bundesarchiv, Koblenz, West Germany; Major Antti Numminen, Finnish Army Instructor, Battle School, Tuusula, Finland; Lieut. Colonel Risto Pajari, Finnish Air Force (Ret.), Helsinki; Markku Palokangas, War Museum, Helsinki; George A. Petersen, Springfield, Virginia; Commodore Eino Pukkila, Finnish Navy (Ret.), Helsinki; Professor Dr. Jürgen Rohwer, Bibliothek für Zeitgeschichte, Stuttgart; Georges Roland, E. C. P. Armées, Paris; Bertil Rubin, AB Text & Bilder, Malmo, Sweden; Axel Schulz, Ullstein Bilderdienst, Berlin (West); Major Matti Vuolevi, Finnish Army, The Photo Center of the Finnish Defense Forces, Helsinki; Lieut. Colonel Anssi Vuorenmaa, Finnish Army, War Museum, Helsinki; Major Hans Wind, Finnish Air Force (Ret.), Tampere, Finland; Professor Earl F. Ziemke, University of Georgia, Athens, Georgia.

The index for this book was prepared by Nicholas J. Anthony.

Numerals in italics indicate an illustration of the subject mentioned.

Printed in U.S.A.